ADULT COGNITIVE DEVELOPMENT

ADULT COGNITIVE DEVELOPMENT

Methods and Models

*Robert A. Mines
and Karen S. Kitchener*

PRAEGER SPECIAL STUDIES • PRAEGER SCIENTIFIC

New York • Philadelphia • Eastbourne, UK
Toronto • Hong Kong • Tokyo • Sydney

Library of Congress Cataloging-in-Publication Data
Main entry under title:

Adult cognitive development.
  Bibliography: p.
  Includes index.
  1. Cognition. 2. Cognition — Research.
3. Young adults — Psychology. I. Mines,
Robert A. II. Kitchener, Karen S.
BF311.A3 1985   153   85-16969
ISBN 0-03-070652-1 (alk. paper)

Published in 1986 by Praeger Publishers
CBS Educational and Professional Publishing, a Division of CBS Inc.
521 Fifth Avenue, New York, NY 10175 USA

Printed in the United States of America on acid-free paper

INTERNATIONAL OFFICES

Orders from outside the United States should be sent to the appropriate address listed below. Orders from areas not listed below should be placed through CBS International Publishing, 383 Madison Ave., New York, NY 10175 USA

Australia, New Zealand
Holt Saunders, Pty. Ltd., 9 Waltham St., Artarmon, N.S.W. 2064, Sydney, Australia

Canada
Holt, Rinehart & Winston of Canada, 55 Horner Ave., Toronto, Ontario, Canada M8Z 4X6

Europe, the Middle East, & Africa
Holt Saunders, Ltd., 1 St. Anne's Road, Eastbourne, East Sussex, England BN21 3UN

Japan
Holt Saunders, Ltd., Ichibancho Central Building, 22-1 Ichibancho, 3rd Floor, Chiyodaku, Tokyo, Japan

Hong Kong, Southeast Asia
Holt Saunders Asia, Ltd., 10 Fl, Intercontinental Plaza, 94 Granville Road, Tsim Sha Tsui East, Kowloon, Hong Kong

Manuscript submissions should be sent to the Editorial Director, Praeger Publishers, 521 Fifth Avenue, New York, NY 10175 USA

This book is dedicated to Kathy, Mike, and Matt,
and to Richard, Greg, and Brian.

Acknowledgments

We would like to thank the Frost Foundation for its support of the Young Adult Development Conference at the University of Denver in 1982, from which this book was developed. The University of Denver Faculty Senate and Mines and Associates: Counseling Psychology Services provided funds supporting the manuscript production.

We especially want to thank Ms Coleen Hiett and Ms Cheryl Merrill for diligent and thorough work on the indexing of this book.

Contents

List of Tables

List of Figures

Introduction:
Convergence and Divergence in Models
of Young Adult Cognitive Development

Inhelder and Piaget's (1958) work on formal operations has profoundly influenced the study of adolescent and adult cognitive development for the last twenty-five years. The work in this book is no exception. The majority of the authors in this volume accept the primary assumptions of the organismic tradition and, as a result, owe a debt to Piaget as the leading proponent of this view in the twentieth century.

The organismic theory at its core assumes that the organism is actively involved in the construction of cognitive operations which shape how it views the world. It is an interactionist position that sees the organism neither as a tabula rasa on which the environment writes nor as innately determined. As Overton (1984, p. 204) has suggested, this view of nature regards activity, change, and organization as essential and a "necessary feature of the cosmos and not simply the product of contingent, accidental features. Accidental features can here affect activity, organization, and change but they cannot explain them." These assumptions characterize the basic view of human nature for the writers in this volume. (See Overton, 1984, for an argument for including dialectics within this theory.) The chapters are especially linked to Inhelder and Piaget's explication of formal operations as the final stage of development. The authors are either offering elaborations of the model or reacting to the failures and limitations of it.

On the other hand, it would be unfair to characterize this book as focusing on postformal operations. In fact, several viewpoints about formal operations are expressed by the authors: (1) formal operations is the pinnacle of intellectual development, but it is not attained by all adults, at least not in all areas; (2) formal operations is one step in a sequence of intellectual development, but not the ultimate one; (3) formal operations describes only one aspect of development (i.e., the ability to use hypothetico-deductive reasoning); it does not fully account for reasoning in other domains (e.g., ethics, epistemology) which is developing sequentially but may not be developing in synchrony with formal operations; (4) while the paths of development may have similar forms (e.g., from simple, single, undifferentiated categories to complex, differentiated ones), the actual categories (concepts) that develop in the individual are profoundly influenced by the environment and historical time. What these authors have in common is the struggle to describe and understand complex reasoning and creativity in adults and how this is both related to and different from the thinking styles of children and adolescents.

These are not the only authors struggling with this issue. In fact, there is a line of often unacknowledged predecessors going back at least twenty years, who have argued that cognitive operations and, as a result, conceptual systems change in the young adult and adult years (Broughton, 1975; Harvey, Hunt, and Schroder, 1961; Perry, 1970; Riegel, 1973). What is interesting about this early group of theorists is the overlap in their descriptions of and assumptions about development. For example, while different vocabularies are used and different content areas explored, generally development is described as progressing from singular and absolute categories to multiple but unintegrated categories. Frequently, they and others (Kohlberg, 1973) have also noted the relativizing of thinking processes as an intermediary step in the sequence.

More recently (Commons, Richards, and Armon, 1984) a plethora of new models describing the development of adult reasoning have been postulated, some of which acknowledge and move beyond their predecessors and some of which do not. However, generally the data base against which both the older and the more recent theories might be evaluated and refined is very small or nonexistent. While all of the theories postulate stages or levels of cognitive development which are uniquely characteristic of the reasoning of late adolescents and young adults, few have actually tested their assumptions or they have been tested with single, small samples. In other words, more attention has been paid to model development than model validation. Further, little thought and almost no empirical studies have been made of how this line of research relates to older, more established models of intelligence in adulthood, i.e., intelligence as a general construct (Spearman, 1927), intelligence as a multifactored trait (Guilford, 1959; Thurston, 1936), intelligence as crystallized or fluid abilities (Cattell, 1963).

In many ways, the current status of the theory validation is understandable. The field is really in its infancy. In addition, the models are frequently complex and assessment is time consuming, expensive, and idiosyncratic. It has been difficult for researchers, other than the models' authors, to use the assessment methods or scoring. As a result, the research base has been neither expanded nor replicated.

It is not too difficult to observe that organismic models have been treated with suspicion and skepticism, both within developmental psychology as well as psychology as a whole. If the field of young adult cognitive development is going to be treated as more than a ''flash-in-the-pan'' phenomenon, it must pay more attention to theory validation. It is, therefore, the purpose of this book to present theories of young adult cognitive development which have begun systematic research programs against which the validity of the models may be evaluated.

The models presented in this book must first be evaluated in light of the current status of the organismic theory in general. Broughton (1984), for example, has claimed that the whole organismic theoretical tradition is intellectually bankrupt and what is needed is a revolution in thinking about development in the Kuhnian sense. Kuhn (1962), a historian of science, argued that science was best understood as progressing through periods of stability in which one view of the world or paradigm was taken to be so fundamental that it was beyond empirical evaluation and through periods of chaos in which all assumptions and methodologies were questioned. These periods of chaos were revolutionary in that they fundamentally changed the questions considered legitimate for scientific inquiry. During periods of stability, most scientists engaged in what he called normal science, a process of articulating the favored paradigm more explicitly. From this perspective, this book would merely represent the redundancy of "normal science."

Many, however, have questioned whether Kuhn's characterization of scientific change, as occurring via occasional extensive or revolutionary revisions in scientific worldviews, is an accurate one (Suppe, 1977). Lakatos (1978), for example, characterized science as consisting of either progressive or degenerating research programs. The major criterion of progressive research programs is their ability to predict or explain new phenomena, i.e., to account for anomalies which other research programs cannot explain. Progressive science solves new problems. By contrast, if a theory does not lead to new predictions or if changing the theory leads to more problems than it solves, then the theoretical program is degenerating and no longer useful.

According to Lakatos, progressive programs protect their "hard core" assumptions while revising their "belt of auxiliary hypotheses" in order to generate more complex and adequate theories. Suppe has suggested that when scientific theories are being actively developed, it is typical that the people working on them think they are false. "What is to the point is to use observation and experiment to discover shortcomings in the theory, and to discover how to eliminate known artificialities, distortions, oversimplifications, and predictions of reality that the theory affords" (Suppe, 1977, p. 706). Using either Lakatos' or Suppe's criteria, the models presented in this book are in the process of active, progressive development while maintaining the core assumptions of the organismic theory. They have attempted to refine and revise Piaget's conceptualization of the stages of development in order to account for the anomalies observed in testing its original formulation. Rest's article in this book testifies most strongly to this assertion. As he notes elsewhere (Rest, 1983), Kohlberg's model of moral development generated more research of moral thought and moral behavior in the last two decades than were produced in the prior five. Further, the observed anomalies between the theories' predictions and actual observations have forced those such as Rest to reformulate the model of morality without abandoning core assumptions.

Taking these arguments one step further, one way for the reader to evaluate the theories in this book is to judge the extent to which the theories generate new, unique predictions and account for anomalies unaccounted for by other theories. Older, more basic criteria for evaluation also include logical consistency, completeness of the model, variety (heterogeneity) of the evidence, explanatory power, precision of predictions, and fit with existing evidence.

As Mines makes clear in the final chapter of this book, how a construct is measured provides a bridge between a theory and actual observations. Evaluating a research program must also include an evaluation of the validity of the assessment procedure. Questions that should be asked are: Do the assessment procedures meet the assumptions of the model? How well do the assessment procedures represent the construct being evaluated? Is the construct being fully measured? Is the index used to represent the construct theoretically valid? and so on. In other words, the methodology employed directly influences the quality and meaningfulness of the data generated.

As Lakatos has pointed out, there are frequently many competing theories that exist at any point in time. The fact that they exist does not mean they are equally useful or valid. However, if the data are not in the public domain, they cannot be judged or evaluated. As a consequence, a second purpose of this book is to provide a public arena through which the theories can be examined and critically evaluated.

In addition to the theoretical coherence of the models, the reader should consider other issues when comparing the models in order to understand their relationship to each other. Other issues to be considered include the scope of the cognitive processes described, the descriptive goals of the model, and the nature of the subject matter under investigation.

The scope of the cognitive processes, described by the models in this book, varies. Some of the models, such as Fischer's, describe very specific skills that apply to specific content domains, e.g., mathematical skills. These specific skills with a developmental basis reflect microdevelopmental processes. By contrast, models such as Basseche's dialectical reasoning describe a macrodevelopmental process that encompasses the totality of skills and reasoning processes required to think dialectically, as well as their systematic interrelationship.

The goals of the models also differ. Some give priority to describing individual development, while the focus of others is on the description of more general developmental patterns. Traditionally, in psychology this split has been characterized as the ideographic versus nomothetic distinction. For example, Gruber's work is very ideographic. He uses a methodology which is useful for describing a particular, exceptional individual, but which has little or no bearing on the description of general developmental trends. The other models have a range of nomothetic explanatory potential. However, their assessment methodology is not refined sufficiently, at this point, to have an impact on ideographic descriptions. The nomothetic potential varies as a function of the scope of each model and the data base upon which the model has been validated.

Contemporary philosophy of science holds that all research methods are incomplete. Each abstracts from the object or characteristic under study limited information; thus each may bring a useful but different perspective on the object of inquiry (Polkinghorne, 1983). The best methodology is one that adequately answers the questions asked and adequately reflects the subject matter under study. In this book, the object of inquiry is young adult cognitive development. The development of human cognition takes place through complex and multileveled interactions with the environment. Each model must be understood and evaluated by the extent to which it brings a useful and valid perspective on this subject matter.

The remainder of this Introduction reviews the models of young adult cognitive development presented in this volume.

In her chapter on formal operational thinking adults, King reviews the key features of formal operational thought as a basis for understanding its role as a seminal theory of young adult cognitive development. In addition, she reviews and critiques the growing body of research on formal operational thinking in adulthood. She notes that comparatively little research has been conducted on formal reasoning in adults, since theoretically, the attainment of this stage is accomplished in adolescence. Given the studies that do exist, however, she concludes that a sizable proportion of the normal, adult population does not reason at formal levels when tested on formal operational tasks. She continues by discussing several possible interpretations of this finding. She notes that the failure to standardize assessment procedures hampers attempts to draw reasonable conclusions across studies. Lastly, King provides an overview of new theoretical developments which have grown out of attempts to understand the construct of formal operation and problems in assessing it, thereby tying her discussion to the focus of several subsequent chapters.

Arlin's chapter focuses on the emergence of strategies and structures in young adults which underlie great discoveries in art and science. She suggests that while on a surface level, discovered problems in these two fields have nothing in common, it may be that at a deeper level they are based on similar cognitive developmental processes. She argues that the problem-solving strategies of the formal operations stage are necessary but not sufficient to account for the development of the questioning orientation necessary for the discovery of new problems. Rather, problem finding can only be accounted for by the emergence of a fifth stage of cognitive development. This fifth stage, which she proposes, is more than just problem finding, however. It is characterized by what Apostle (1979) calls the contractions and expansions of logical systems. Lastly, Arlin discusses her current research program, focusing on the relationship between formal operations and the emergence of contractions and expansions of thought in young artists and scientists.

Basseches, like Arlin, is interested in postformal operational thinking. His characterization of postformal development, however, is based on the concept of a dialectic. Dialectical thinking, he argues, is a form of cognitive organization which creates a new level of equilibrium in thought structures, transcending those provided by formal operations. Once these structures develop, he claims they provide a basic cognitive approach to problems in science, the arts, and social service, as well as those in day-to-day life. He suggests, for example, that dialectical structures provide a basis for Loevinger's autonomous level of ego development and Kegan's interindividual ego stage. He suggests that dialectical thinking is important because it allows individuals to embrace, rather than deny, contradictions in their own thinking or between their own thinking and that of another. In this chapter, Basseches reviews the schemata which make up dialectical operations and the evidence for their appearance. Lastly, he suggests the potential environmental influences that may stimulate development.

In their chapter, Fischer and Kenny discuss the evidence for discontinuities in the development of abstractions. Discontinuities are sudden alterations in the pattern of developmental change. They propose that with the emergence of a new cognitive-developmental level, a spurt in performance should be observed. For spurts to occur reliably, they argue that people must perform at or near their optimal level, the most complex skill they can control. Environmental conditions determine when people perform at their optimal level as well as the areas in which abstract skills emerge.

Second, Fischer and Kenny review the evidence for slow, gradual change in adult thinking and then use the optimal level hypothesis to predict and explain how spurts appear and disappear. They suggest that it takes work to build skills, and that skills have to be actively constructed. The environment must provide a context to induce and support the new skill and the person must practice the skill to a level of mastery.

Third, Fischer and Kenny review the theory and research on the development of levels of abstractions for education, based on skill theory.

In contrast to Arlin and Basseches, Kitchener claims in her chapter that the Reflective Judgment model, which describes the development of epistemic assumptions, is neither reducible to formal operations nor is it postformal in the sense of being superimposed upon the development of formal operations. Rather, she suggests that formal operations and reflective judgment are two different, but important, interrelated aspects of intellectual development. Neither one fully accounts for the development of the other, nor for what is broadly meant by intellectual development. Her claim is closer to that of Fischer and Kenny's, i.e., that there are several different threads or sets of cognitive assumptions which are developing but at different rates.

In her chapter, Kitchener relates the development of Reflective Judgment to the concept of epistemic cognition and notes the importance of epistemic assumptions in differentiating puzzles and wicked-decision problems. She suggests that epistemic assumptions provide individuals with a framework through which they monitor the nature of problems and the way in which solutions are knowable. She then goes on to elaborate the theoretical rationale and empirical support for the Reflective Judgment model.

In Rest's chapter on moral development in young adults, he first suggests that moral development includes an ensemble of four processes. The first involves interpreting the situation as a moral one. The second includes what is usually thought of as the cognitive-developmental component of moral development: moral judgment. The third aspect involves deciding what to do in the situation by selecting among competing values. The fourth component refers to processes usually thought of as "ego strength" or "self-regulation" skills. He suggests that if one is to understand moral development at any age, research must attend to all components. He also notes, however, that almost all research on moral development in young adults explores the second component only.

The second part of this chapter explores the research on moral judgment in young adults. He points out that while there is definite development in moral reasoning, it is strongly linked to formal education. In young adults, it is linked to higher education. Lastly, he discusses the difficulty in determining why higher education is so consistently and strongly associated with increases in moral judgment and notes that searches for singular causes of development will probably be futile.

Gruber asks the difficult developmental question: Which way is up? He is interested in studying maximal performance in exceptional individuals as a means of understanding optimal development. He differs from the other authors in both his focus and methodology. Gruber raises and discusses a number of issues in young adult cognitive development. First, developmental progress may not be linear but may occur along many developmental lines. He suggests that one person's progress is another person's stagnation. This complexity makes the concept of progress more difficult than is commonly understood. Second, Gruber is interested in studying maximal performance rather than in establishing species-typical norms. He argues that traditional research methodologies are not adequate for research on such topics. He discusses the case study, among other alternatives, as particularly suitable for studying exceptional performance. Third, the issue of what can be learned from intensive case studies of creativity that might be relevant to understanding ordinary development is raised. He defines and discusses the Evolving Systems Approach (ESA) to creativity. Gruber proposes that ESA is both a phenomenological and a constructionist approach, and he uses the ESA to connect the study of creativity to the study of ordinary lives. Lastly, in order to place developmental theory in a historical perspective, Gruber examines the relationship of young adult cognitive development and the danger of self-extinction of our species.

In order to validate theory, methodology must be comprehensive and appropriate. In the final chapter of this book, Mines discusses theoretical, psychometric, and methodological considerations in young adult cognitive developmental research. In the theory section, the issues of presence, direction, and rate of change; continuity versus discontinuity of change; sequences of unequal length; age/education level confounding; quantitative versus qualitative change; and the hierarchical arrangement of stages are reviewed and applied to the state-of-the-art research in this area. Second, Mines reviews psychometric concerns including the unit of analysis, scales of measurement, scoring methods, measurement tasks, and natural versus optimal conditions for assessment. Under each topic, current research on the models is evaluated and general research design issues are discussed. Mines concludes with the admonition that research needs to be ecologically valid—that the field consider how adults think about important issues such as nuclear war and starvation, rather than fall into the trap of opting for strong internal validity while studying trivial phenomena.

1

Formal Reasoning in Adults: A Review and Critique

Patricia M. King

The contribution of Jean Piaget to the field of adult cognitive development should not be underestimated. His theoretical concepts, methodologies, and educational applications have served to stimulate the collective imagination of hundreds of theorists, researchers, and teachers. The subsequent flurry of activity in Piagetian-based theory, research, and educational practice has dramatically increased our understanding of adult cognition. However, as Neimark (1979) notes:

> While there is an increasing acceptance of the existence of a level of adult thought qualitatively different in structure and properties from the stage of concrete operations, there is also a great deal of healthy skepticism as to its generality, the methodology of its assessment, and the theoretical characterization of its essential ingredients. (p. 61)

Until Piaget's formulation of the period of formal operations, few theoretical models were available as explanations for the distinctive characteristics of adult thinking. This theory has served as a catalyst for the creation of a sizable and growing body of theories that now increase the explanatory power of our observations. Members of this next generation of theories are based at least in part on major Piagetian assumptions (e.g., Arlin, 1975; Broughton, 1978; Ennis, 1976; Kitchener & King, 1981; Perry, 1970; Sinnott, 1984). (Several of these models are described elsewhere in this volume.) As Keating (1980) has observed: "...Piaget's theory of formal operations is to be given most of the intellectual credit for initially raising the important questions that remain the focus of attention in this area" (p. 225).

Source: Chapter prepared for R. A. Mines and K. S. Kitchener (eds.), *Adult Cognitive Development.* Praeger Press, 1985.

This chapter will first describe the key features of formal operational thought as the basis for understanding its role as a seminal theory of adult cognitive development. The second major section will review the growing body of research on formal operational thought in adulthood; this will be followed by an overview of new theoretical developments that have grown out of the recent research findings.

PIAGET'S THEORY OF THE DEVELOPMENT OF FORMAL REASONING

In Piaget's theory, human development is posited as moving through a sequence of four major and qualitatively distinct periods. These periods are sensorimotor (birth to two years), preoperational (two to seven years), concrete operational (seven to eleven years), and the formal operational period (eleven years and above). The focus of this review of the Piagetian literature will be on the formal operational period (Inhelder and Piaget, 1958). Flavell (1963) has called this period "the crowning achievement of intellectual development, the final equilibrium state towards which intellectual evolution has been moving since infancy" (p. 202). The degree to which formal operational thinking is actually observed among adults is discussed below, following a more detailed description of the theory.

The most central feature of formal operational thought, from which all other characteristics are derived, is found in its orientation toward the possible and hypothetical. In contrast to concrete operations, a new relationship exists between the real and the possible, and actuality is subjugated to possibility. Reality is no longer seen just as "what is," but now belongs within a larger context, the "is" portion of the "might be" totality (Flavell, 1963, p. 205).

Three major characteristics are derived from this central feature. First, the process that most adequately characterizes reasoning from the possible to the actual is *hypothetico-deductive* reasoning, where predetermined hypotheses may be disconfirmed by reference to relevant data. The second characteristic is *propositional* thinking. Whereas the concrete operational thinker is only able to organize (e.g., classify or seriate) objects or events, the formal operational thinker can also construct propositions about these data and explore ways in which they are logically related (e.g., by disjunction). The third major characteristic of this period is the ability to systematically generate a listing of all relevant variables, both individually and in all possible *combinations*. This strategy ensures that a complete listing of "the possible" is available, a list from which "the real" may be identified. These characteristics gain cohesiveness when seen as an approach to problem solving.

> We see, then, that formal thought is for Piaget not so much this or that specific behavior as it is a generalized *orientation,* sometimes explicit and some-

times implicit, towards problem-solving: an orientation towards organizing data (combinatorial analysis), towards isolation and control of variables, towards the hypothetical, and towards logical justification and proof. (Flavell, 1963, p. 211)

This orientation to problem solving in many ways seems obvious; it is used by mature problem solvers in everyday transactions. For example, determining whether it is a burnt-out light bulb or a dead battery which is causing a malfunction in a flashlight requires isolation and control of variables and verification of the conclusion (e.g., whether the light goes on when the bulb is changed). Piaget's theory explains the observance of these new characteristics (hypothetico-deductive reasoning, propositional thinking, and the ability to generate all possible combinations of variables by reference to two logical-mathematical models, the combinatorial system and the INRC group of transformation).

The combinatorial system. As noted above, the formal thinker has a predisposition toward identifying and an ability to identify all possible factors and combinations of factors relevant to a given problem. These factors are not generated randomly, but, according to Piaget, constitute a lattice, and formal operations are postulated to have a lattice structure. A lattice structure consists of a set of elements as well as a relation between two or more elements (Flavell, 1963). This structure is exemplified in the Pendulum task, where the subject is asked to find out which of four factors accounts for a pendulum's speed of oscillation: length of the string, weight of the attached objects, height at which the string is released, and the force with which the strings are pushed. For purposes of this example, we will consider only the effect of one of the factors, weight. Let p=fast oscillation, $\bar{p}$=slow oscillation, q=heavy weight, and $\bar{q}$=light weight. This yields four base associations $(p.q, p.\bar{q}, \bar{p}.q, \bar{p}.\bar{q})$ and sixteen possible combinations of these four base associations. The combinations are signified by the symbol "v" placed between any two pairs of base associations. The formula describes what is known when the information about the effects from the two base associations is combined. The combinations are as follows:

(1)	O	(complete negation)
(2)	A	$p.q$ fast oscillation/heavy weight
(3)	B	$p.\bar{q}$ fast oscillation/light weight
(4)	C	$\bar{p}.q$ slow oscillation/heavy weight
(5)	D	$\bar{p}.\bar{q}$ slow oscillation/light weight
(6)	AB	$(p.q)$ v $(p.\bar{q})$ fast oscillation/heavy or light weight
(7)	AC	$(p.q)v(\bar{p}.q)$
(8)	AD	$(p.q)v(\bar{p}.\bar{q})$
(9)	BC	$(p.\bar{q})v(\bar{p}.q)$
(10)	BD	$(p.\bar{q})v(\bar{p}.\bar{q})$
(11)	CD	$(\bar{p}.q)v(\bar{p}.\bar{q})$
(12)	ABC	$(p.q)v(p.\bar{q})v(\bar{p}.q)$
(13)	ABD	$(p.q)v(p.\bar{q})v(\bar{p}.\bar{q})$

(14) ACD $(p.q)v(\bar{p}.q)v(\bar{p}.\bar{q})$
(15) BCD $(p.\bar{q})v(\bar{p}.q)v(\bar{p}.\bar{q})$
(16) ABCD $(p.q)v(p.\bar{q})v(\bar{p}.q)v(\bar{p}.\bar{q})$

If one constructed only a partial set of combinations, the results might be quite misleading. For example, knowing only combination 8, AD, that the string with the heavy weight swings fast and that the string with the light weight swings slowly, weight appears to be a significant factor. However, knowing only combination 6, AB, that the speed is the same regardless of weight, suggests quite a different interpretation. It is when the effects of the entire set of combinations are known that one has sufficient data from which to deduce a correct, causal interpretation. But in order to do so with a high degree of certainty, one needs a complete list of the possibilities. It is the lattice structure, according to Piaget, that allows the individual to generate this listing of possibilities of elements and their relations.

The INRC group of transformations. While the child at the level of concrete operations can think intrapropositionally, that is, within a proposition, the formal operational thinker can also reason about the relationships between sets of propositions, or interpropositionally. The second logical model used by Piaget and Inhelder to describe the structure of formal operations is called the INRC group, or four-group. This model describes the interpropositional relationships.

Consider the operations p and q which have exactly equivalent outcomes or effects. Two operations, p* and q* nullify p and q, respectively. There are four possible transformations with this set of operations.

1. Identity (I): $I(p)=p$; $I(q)=q$; $I(p^*)=p^*$; $I(q^*)=q^*$
2. Negation (N): $N(p)=p^*$; $N(q)=q^*$; $N(p^*)=p$; $N(q^*)=q$
3. Reciprocal (R): $R(p)=q^*$; $R(q)=p^*$; $R(p^*)=q$; $R(q^*)=p$
4. Correlative (C): $C=NR$ (the product of negation and reciprocal) $C(p)=q$; $C(q)=p$; $C(p^*)=q^*$; $C(q^*)=p^*$

Using this model to explain a scale balance task, for example, the balance can be tipped either by adding weight to the pan on one side of the balance (p) or by moving the weight farther from the fulcrum (q); following this notation, the corresponding opposite actions are removing weight from the pan (p*) and moving the weight close to the fulcrum (q*). To illustrate negation in this example, the inverse of adding weight (p) is to remove weight (p*), $[N(p)=p^*]$, and the negation of moving the weight farther away from the fulcrum (q) is to move it closer to the fulcrum (q*), $[N(q)=q^*]$. The reciprocal produces the same ultimate effect as negation, but does so not by reversing the operation itself (as in negation) but by creating an equivalent counterforce. As stated above, $R(p)=q^*$. In the balance example, the effect of adding weight to one side of the balance (p) can be counteracted by moving the weight on the other side of the balance farther away from the fulcrum, thus restoring the original balance. The INRC group, then, provides a description of the ways four operations (p, q, p*, and q*) interrelate as a system. The power of this system in understanding adolescent thought is succinctly stated by Flavell (1963):

> This group is taken as a cognitive model because the adolescent behaves as if he understood precisely these same interrelations, and as if this understanding served as a guiding conceptual framework in solving problems entailing such systems. (p. 219)

Piaget suggests a close, causal relationship between the development of the major formal operational characteristics (described above) and the acquisition of the combinatorial system and the INRC group: "The development of propositional logic brings in its train a grasp of certain interpropositional relations (whose structure the logical INRC group describes)" (Flavell, 1963, p. 220). However, as Flavell (1963) also notes, "it appears that Piaget believes that the causal relation also works in the other direction, i.e., the understanding of the negation-reciprocal coordination facilitates the mastery of propositional operations" (p. 220). Whatever the direction of the causal relation, these constructs have proven very useful in understanding increasingly complex forms of thinking and problem solving that are typically observed in adults but not in children.

Does formal operational thinking actually characterize adult thinking? As a first step toward answering this question, let us consider the following question: To what degree do adults demonstrate their understanding of formal operational concepts and their mastery of tasks requiring the use of these concepts? The empirical evidence relevant to these questions will now be reviewed.

RESEARCH ON FORMAL OPERATIONAL THOUGHT IN ADULTHOOD

Comparatively little is yet known about patterns of adult reasoning in general and of formal operational reasoning of adults in particular. It is not surprising that little research has been conducted on formal reasoning in adults, given that the attainment of this stage is theoretically accomplished during adolescence and is therefore not a variable of relevance to those conducting research on adult thought. But there are several reasons for investigating the level of attainment of formal reasoning capabilities in adults. First, the question must be articulated before the theoretical assumption can be explicitly tested. Presumably this was Lovell's (1961) rationale for including adults in his major replication study of Inhelder and Piaget's (1958) work. The second reason grows out of the research that has been conducted regarding attainment of formal operational abilities, which indicates that only a moderate (and frequently a small) proportion of adolescents reason formally. Researchers have subsequently questioned what proportion of the normal adult population reasons at a formal level. Such data on adult reasoning could serve as a baseline with which to compare data on adolescent reasoning. And third, also in response to this evidence, it seems reasonable that adolescents might function at different stages on different tasks because their formal reasoning structures are relatively new and have not yet stabilized. This would account for the transitional reasoning and variability of reasoning across tasks observed among adolescents. Using this logic, adults would be expected to consistently demonstrate formal reasoning because their formal operational structure would be more stable.

While there are a growing number of studies addressing the issue of formal reasoning among adults, there currently exists no comprehensive review of this portion of the formal operations literature. Table 1.1 lists twenty-five studies which have reported the proportion of adult subjects eighteen years of age and older using formal reasoning strategies. Many other studies which tested adult subjects using formal reasoning tasks have also been conducted (e.g., Ackerman, 1978; Chap and Sinnott, 1977–78; Clayton and Overton, 1976; Demetriou and Efklides, 1979; El-Gosbi, 1982; Ellis, 1978; Goolishian, 1981; Hargrove, 1977; Hill, 1981; Moshman, 1979; Muhs, Hooper, and Papalia-Finlay, 1980; Parete, 1979; Podgoretskaya, 1979; Sheehan, 1977; Vu, 1978; White and Ferstenberg, 1978). These studies were not included in Table 1.1 because the nature of the research question or the manner in which the scores were reported precluded determination of the incidence of formal operational reasoning.

It is apparent from Table 1.1 that a rather large proportion of adults do not evidence formal thinking, even among those who have been enrolled in college. This proportion varies across different tasks and studies, covering the full range of possible scores in this table, from Lovell's (1961) 0 percent on the balance task to Broughton's (1975) 100 percent on the chemicals and pendulum tasks.

The rather wide variety of tasks used by researchers to measure formal reasoning should also be noted. An investigator's rationale for choice of task(s) is seldom given, and as Neimark (1975a) has pointed out "...there is no good theoretical rationale for selecting among the tasks" (p. 559). In addition, there currently exists no standard subset of formal operations tasks from which one can derive an overall assessment of formal operational level. In lieu of such a standard procedure, there exists no well-accepted way of determining what combination of tasks, or even how many formal tasks, to use in a formal reasoning study. In Table 1.1, for example, from one to five tasks were administered in a single study, utilizing eleven of the fifteen tasks described by Inhelder and Piaget (1958). The pendulum and chemicals tasks were used most frequently (fourteen and ten times, respectively), with two tasks being used only once (equality of angles of incidence and reflection and the law of floating bodies). Fourteen additional tasks were used in these studies to measure formal properties (DeLisi & Staudt, 1980; Dulit, 1972; El-Sowygh, 1982; Kuhn & Brannock, 1977; Roberge and Flexer, 1979; Schwebel, 1975; Sinnott, 1975; Sinnott and Gutt-

TABLE 1.1. Incidence of Formal Operational Thinking by Adults

Study	Sample	Tasks	Transitional[1]	Formal
Arlin (1975)[2,3]	60 college sophomores	chemicals pendulum shadows		52%
Bart, Frey, and Baxter (1979)[2]	34 collegiate gymnasts	balance horizontal plane pendulum invisible magnetization correlations		71% 91% 97% 97% 35%
	22 nursing students	balance horizontal plane pendulum invisible magnetization correlations		23% 64% 95% 95% 50%
Broughton (1975)[2,3]	6 college students 6 graduate students	chemicals pendulum		100% 100%
DeLisi and Staudt (1980)[2]	10 male junior or senior college students, physics majors	pendulum political socialization literary style analysis		90% 60% 40%
	10 male junior or senior college students, political science majors	pendulum political socialization literary style analysis		50% 80% 40%

TABLE 1.1. *(Continued)*

Study	Sample	Tasks	Transitional[1]	Formal
	10 male junior or senior college students, English majors	pendulum political socialization literary style analysis		40% 40% 90%
Dulit (1972)[2]	12 adults, 20–55 years old	shadows chemicals		33% 25%
El-Sowygh (1982)[2]	81 male college students from Saudi Arabia in Colorado colleges	Piagetian Objective Formal Test	40%	46%
Elkind (1962)	240 college students, 17–37 years	conservation of volume		58%
Haan, Weiss and Johnson (1982)[2,3]	62 50-year-old males 66 50-year-old females	pendulum correlations	47% 44%	27% 20%
Kitchener and King (1981)[2]	20 college juniors 20 graduate students 20 college juniors 20 graduate students	chemicals pendulum	15% 20% 20% 25%	60% 55% 40% 45%
Kuhn and Brannock (1977)[2]	20 college freshman	plant problem pendulum	25%	65% 75%
Kuhn, Langer, Kohlberg, and Haan (1977)[2]	51 16–20-year-olds 52 21–30-year-olds 130 45–50-year-olds	pendulum	34% 26% 29%	36% 39% 35%

Study	Sample	Concept/Task		
	51 16–20-year-olds	chemicals	45%	14%
	52 21–30-year-olds		49%	30%
	130 45–50-year-olds		45%	25%
Lovell (1961)[2,4]	10 training college students	chemicals	12%	60%
		pendulum	12%	71%
		invisible magnetization	26%	29%
	3 adults, 25–32 years	motion on a horizontal plane	0%	53%
		balance	60%	0%
McKinnon and Renner (1971)[2,3]	131 college freshmen	conservation of volume	25%	25%
		equality of angles of incidence and reflection		
		law of floating bodies		
		rods flexibility		
		pendulum		
Pitt (1976/1977)[2]	14 college juniors	chemicals	14%	71%
	7 science professors		0%	100%
Renner and Lawson (1973)[2]	185 college freshmen	conservation of volume		72%
		pendulum		42%
	44 law students	conservation of volume		86%
	22 law students	pendulum		70%
Roberge and Flexer (1979)[2]	72 adult males and females, 22–48-years-old	combinations		85%
		propositional logic		65%
		proportionality		53%
Ross (1973)	65 undergraduate students	balance	51%	17%
		pendulum	22%	31%
		correlations	89%	9%
		chemicals	71%	5%

TABLE 1.1. *(Continued)*

Study	Sample	Tasks	Transitional[1]	Formal
Schwebel (1972)[2,3]	58 college freshmen	rods flexibility balance hauling weight on an inclined plane shadows chemicals		83%
Schwebel (1975)[2,3]	30 female college freshmen 30 male college freshmen	rods balance scale truck	63% 63%	10% 30%
Sinnott (1975)[2,3]	30 men, 30–82-years-old	combinational and proportional reasoning familiar materials unfamiliar materials		73% 67%
	30 women, 30–82-years-old	familiar materials unfamiliar materials		87% 60%
Sinnott and Guttmann (1978)[2,3]	447 age 60 years and older	baking a cake *or* mixing paint problems		55%
Storck, Looft and Hooper (1972)[2]	24 adults, $\bar{X}$ age = 65.8 years	conservation of volume		29%
Tomlinson-Keasey (1972)[2,3]	female college students female adults	rods flexibility pendulum chemicals	23% 17%	67% 54%

Study	Sample	Tasks		
		balance		
		hauling weight on an inclined plane		
Tomlinson-Keasey and Keasey (1974)[2,3]	24 female college students	pendulum	22%	70%
		balance		
		rods flexibility		
Towler and Wheatey (1971)	71 female college students, 17–27 years; Median = 18 years	conservation of volume		61%

[1]No transitional score is listed where authors reported only formal levels.
[2]For further information, see Notations, Table 1.1.
[3]Reported scores were averaged across tasks.
[4]Reported scores were averaged across samples.

Notations, Table 1.1.
(Listed by Study)

Arlin (1975)—The formal operations level criterion was a score at the formal level on at least two of the three tasks.

Bart, Frey, and Baxter (1979)—Calculations are based on data given in Table 1, p. 255.

Broughton (1975)—Total sample size was 36, including eight students each in 4th, 8th, and 12th grades.

DeLisi and Staudt (1980)—The political socialization concepts task was adopted from Adelson, Green and O'Neil (1969). The literary styles analysis task was based on the work of Gardner and Lohman (1975).

Dulit (1972)—Total sample size was 96, including 84 14–17 year old adolescents. A paper and pencil simulation of the chemicals task was developed by the author and used for this study.

El-Sowygh (1982)—The Piagetian Objective Formal Test is based on the work of Burney, 1974.

Notations, Table 1.1. *(Continued)*

Haan, Weiss, and Johnson (1982)—Total sample size was 225 adolescents and adults; formal operations data needed for this table were reported only for the subsample of 50-year-olds. The number of males in this subsample was incorrectly listed in Table 4 (p. 252) as 72 rather than 62 (N. Haan, personal communication, December 13, 1983).

Kitchener and King (1981)—Total sample size was 60, including 20 junior high school students. Subsamples were matched by individual on MSAT scores. Formal reasoning scores for each group are reported in King (1978). Rating rules for chemicals task were based on rules developed by Dale (1970). Mecke and Mecke's (1971) scoring system was used for the pendulum task.

Kuhn and Brannock (1977)—Total sample size was 80, including 60 4th, 5th, and 6th graders. The plant problem was designed by the authors to assess isolation of variables. Proportion of subjects reasoning on the transitional level is not reported for the chemicals tasks.

Kuhn, Langer, Kohlberg, and Haan (1977)—Total sample size was 265, including 32 10–15-year-olds. Scores listed are approximations taken from Figure 4, p. 115; exact percentages were not specified.

Lovell (1961)—Total sample was 200, 8–32-year-olds. For chemicals task, n=39, including "grammer school" subjects (comparable to American junior and senior high school students), as well as "training college" subjects (students enrolled in professional teacher education programs), frequently teacher education programs), and adults. Exact size of each group is not given. For the invisible magnetization task, n=38, including grammer school students, training college students, and adults. For the motion on a horizontal plane task, n=28, including grammer school students and adults. Exact size of each group is not given. For the balance task, n=10, including training college students only.

McKinnon and Renner (1971)—A score of 0–4 was possible for each subject on each of five tasks. The total score earned determined subjects' stage score, as follows: 0–9: concrete operational; 10–13: transitional; 14–20: formal operational.

Pitt (1977)—Total sample size was 35, including 14 10th grade high school students. Stage score was assigned using Dale's (1970) scoring rules.

Renner and Lawson (1973)—Total sample size was 381, including 99 11th grade students and 97 12th grade students.

Roberge and Flexer (1979)—The formal operations level criterion was a score at the formal level on at least two of the three tasks. Total sample size was 144, including 72 early adolescent males and females. Researchers constructed paper-and-pencil tests to assess comprehension and/or application of the three Piagetian operations listed. To be classified as formal, a subject had to correctly answer at least 75% of the items for a given measure.

Schwebel (1972)—The shadows and chemicals tasks were also used in the study, but incidence of formal operational thinking could not be determined from their report.

Schwebel (1975)—The SAT-V and SAT-M scores were each almost a standard deviation above the national mean for each of six groups. The males scored significantly ($p < .01$) higher than the females on the SAT-M; however, this factor was not statistically controlled.

Sinnott (1975)—Paper and pencil written formals were designed by the author to measure combinational and proportional reasoning in both familiar and formal (unfamiliar) versions. The formal operations level criterion was to earn a passing score on each test. "Subjects were given a passing score if they either gave the correct answer, or explained their manner of reaching an answer in such a way as to show that they could have given the correct answer if it were not for arithmetic error or an oversight" (p. 434).

Sinnott and Guttmann (1978)—The baking a cake or mixing paint problems were designed by the authors to assess manipulation of proportional relationships.

Storck, Looft, and Hooper (1972)—This task was based on Lovell and Ogilvie's (1961) description. Formal operations level criterion was not specified; the figure reported here is based on the number of subjects passing 7 or more of the 9 subtrials.

Tomlinson-Keasey (1972)—Total sample size was 89, including 6th grade girls. Exact number of subjects per group is not given.

Tomlinson-Keasey and Keasey (1974)—Total sample was 54, including 30 6th grade girls. The formal operations level criterion was a score at the formal level on at least two of the three tasks.

man, 1978). Some of these additional tasks represent paper-and-pencil adaptations of the original Inhelder and Piaget (1958) tasks (e.g., Dulit, 1972), while others are adaptations to new content areas (e.g., Kuhn and Brannock's, 1977, plant problem). This information is given in the Notations for Table 1.1, which also lists additional information on sample characteristics, scoring rules used, formal level criteria used, etc. (A ''2'' appears on the table near the author's name when a notation has been added.)

There is also a considerable variability in the degree of specificity with which the results are reported regarding subject performance across tasks. Only fifteen of the twenty-five studies summarized in Table 1.1 reported separately the results for the individual tasks. The remaining ten studies in this group reported only composite scores. (These are noted with the notation ''3'' on Table 1.1.) Of these, only four (Arlin, 1975; Schwebel, 1972; Sinnott, 1975; and Tomlinson-Keasey and Keasey, 1974) reported the criteria by which formal operational level across tasks was determined (e.g., performing at a formal operational level on two of the three tasks administered). Because of the differences in criteria used to arrive at an overall score, the comparability of results across studies is difficult to ascertain. Valuable information on task variability is masked by this procedure.

While most studies test each subject on more than one task, only six of the twenty-five studies described here (Kitchener and King, 1981; Kuhn, Langer, Kohlberg, and Haan, 1977; Lovell, 1961; Roberge and Flexer, 1979; Ross, 1973; Schwebel, 1975) address the question of intrasubject variation across the tasks by reporting intertask correlation coefficients. Bart, Frey, and Baxter (1979) addressed this question more precisely by reporting all eleven task response patterns that were observed after administering five formal operations tasks. This procedure yielded information on the proportion of subjects in each subsample who scored at the formal level on each task and on each combination of tasks. This approach is extremely informative, and its use should be strongly considered by other researchers.

Information on subject variability across tasks is particularly important for researchers investigating the difficulty level of individual tasks as a task demand variable (discussed below). Further, such information is very helpful in establishing criteria for selecting which task(s) to use in future studies.

Predictably, Table 1.1 reflects a great diversity of adult samples, where the age range varied from eighteen to seventy-nine years. The description of the sample characteristics was often lacking. Some researchers either omitted the number of subjects per age group (e.g., Lovell, 1961; Tomlinson-Keasey, 1972), or described the groups with a label that is not necessarily indicative of age (e.g., Lovell's [1961] ''training college'' students; Tomlinson-Keasey's [1972] ''women''; or Elkind's [1962] ''college students''). Elkind's students, for example, spanned an age range of two decades. Such labelling makes it difficult to categorize the results using even a very general distinction such as early and middle adulthood, which in turn makes it more difficult to identify developmental trends in the data.

It is also important to note in summarizing these studies that none in this group utilized a longitudinal design, a problem which is typical of the research on formal operations in general. Longitudinal studies of the development of formal reasoning have been done with children (e.g., Neimark, 1975b), but this research methodology has not been extended to the adult years.

In spite of these methodological limitations, the conclusion stated above still seems reasonable: A sizable proportion of the normal adult population does not reason at formal levels when tested on formal operations tasks. The rates of successful performance (i.e., scoring at the fully formal level) averaged 40–70 percent for the college students and adults tested in these samples. Further, the successful performance rate for about one-third of the samples tested was below 30 percent. These data are clearly a challenge to the assumption of the universality of attainment of the formal operations level.

Many researchers, inluding Piaget himself, have attempted to explain these findings. Piaget (1972) addressed the issue of the degree of attainment of formal operational thinking by late adolescents in light of several studies in which the age norms were different from those found in his own studies. He explains the variance in levels of reasoning by reference to the increasing differentiation of aptitudes:

> All normal subjects attain the stage of formal operations or structuring if not between 11–12 to 14–15 years, in any case between 15 and 20 years. However, they reach this stage in different areas according to their aptitudes and their professional specializations (advanced studies or different types of apprenticeship for the various trades): the way in which these formal structures are used, however, is not necessarily the same in all cases. (pp. 9–10)

Piaget suggests that if the experimental situation does not correspond to subjects' aptitudes and interests, some subjects might appear to be reasoning at a concrete level, whereas a formal level would more accurately reflect their level of thinking in their particular fields. This hypothesis is strongly supported by DeLisi and Staudt's (1980) study of formal reasoning by college men in three academic majors (physics, political science, and English). They administered three formal reasoning tasks that were selected because of their correspondence to each of the academic majors listed above: the pendulum problem, political socialization concepts task, and a literary analysis task, respectively. They found nonsignificant main effects for major and task, but a significant ($p < .01$) major × task interaction. The proportion of students within each major who scored at the formal operational level was consistently higher than that of their counterparts on the task whose content corresponded to their major field of study. These authors conclude, as Piaget suggested, that "adults can be expected to function at their highest levels of thought when working on content which fits their aptitudes and interests'' (DeLisi and Staudt, 1980, p. 207).

Flavel and Wohlwill (1969) have addressed this type of intrasubject variability by reference to the ''competence-performance distinction'' (p. 69): What one is fundamentally capable (competent) of doing as distinguished from how one acts (performs) in a given situation. The content area of the task used, then, may act as a performance variable which may interfere with making an accurate competence assessment of a subject's reasoning level. Piaget thus explained the discrepant findings as ''false negatives'' due to characteristics of the testing procedures, an interpretation that remained consistent with the hypothesized universality of formal operational thinking among postadolescents.

Another interpretation consistent with the assumption of universality is provided by Mortorano (1975), who argued that variability across content domains is more likely true for transitional subjects who are presumably in early adolescence than for subjects with a well-integrated formal structure. The data on adult formal reasoning levels reported in Table 1.1, however, do not support this interpretation. As Keating (1980) notes, ''task variables seem to operate in highly similar fashion regardless of the age of the subject'' (p. 216).

The task demand variable has received a great deal of attention as an explanatory variable. Flavell and Wohlwill (1969) cite several factors related to task difficulty:

> ...the stimulus materials and their familiarity, the manner of presentation of the relevant information and the amount of irrelevant information from which it has to be abstracted, the sheer magnitude of the information load placed on the child in dealing with the problem, the role played by memory and sequential processing of information, and so on. (p. 99)

Building on the work of Wohlwill (1973) and his own studies of developmental assessment, Rest (1979a) has suggested that the observed variability in subject performance across tasks is inconsistent with a simple stage model of development, typically characterized by emphasis on qualitative differences only, a very high degree of stage unity, step-by-step invariant sequence, and error-free, context-independent assessment. He proposes a more complex developmental model that helps account for subject variability across tasks. This model provides a framework for understanding the results summarized in Table 1.1. As Rest (1979a) notes, ''The question of developmental assessment should not be, 'What stage is a person in?' but rather, 'To what extent and under what conditions does a person manifest the various types of organizations of thinking?' '' (p. 63).

For example, Sinnott's (1975) and Kuhn and Brannock's (1977) research on the use of familiar materials or contexts examines the role of experience and the influence of the cultural milieu as conditions affecting formal operational thinking. Researchers who have offered variations on or alternatives to the traditional

Inhelder and Piaget (1958) tasks also offer ways of exploring factors that contribute to subject variability in performance. While this type of "creative assessment" is a nightmare for the researcher trying to identify trends across studies, these developments nevertheless serve several purposes: they indicate the need for more sophisticated assessment methodologies, they chart progress toward the refinement of existing procedures and they show, as Rest (1979a) has noted, that the developmental "baby" need not be thrown out with the developmental assessment "bathwater."

NEW THEORETICAL DEVELOPMENTS

It is difficult, if not impossible, to separate the complexities of developmental assessment and analysis from the theoretical assumptions in which assessment procedures are grounded. Thus, while problems seemingly related to assessment difficulties spur researchers to develop better assessment tools, they also spur theorists to question and reevaluate their assumptions and to posit better definitions or more explicit descriptions. And so it has been with formal operations research.

Ironically, it was Inhelder and Piaget themselves who first noted what has become a major point of controversy in discussions about the explanatory power of the formal operations construct. As Keating (1980) so aptly points out:

> A point made by Piaget, but not often noted by Piagetian commentators, is that although the acquisition of formal logic by the adolescent underlies many of the observable changes in adolescent thinking, it does not account for all of them: "There is more to thinking than logic" (Inhelder and Piaget, 1958, p. 335, quoted by Keating, p. 212).

Yet the focus of the model on logical-algebraic thinking and hypothetico-deductive reasoning has led some researchers (Braine and Rumain, 1983; Ennis, 1975; Falmagne, 1975, 1980; Leiser, 1982) to question Piaget's intent in using a theoretical model based in formal logic, and to suggest new ways of interpreting Piaget's model that retain a scheme that generates all possible hypotheses and yet is free from the logical inconsistencies that appear in Piaget's model. For example, depending on the interpretive scheme used to understand the intent of Piaget's logic, it can be argued that the logic in Piaget's model requires the existence of cases that intuition does not require, and further, that the logical operations of implication and converse implication are incompatible. (The interested reader should consult Braine and Rumain [1983] for an extended discussion of these problems.) Falmagne (1975, 1980) has carried this argument further by noting that the Inhelder and Piaget (1958) tasks "...explore a scientific type of reasoning; they involved obtaining and interpreting evidence, and study the child as scientist rather than the child as logician" (quoted from Braine and Rumain, 1983, p. 316). He notes here, for example, that while logic plays an important part in interpreting scientific evidence, its role is insignificant in determining which data to gather, a critical function for a successful scientist. Thus, this criticism of Piaget's emphasis on a logical model stems from the inconsistencies with assumptions that are based on "pure logic" and the subsequent realization that "logical reasoning" does not adequately describe scientific reasoning.

Neimark (1979), in her most recent review of formal operations research, presents a very different approach in summarizing the criticisms arising from the model's emphasis on the logical reasoning. As she notes,

> Several authors have, rightly, noted that a narrow focus upon hypothetico-deductive reasoning overlooks all the richness and complexity of thought during early and middle adulthood which arises from dealing with attendant practical, social, and philosophical problems. (p. 61)

Whether adults do in fact experience further structural development beyond formal operations (perhaps through successfully dealing with the types of problems Neimark describes) is a question that has emerged among several researchers and theorists (e.g., Arlin, 1975, 1977; Broughton, 1978; Gilligan and Murphy, 1979; Kitchener and King, 1981; Richards and Commons, 1984; Riegel, 1973; Sinnott, 1984). In noting the types of recent theoretical advances made in the field of cognitive development, Flavell and Markman (1983) observed that:

> One of the more striking changes is the movement away from orthodox Piagetian theory. It is a tribute to Jean Piaget's greatness that almost everything people think and do in this field has some connection with questions that Piaget raised... Although investigators continue to address these fundamental Piagetian questions of cognitive development, the nature of the answers has changed greatly. (pp. viii–ix)

The nature of the questions, however, has also changed. For example, Siegler's (1976) work on a rule-based model of information processing exemplifies the shift in researchers' questions from observations about performance to observations about rule systems used to guide predictions and subsequent performance. Wood's (1983) use of an inquiring systems approach (Churchman, 1971) to analyze different types of problems exemplifies a refinement in thinking about the basic nature of problems themselves, or how we define their solutions.

This relatively new focus on different strategies used to solve problems has led to several new developments and insights in the field of metacognition (e.g., Flavell, 1979; Kitchener, 1983a). Kitchener (1983a), for example, has posited a three-level model of cognitive processing. At level 1, individuals engage in such cognitive tasks as computing, memorizing, reading, perceiving, acquiring language, etc. Level 2, metacognition, is defined as "the processes which are invoked to monitor cognitive progress when an individual is engaged in level 1 cognitive tasks..." (p. 225). Level 3, epistemic cognition, is defined as "the process an individual invokes to monitor the epistemic nature of problems and the truth value of alternative solutions. It includes the individual's knowledge about the limits of knowing..., the certainty of knowing..., and the criteria for knowing" (pp. 225–26). The reasoning strategies that exemplify formal reasoning are characteristic of level 2 processes, such as planning what combinations of chemicals to mix in the chemicals tasks. Several of the criticisms of the limits of formal logic in adequately describing adult thought (e.g., Neimark, 1979, quoted above) do so on level 3 grounds: Not all problems faced by adults can be resolved using formal logic, even flawless logic. As Kitchener (1983a) notes in describing epistemic cognition, "It is knowledge of whether our cognitive strategies are sometimes limited, in what ways solutions can be true, and whether reasoning correctly about a problem necessarily leads to an absolutely correct solution" (p. 226). The wisdom of Inhelder and Piaget (1958) has now come full circle: There is in fact more to thinking than logic.

It is important to note that these new developments by American psychologists are not inconsistent with recent research by members of the Genevan School, including Piaget and Inhelder. As Bullinger and Chatillon (1983) note, research from the Genevan School is increasingly focused on the relationships between representation and action at different points in development. "The study of strategies for solving problems attempts to specify the manner in which subjects do or do not make use of the mental means available to them to produce an action within a defined task" (p. 232). This emphasis on the study of reasoning strategies and their acquisition reflects a shift in the central concern of the Genevan researchers away from the initial formulations which investigated how Piaget's theory of formal operational thought could be used to describe the observed changes in the quality of thought occurring at about the time of adolescence. Gallagher and Reid (1981) have termed this a shift from stress on structures related to stages (Piaget, 1953) to stress on mechanisms (e.g., Sinclair, 1977). The stress on mechanisms is one where questions of reasoning processes and strategies are of central concern, a focus which is similar in intent to that of Siegler (1976).

Further, the Genevans are also interested in questions of metacognitive analyses (although they do not appear to use this term for it). As Bullinger and Chatillon (1983) point out,

It is not sufficient that the child has acquired a certain instrument of knowledge or reasoning mechanism for her to know how to use them. We also need to ask about *the manner in which she chooses or actualizes a given structure rather than another to assimilate the situation facing her* [italics added]. In the generally complex assimilation process, it is also appropriate to analyze what role each particular form of reasoning plays in the set of solution processes. (p. 233)

In other words, we need to investigate the metacognitive as well as cognitive strategies used to resolve given problems. These examples show that the American and Genevan schools, with their different histories, methodologies, and priorities, have nevertheless converged in their identification of new directions to be explored.

SUMMARY

Inhelder and Piaget's (1958) publication of *The Growth of Logical Thinking from Childhood to Adolescence* sparked a remarkable amount of interest in questions related to cognitive development, especially among adolescents and adults. Twenty-five years later, it is sometimes difficult to distinguish between Piagetian research and Piagetian-inspired research in this area, a testament to his pervasive influence on the field. During this period of time, we have witnessed some dramatic changes in both the nature of the questions being asked and the answers being offered. Foundational assumptions such as stage unity across tasks and universality of attainment of formal operations have been strongly challenged by research findings, resulting in new theoretical propositions and hypotheses that take these "unpredicted" findings into account. Perhaps more predictably, methodological issues (e.g., use of familiar tasks or familiar content areas) continue to serve as catalysts for raising and answering new theoretical questions.

A central issue to be addressed now is the role of formal reasoning in accurately describing adult thought and its evolution. Formal reasoning has emerged as one component of the complex, interrelated system of components differentiating it from childhood and adolescent reasoning. Whether formal reasoning functions as a necessary but not sufficient condition for higher order reasoning, whether it represents one of several aspects of thinking that develop in a parallel fashion, or whether the true relationship has yet to even be hypothesized cannot be ascertained at this time. What can be said is that we are now aware of many methodological constraints that cloud our vision (many of which we know how to alleviate) and have several new theoretical tools to assist us in improving our understanding of adult reasoning. As Broughton (1984) has aptly reminded us, "The issue is not one of the stage 'beyond formal operations'; it is one of the stage 'beyond Piaget' " (p. 411).

Nevertheless, within the component of adult reasoning that Piaget's theory of formal operations does describe, much is left to be learned. The conditions under which adults access formal reasoning structures, the types of problems they identify as being amenable to logical resolution, and the role of content familiarity in adults' mastery of formal reasoning problems are only a few of many fertile areas for future research.

There is definitely a need as well for further investigation into assessment procedures themselves. As noted earlier in this review (see Table 1.1), the number of formal reasoning tasks that researchers are using is now equal to (and likely greater than) the number of tasks developed by Inhelder and Piaget. The type and variability of tasks across content areas and type of tasks (e.g., production, recognition, pencil-and-paper) as well as some provocative results based on their use (e.g., DeLisi and Staudt, 1980; Sinnott, 1975) offer researchers the opportunity to use these new assessment tools and methodologies to raise and answer previously undefined questions, both theoretical and empirical.

Lack of standardization of assessments procedures across studies continues to hamper attempts to draw reasonable conclusions about our knowledge base of adult formal reasoning. However, utilizing procedures discussed earlier in this review (e.g., reporting specific scoring rules used, reporting criteria for determining formal reasoning level, and reporting results for each task separately, even when a composite score is also reported) would greatly assist other researchers in evaluating new measures, in selecting which tasks to use and ultimately, in improving the level of standardization of assessment procedures.

A dramatic shift, or family of related shifts, that has been observed in the last twenty-five years is reflected in our new ability to ask more precise questions about mechanisms or processes of adult thought. Siegler's (1976) rule-based model of information processing, Kitchener's (1983a) three-level model of cognitive processing and Rest's (1979a) insights about simple and complex stage models each exemplifies the greater precision that has been achieved in articulating new research questions. In spite of these developments and the serious questioning of some of the major assumptions of his original theory, Piaget's theory of formal operational thinking nevertheless continues to serve as an important foundation, albeit an historical if not a complete theoretical foundation, for current research on adult intellectual thought.

2

Problem Finding and Young Adult Cognition

Patricia Kennedy Arlin

The early work on problem finding was directed toward the identification of those cognitive process variables which would best predict the quality of questions one raises in ill-defined problem situations (Arlin 1974, 1975–76; Mackworth, 1965). The origin of the term problem finding is somewhat obscure. The sociologist Merton (1945) used the term problem finding to describe the unique contributions of scientists whose questions brought about major shifts in thinking within their disciplines. Getzels (1964) described eight types of problems and processes of solution along a continuum from ''presented problem situations'' to ''discovered problem situations.'' The former begins with problems for which both the solution and the means of obtaining that solution are known to both the presenter and the solver. The latter are problems for which there is no known method of solution nor is there a known means of evaluating the correctness of the solution once it is obtained. Gradually these ''discovered problems'' become problem finding for Getzels.

Getzels and Csikszentmihalyi (1965) used this notion of ''discovered problems'' to characterize the creative productions of young artists. They suggested that the artist's ''concern for discovery'' as represented through the artist's own work, in selecting objects for and completing a still life drawing, are directly related to the subsequent judgments of the creative and overall aesthetic quality of that work.

Their early work with artists and their discovered problems evolved into a ten-year study of problem finding in art (1976). They defined problem finding as functioning effectively in a discovered problem situation (p.82). While the work of Getzels and Csikszentmihalyi provides a type of process model of problem finding, it was in Mackworth's (1965) work that an attempt was made to provide an operational definition of problem finding. Mackworth's definition contrasted problem finding with problem solving.

Mackworth defined problem solving as the ''selection and use of an existing program from an existing set of programs." He defined problem finding as "the detection of the need for a new program by comparing existing and expected future programs (i.e., to devise new programs)." The outcome of the problem solving process was "the discovery of one specific acceptable answer to one well-defined problem." The outcome of problem finding was "the discovery of many general questions from many ill-defined problems" (p. 57).

It was Mackworth's emphasis on "the question" in problem finding which led me to search for a cognitive process model of problem finding. The role of "the question" in art and in science in the formulation of problems seemed fundamental to great discoveries in both fields. Wertheimer (1945) hinted at this when he commented:

> the function of thinking is not just solving an actual problem but discovering, envisaging, going into deeper questions. Often in great discovery the most important thing is that a certain question is found. Envisaging, putting the productive question is often more important, often a greater achievement than solution of a set question. (p. 123)

This type of questioning seems to be peculiar to adult thinking if it occurs at all. An intriguing issue is the issue of why there are so few "productive questions" within the disciplines. A second issue immediately follows on this first. What types of cognitive processes are involved in generating productive questions and to what extent are these processes also developmental processes?

During the past ten years I have used three models in an attempt to describe these processes. The first model involved classical cognitive variables and their interrelations. The second model was a cognitive developmental model which contained stage-related properties. The third model was an information processing model. Each of the three models represents either a structural or a strategic model of problem finding. The new model proposed here is a model which unifies strategies and structures in the differentiation of young adult cognition from adolescent cognition. It is a model which redefines problem finding as one dimension of young adult cognition rather than as synonymous with it.

Each of the three early models made its own unique contribution to the problem of the separation of adolescent cognition from young adult cognition. This separation is substantial enough to warrant the use of stage terms in the description of the differences.

The contributions of each of these three models will be described in turn. Then the current working model will be described along with the program of research that it inspires.

The first model: a cognitive processes model. This model was built upon Getzels and Csikszentmihalyi's (1965) description of "discovered problems" and Mackworth's (1965) definition of problem finding in terms of the discovery of generic questions. The first cognitive model of problem finding which I used included selected variables drawn from Guilford's (1959) "structure of the intellect model''; Schroeder, Driver, and Steufert's (1967) levels of information processing and Inhelder and Piaget's (1958) formal operational schemes (Arlin, 1975–76).

The initial test of the model involved the presentation of a stimulus array. The array was made up of a set of objects that Dunker (1945) used in his studies of problem solving. Some of the objects were an index card with a dime-sized hole in its center, a C-clamp, a coin, and two six-foot long cords. The reason for selecting objects traditionally used in problem solving research for this study of problem finding was that an argument could be made that these objects were problem-rich objects. They could provide a basis for the question-asking task which provided the main measure of problem finding. Given Mackworth's definition of problem finding, the opportunity for subjects to ask questions seemed essential for the study. This array of objects served as the ''input'' for the model of problem finding.

The outputs of the model were the various organizations of information that could be inferred from the types of questions posed and the types of cognitive operations that correlated with these outputs. At each major point along the problem finding process failure to employ a mainline process, such as the integration of information, results in the production of a lower level question which is designated as an output. The failure to integrate information results in the output of ''classes'' type questions. If each of the mainline processes is in evidence, the final output is problem finding, if not, the resulting outputs are in the form of lower level questions. The products categories from Guilford's ''structure of the intellect model'' were those used originally to distinguish one question from another. Each category was viewed as a way in which the information a person takes in from the stimulus array is organized and processed and finally produced in the form of a question.

While the model was a simplistic one it became the basis for further explorations of problem finding and problem defining. Two observations were made across subjects and contexts on the basis of the initial study. There was, for adolescents and young adults, a consistent negative correlation between the quality and quantity of questions any one individual would pose. This was of the order of $r = -.60$. For children under the age of twelve the opposite was true (Arlin, 1974, 1975–76, 1977). The second most powerful predictor of quality after question quantity was the individual's performance on three of Inhelder and Piaget's (1958) formal tasks. While some of the typical divergent thinking factors accounted for a small percentage of the variance in problem-finding performance, the ability to reason using the formal operational schemes, appeared as the single, most important cognitively related variable.

Thus this first model led to the question of the role of developmental variables in problem finding. It resulted in emphasis being shifted from a description of cognitive process variables that might be involved in problem finding to a search for developmental prerequisites and to a cognitive developmental definition of problem finding.

The second model: a cognitive developmental model. It became clear upon replication of the earlier studies that formal operational thought might not relate only to problem-finding performance, but that it also might be the necessary but not sufficient condition for it (Arlin, 1975, 1977, 1984a). The possibility of this relationship led to an argument for structural development beyond formal operations. I chose to characterize this development as the problem-finding stage or "fifth stage" (Arlin, 1975). I described this new stage in terms of the processes associated with discovered problems (Getzels, 1964; Getzels and Csikszentmihalyi, 1965, 1976); the raising of many general questions from many ill-defined problems (Mackworth, 1965); and the slow cognitive growth represented in the development of significant scientific thought (Gruber, 1973). While the very notion of a stage is a controversial one, the possibility of characterizing processes and structures "beyond formal operations" has been proposed by Neimark* in her description of wisdom as well as by Meechan (1983); by Case (1978) in terms of "third order operations" as well as by Commons, Richards, and Kuhn (1982) who term these third order operations, "metasystematic" reasoning; and by Riegel (1973) and Basseches (1980) who describe the fifth stage as the stage of dialectic operations.

There is another rationale for separating out the processes associated with problem finding from those associated with formal operations. A careful analysis of Inhelder and Piaget's (1958) description of hypothetico-deductive reasoning in the formal operational stage leads to the recognition that in each instance they are describing subject's responses to problems which have been presented to them for a solution. These formal operational problems are archtypical examples of Getzels (1964) "presented problems." "Discovered problems" are simply not accounted for in the traditional Piagetian framework. Each formal operational task requires the discovery of one specific answer to one well-defined question. Hence, in Mackworth's (1965) terms, subjects are engaged in sophisticated problem-solving situations.

The distinction made by Getzels and Csikszentmihalyi as well as by Mackworth, between the formulation, finding, or definition of the productive question or problem and the solution of that problem once formulated, is an important distinction to be made within cognitive developmental models of adolescent and young adult thought.

The third model. a cognitive science model. Several inferences can be made from both the classical and the cognitive developmental representations of problem finding. These inferences serve as bridges to a representation of problem finding that is firmly based in cognitive science. These inferences can be grouped as: (1) inferences about the organization of information within a problem space; (2) inferences about formal operational schemes functioning as operators on ele-

---

*Edith Neimark, discussant comments in symposium: "New perspectives on formal operations reasoning" (R. S. Siegler, Chair), at the Biennial Meeting of the Society for Research in Child Development, Denver, Colorado, March 1975.

ments within a problem space; and (3) inferences about the special role of the formal operational scheme of the coordination of two or more systems (or frames) of reference (Inhelder and Piaget, 1958), as both a process for restructuring the original problem space and as the product of that restructuring.

The type of model of problem finding which emerges within a cognitive science framework involves the application of the concept of frames (Minsky, 1977); levels of organization; the definition of specific operators and the displacement of concepts (Schon, 1963). Anomalies, conflicts, and discrepancies introduced in the initial phase of search within a problem space may hold the key to the processes of problem finding in that space. The types of questions raised, in the face of discrepant information, may define the existing problem space or require the restructuring of that space. This restructuring may result in either a redefinition of the original problem or in the construction of a new problem space which may be the "discovered problem."

Sternberg and Davidson (1983) in their information processing description of "insight in the gifted" seem to hint at a similar set of processes. They define insight in terms of three kinds of skills:

> (a) selective encoding, by which relevant information in a given context is sifted from irrelevant information; (b) selective combination, by which relevant information is combined in a novel and productive way; and (c) selective comparison, by which new information is related in a novel way to old information. (p. 51)

The possibility exists that Mackworth (1965), Schon (1963), and Sternberg and Davidson (1983) are each describing the basic process of problem finding within their own frameworks. But the developmental question still remains, through what mechanisms are these processes and skills acquired? This question leads to the necessity of combining models of structures with models of strategies into one model of young adult cognition.

TOWARD A UNIFIED MODEL

Each of the previous three models represented an attempt to describe the problem finding process. More recently, I have returned to the Piagetian model and to the adoption of a broader view of a fifth stage or a stage of postformal thought (Arlin, 1984a). This return provides the opportunity to consider a unification of strategies and structures into a more comprehensive view of adult cognition for which problem finding is simply a part of a greater whole.

> Apostle (1979) provides the basis for this reformulation:
> I think something that has to happen after the formal stage has been reached is the combination of different spaces of possibilities.... [This involves two

simultaneous moves]...contractions and expansions. [Both] consist in the comparison of different types of universal logical possibilities.... These contractions and expansions consist in the comparison of different types of universal logical possibilities and these comparisons...would be the combination, the synthesis of very many INRC groups with each other. (p. 11)

Apostle's description of postformal thought seems to suggest a basic contradiction. The contradiction is that postformal thought can be characterized as representing both contractions of logical systems and expansions of those same systems. There is a way in which Apostle's description can be seen to employ Bohr's (1934) "principle of complementarity" with respect to psychological phenomena rather than physical phenomena. In other words, what appear to be apparently paradoxical, contradictory accounts of adult cognition (contractions and expansions) should not divert our attention from the wholeness and richness of that cognition. The inherent contradiction in studying adult cognition is the type of contradiction that lies at the heart of major breakthroughs in science.

The apparent contradiction of postformal thought being both a contraction and an expansion of logical systems as described by Apostle suggests a type of relativity of thought. Such thought is relative in the sense that in one context it can best be characterized as a contraction of logic, and in another context, it is best characterized as an expansion of thought. There is a second sense in which postformal thought can be described as a type of relativity of thought. It appears that some adults characterize their own knowing in relative terms. They recognize that all knowledge is relative. They can make decisions on the basis of available information, but they remain receptive to new information which may alter their view. This type of relativity of thought may represent optimal adult thought. Such relativity of thought simply is not present in descriptions of adolescent cognition (Arlin, 1984a; Kramer, 1983; Murphy and Gilligan, 1980). It is the type of relativity of thought alluded to by Sinnott (1981); Labouvie-Vief (1982) and Meechan (1983).

Apostle's conception of postformal thought can be seen as an extension of the classical Piagetian position. This extension is accomplished if one studies the possibility of the formal scheme of "the coordination of two or more systems of reference" (Inhelder and Piaget, 1958) functioning as a bridge between formal and postformal thought as I have suggested elsewhere (Arlin, 1984a).

This relativity of thought is not only consistent with the general Piagetian model but it is also consistent with alternative descriptions of adult thought which often appear to be contradictory. If "contractions" and "expansions" are characteristic of relativistic, flexible, postformal thought then various conflicting statements on the nature of young adult thought can be reconciled and the diverse characteristics of that thought can be unified.

A partial list of the contractions and expansions which are used to characterize young adult thought form the framework for the search for structures and strategies associated with postformal thought. Apostle's concept of "contraction" is used here to represent findings in research on adult cognition which suggest less than optimal performance in the use of logical, rational systems of thought. The list of contractions includes:

1. Problem solving which often requires procedures of search which use classificatory and serial abilities and skills rather than combinations of all possible values of variables and their relations (Apostle, 1979; Simon, 1978, 1979);
2. Decision making by adults which often is compromised by both faulty logic and simplified representations of reality (Shaklee, 1979; Slovic, Fischoff, and Lichtenstein, 1977). A good example of this type of decision making is Simon's (1957) concept of "bounded rationality" whereby adults appear to make decisions on a less than rational basis.
3. Discovery-oriented behaviors of scientists (and artists) which often involve overgeneralization and the conscious ignoring of negative instances in the search for new explanations (representations) of phenomena (Karmiloff-Smith and Inhelder, 1974).

Other research on adult cognition results in a list of expansions and/or extenstions of logical systems. These expansions suggest a type of performance which extends a logical system(s) beyond normal limits and which may represent the creation of new systems of thought. Some of the expansions associated with the stage of postformal reasoning include:

1. Problem finding which may represent one dimension among the several that are unified structurally;
2. Metasystematic reasoning across systems as opposed to hypothetico-deductive reasoning within one system, which requires what Commons, Richards, and Kuhn (1982) have described as third order operations;
3. Dialectic operations which are directed at the creation and tolerant coexistence of inconsistence rather than its removal (Riegel, 1973);
4. Displacement of concepts and the use of metaphor as a process of thought (Schon, 1963).

This partial list of "contractions" and "expansions" which simultaneously characterize adult cognition provides a framework for research on postformal thought and leads to the definition of a course of action in the search for structures. It also leads to the attempt to develop a comprehensive model of young adult cognition which unifies both structures and strategies.

Any unified model of postformal thought must take into account the "contractions" represented in problem-solving, decision-making, and discovery-oriented behaviors as well as the "expansions" represented in problem finding, metasystematic reasoning, dialectical operations, and the displacement of concepts. If a model of the postformal or fifth stage in cognitive development can encompass the "contractions" represented in some forms of problem-solving, decision-making, and discovery-oriented behavior as well as the "expansions" represented in problem finding, metasystematic reasoning, dialectical operations, and the displacement of concepts, the next step is to show how these contractions and expansions evolve and merge into a picture of young adult cognition. It is the problem of determining if there is a ''structure d'ensemble'' that provides the scaffolding for young adult cognition.

CURRENT RESEARCH

The context of my present research efforts is problem-solving and problem-finding behavior in art and in science as elicited from young students working within these disciplines who are fifteen to twenty-one years of age.* The study provides an opportunity to observe the emergence and blending of these contractions and expansions in thought. If the onset of formal operations spans the years of eleven to fourteen, and if the full consolidation of formal operations may require several years, the fifteen-year-old should be the ideal subject to begin a study of his/her acquisition, consolidation, and integration of the formal operational schemes. The argument is not that all fifteen-year-olds will be formal operational. It is rather that at age fifteen one has an opportunity to observe a fair proportion of persons who have the potential for this type of thought. By twenty-one years there should be some evidence of the emergence of new thought forms characteristic of young adults if the argument for a postformal stage is valid. A number of studies suggest that significant differences in performance exist across these age groups and indicate that the shift from an absolute to a relative point of view begins to take place (Kramer, 1983; Murphy and Gilligan, 1980; Perry, 1970).

The study is now in its third year. The design of the study is a modification of the Nessleroade and Baltes (1974) longitudinal-sequential design. The three age groups used in the study began the study at ages fifteen, seventeen, and nineteen years. At the conclusion of the study these same subjects will be seventeen, nineteen and twenty-one respectively. Through the use of this design it is possible to observe not only interindividual but also intraindividual changes occurring in the transition from formal to postformal thinking in fifteen to twenty-one year olds.

The general hypothesis is that across the age range of fifteen to twenty-one years, both interindividually and intraindividually the emergence, consolidation, and integration of the formal operational schemes will precede the emergence of the schemes, operations, and strategies associated with postformal thinking. Implicit in this hypothesis is the strategic role of the Piagetian formal scheme of the coordination of two or more systems of reference. The presence of this scheme should signal the emergence of relativistic, postformal thinking. In its

*This research is supported by a three-year grant from the Natural Science and Engineering Council of Canada.

absence, there should be little evidence of any of the "expansions" and "contractions" of thought associated with the new stage. The data generated by a series of tasks, observations, and interviews and their associated scoring procedures will yield information with respect to the list of "contractions" and "expansions" associated with postformal thought as well as developmental information with respect to the emergence and consolidation of the formal operational schemes.

The tasks consisted of (1) a group-administered test of formal reasoning (Arlin, 1984b) which provides data on the subject's performance on the eight formal operational schemes described by Inhelder and Piaget (1958). On the basis of this test a subject can be assigned an operational level from Concrete to High Formal and her specific performance on each of the schemes can be profiled; (2) a group-administered, problem-finding task (Arlin, 1975–76) which yields both a quality and a quantity score for the questions that subjects raise in completing this task; (3) a group-administered displacement of concept task (Schon, 1963; Arlin*) which is scored in a manner similar to the problem-finding task; (4) individually observed experimental studio-artistic (or laboratory-scientific) problem-formulation and problem-solving task which was adapted from Getzels and Csikszentmihalyi (1976). These observations are quantified in terms of the problem-finding stage, the problem-solution stage, and the subject's overall "concern for problem finding." The scoring scheme for these three phases is the same scheme used by Getzels and Csikszentmihalyi; (5) Individual interviews based on the set of questions employed by Getzels and Csikszentmihalyi (1976) are the last task. The questions in the interview include the following: (a) "Why do you paint?"; (b) "In what ways were your thoughts and working methods different in this experiment from your thoughts and methods when you work on your own?"; (c) "Why did you pick up these objects?" (the objects which were the stimuli for the drawing session); (d) "What meaning does this drawing have for you?"; (e) "Could any of the elements in your drawing be eliminated or altered without destroying its character?"; and (f) "What were you thinking while you were drawing—what was your major concern?" These same questions were adapted to the "design an experiment" task for the science subjects. The interviews were scored on "concern for discovery" as defined by Getzels and Csikszentmihalyi (1976). The interview questions were analyzed for evidence of any of the twenty-four dialectical schemata in the manner described by Basseches (1980); and (g) Commons, Richards, and Kuhn's (1982) metasystematic reasoning task.

The types of tasks chosen provide an opportunity to study the emergence of both strategies and structures associated with postformal thinking. They provide as well a further exploration into the relations between problem solving and

---

*The protocols for the displacement of concepts task and for the other tasks described in this section may be obtained from the author.

problem finding. As an example consider the following responses to the interview question "Why do you do art?" of a small sample of fifteen- and nineteen-year-old artists.

15 Years

(S1) I do art for the fact of accomplishing and creating and in my creating of an image I can express all that I want to express.

(S2) I do art for many reasons, some of which I will explain. First of all it is something that I definitely enjoy. To do something completely original is the best way I can understand myself.... I love to create.... Furthermore, I am somewhat introverted and cannot explain my real feelings I can express them in my sketch book.

(S3) I do art because it's something I create and it gives me a sense of satisfaction when I complete it.... I enjoy the ability to get action and movement in my pictures.

19 years

(S10) There is a real need within me that needs to be expressively fulfilled. I must in my life have personal evidence of my individuality. There have been times wherein I did not do my art and I felt that I was fading, becoming insignificant.

(S11) I paint/draw, because I do it well. I paint/draw, because I can complete it myself, always.

(S12) To remain sane. To explore relationships. To see how the finished product affects me....To be able to manipulate my world.

(S13) "I am emotionally attracted to the effects the act has on my mind. I am thinking in my own way. I am rearranging and manipulating colors...according to innate feelings. I am responding to an inner need. I am sorting, seeking deeper meaning.

While the answers are rich and varied, they can be analyzed from a dialectic perspective, from a problem-finding framework and from the point of view of displacement of concepts. There is absolutism to the responses of the fifteen-year-olds, a single direction between the artist and the object of the artist's work. Contrast this with the interactive and existential responses of some of the nineteen-year-olds. The contrast is compelling.

This absolutism versus relativism in the nineteen-year-olds is particularly evident in their responses to a second question. Sense of discovery, of interacting with the materials, of creative tension is much more in evidence in their responses when they were asked "Could any of the elements in your drawing be eliminated or altered without destroying its character?" The fifteen-year-olds answered in turn: (S1) "No, none of the objects could be changed"; (S2) "Maybe I could have drawn the chest's lid open, elevated by the piece of wood going through the peg''; and (S3) ''For sure. Because I did a few drawings of several different drawings rather than a group.'' All were responding to the question in terms of a still life drawing they had completed under studio conditions as part of the study. While S3 seems to indicate an openness by his ''sure,'' it immediately becomes clear that he has interpreted the question quite differently. He seems to be asking himself the question ''Could I have made any other drawing using these still life subjects than the drawing which I actually produced?'' Some of the nineteen-year-olds responded with a sense of relativism. Their responses were as follows: (S10) ''Sure, I don't consider it finished''; (S11) ''Any of the objects could be replaced with simple geometric forms because I was concerned with getting a dark shadow''; (S12) ''Of course, because my art is a living thing with many interpretations and possibilities.'' These are only a sampling of subtle evidences of possibility of new thought forms in young adulthood. There is a sense of continuity and of discovery in the responses of the nineteen-year-olds which does not seem to be the concern of the adolescent artists.

This foregoing description of tasks and the examples hint at the richness of the data. Given the design, the completed project should provide some insight into how the various contractions and expansions of thought which are descriptive of adult cognition evolve across late adolescence as young artists and young scientists begin to formulate problems for their life's work and for their own lives.

CONCLUSIONS

Pasteur is said to have quipped that great discoveries do not simply happen by chance, they come to the ''prepared mind.'' Possibly that preparation is, in part, a cognitive developmental one in which the sophisticated problem-solving strategies of the formal operational stage are the necessary but not sufficient prerequisites for developing a questioning orientation in the discovery of problems regardless of the discipline in which they are found.

It may be true that on the surface of our experience discovered problems in art and in science may appear to have nothing in common. It may be that at a deeper level there are common cognitive processes, strategies, and structures that make the initial formulations possible. While the surface features of art and of science may appear to have little in common, the underlying rules generating the systems of thought which support them may be fundamentally the same. It is the search for these underlying rules and processes and for their cognitive developmental constraints that I believe characterizes the next step in the study of problem finding and of young adult cognition.

3

Dialectical Thinking and Young Adult Cognitive Development

Michael Basseches

Dialectical thinking—a form of cognitive organization which appears to develop in some individuals during the young adult years—creates in thought a new level of equilibrium transcending those provided by Piagetian cognitive structures. The development of dialectical thinking has profound implications for epistemological and metaphysical reasoning, as well as for individuals' approaches to analyzing various particular phenomena. These phenomena cover the full spectrum of natural science, social science, and humanities subject matters, as well as situations of day-to-day life. Furthermore, Loevinger's (1976) autonomous level of ego development, Kegan's (1982) interindividual ego-stage, Fowler's (1981) conjunctive level of faith development, and the integration of Kohlbergian principles of justice (1971) with the highest level of the morality of responsibility described by Carol Gilligan (1978, 1982), all depend on aspects of dialectical thinking (Basseches, 1984). This chapter will clarify the idea of dialectical thinking, illustrate its relevance to young adult reasoning, and describe the nature of the equilibrium which dialectical thinking provides in mature thought.

Consider the following scenario of young adult life where dialectical cognitive organization would make a difference in the analysis of phenomena. Two nondialectical, but not unusual, ways of thinking about the problem at hand, precede a third, dialectical alternative.

Mark, Howard, and George are college juniors. They are feeling very frustrated about three years of the routine of tests, paper assignments, and grades. They worry that going through this process has taken its toll, undermining their love of learning.

Mark is confused. Based on his own experience, it seems to him that students would learn much more if they were given more freedom to pursue their own intellectual interests, rather than being required to take standardized tests and complete standardized assignments. On the other hand, he assumes that the college is run by experienced educators, who must have determined that the use of tests and assigned papers to measure, and grades to motivate is the soundest educational method.

Howard is angry. He locates the cause of his own demoralization and that of his fellow students in teachers' illegitimate presumption that they can pass judgment on students' ideas. He believes that much of grading is subjective, and that teachers use their power to impose their own personal tastes on what students think and how students write. Although Howard doesn't accept it as educationally legitimate for teachers to dictate what students should learn and then to evaluate them by subjective standards, he does accept that that's the way the system works. He has decided that he wants to make it through the system and has cynically dedicated himself to cultivating the art of giving teachers what they want.

George begins to analyze the problem by locating the college within the larger society of which it is a part. The college is expected to perform a certification function for that society, by providing transcripts which other social institutions can use in their selection processes. But the college is also expected to provide students with a good education. The problem that he and Howard and Mark are experiencing reflects a contradiction between the certification and educational functions of the college. The need to provide certification (grades) to the outside leads the college and its faculty to employ practices which may not be educationally optimal (i.e., standardized assignments). Similarly, the concerns with providing a good education lead to practices which may not be certificationally optimal (i.e., grading students on subject matter where completely objective evaluation is impossible). George reasons that this contradiction will only really be resolved when the basic relationship of the colleges and universities to society is transformed. He decides that he will devote his time at college to trying to learn all he can that might help him contribute to that kind of transformation of educational institutions. He accepts that in the meantime, he will be given standardized assignments and grades and will have to make compromises just as his teachers do between what is educationally and certificationally optimal. But he is resolved not to lose sight of his own educational goals.

A conception of a dialectical philosophical perspective provides a basis for recognizing instances of psychological phenomena of dialectical thinking. The following account of this philosophical perspective is intended to clarify its underlying unity. In describing the dialectical philosophical perspective, this account casts a slightly broader net than many intellectual historians might. For the intellectual historian, actual historical connections among ideas and thinkers may be needed to establish a tradition; here, philosophical and psychological similarities are an adequate basis for grouping ideas and ways of thinking under the heading of the dialectical philosophical perspective.

THE DIALECTICAL PHILOSOPHICAL PERSPECTIVE

The dialectical perspective comprises a family of world-outlooks or views of the nature of existence (ontology) and knowledge (epistemology). These world-outlooks, while differing from each other in many respects, share a family resemblance based on three features—common emphases on change, on wholeness, and on internal relations.

Dialectical ontologies emphasize (1) that what is most fundamental in reality are some ongoing processes of change; (2) that in the course of these ongoing processes of change within existence as a whole, forms of organization emerge which have a coherence that cannot simply be accounted for by the nature of the parts that are organized within these forms (the forms are temporary and may disintegrate or give way to more complex forms of organization); (3) that everything that exists in relationship to other things, and that these relationships are internal to the nature of the things themselves—they are part of what makes the things what they are (and as a thing's internal relations change, its nature changes).

Similarly, dialectical epistemologies emphasize (1) that both individual and collective knowledge are essentially active processes of organizing and reorganizing understandings of phenomena; (2) that in these knowing processes there emerges individual and collective conceptual systems which give the knowledge a coherence that cannot simply be accounted for by the specific concepts, ideas, and facts organized within them; (3) that concepts, ideas, and facts exist in relationships not only to other concepts, ideas, and facts, but also the lives of the knowers who employ them. These relationships determine the meaning of the concepts, ideas, and facts and as these relationships change, the meanings of concepts, ideas, and facts change also.

What ties together the emphases on change, wholeness, and internal relations in dialectical world-outlooks is the concept of dialectic. This concept underlies both dialectical world-outlooks and the particular approaches to analysis which constitute dialectical thinking.

THE IDEA OF DIALECTIC

Dialectic is *developmental transformation (i.e., developmental movement through forms) which occurs via constitutive and interactive relationships.* The phrase, "movement *through* forms" is meant to distinguish such movement from movement *within* forms. To illustrate this distinction, consider what happens when a road is built from one city to another. The road has a certain form to it, and the form of that road regulates the movement of the vehicles which travel between those cities. Thus, we may take this movement of the vehicles as movement within forms. On the other hand, the movement or change associated with the decay of the road, the emergence of trouble spots in terms of accidents or traffic jams, and the process of building a new and better road with a different form to replace or supplement the old road can be seen as a movement through forms. Through the notion of movement through forms, or transformation, the definition of dialectic relies upon and presupposes both the notion of movement and the notion of form and focuses on a particular relationship between them. Describing this movement through forms or transformation as developmental implies that there is a certain direction to it. This direction is usually associated with increasing inclusiveness, differentiation, and integration.

The definition relates this developmental transformational movement to constitutive and interactive relationships. A relationship may be understood as a connection. Although a relationship is often thought of as a connection between things, where the things are taken to exist prior to the relationship, the phrase "constitutive relationship" is meant to indicate the opposite—that the relationship has a role in making the parties to the relationship what they are (cf., "internal relations," above). The adjective "interactive" implies that a relationship is not static but is characterized by motion or action of the parties upon each other.

Our example of the road will also serve to illustrate the concepts of constitutive and interactive relationships. Constitutive and interactive relationships can be identified among the builders of the road, the road itself, and the users of the road and their vehicles. The road is constituted not only by its interaction with road-builders (who build it) but also by its relationship with the vehicles which travel on it. For if no vehicles were permitted to travel on it, it would no longer be a road. It would perhaps be a road that had been converted to a mall. Or if only airplanes travelled on it, it would be a runway rather than a road. Thus, its being a road depends on its particular relationship to vehicles. Likewise, it is clearly relationships with roads that make road-builders *road-builders*. It is also, though perhaps less obviously, relationships with roads that make vehicles *vehicles*. Vehicles are vehicles because they have the capacity to transport one someplace, and the extent to which they have this capacity is dependent on the extent to which suitable thoroughfares exist.

The relationship between the vehicles and the road is interactive, as well as constitutive, in that the vehicles change the road and the road changes the vehicles. This should be clear from the previous discussion of road decay or wear (vehicles changing the road) and of developing trouble spots on the road which cause accidents to the vehicles (the road thus changing vehicles).

As was mentioned earlier, this interaction between road and vehicles leads to the transformation of the whole situation described earlier in terms of the building of a *new* road. This is the sense in which the transformation occurs via constitutive and interactive relationships. Thus, the movement whereby a new road is built as a result of the interactive and constitutive relationships among the previous road, the road-users and their vehicles, and the road-builders, may be seen as an instance of dialectic.

DIALECTICAL THINKING AND DIALECTICAL ANALYSES

Dialectical ontologies view existence as fundamentally a process of dialectic. Dialectical epistemologies view knowledge as a process of dialectic. Because dialectical thinking derives from a general world-outlook, individual dialectical thinkers are likely to view both existence and knowledge dialectically. It is possible to hold a dialectical view of one realm and not the other or to view neither realm as a whole in a fundamentally dialectical way, but to think dialectically about particular phenomena. Most generally, we can say that dialectical thinking is any thinking which looks for and recognizes instances of dialectic, and which reflects this orientation in the way in which it engages in inquiry. Orienting toward dialectic leads the thinker to describe changes as dialectical movement (i.e., as movement that is developmental movement through forms occurring via constitutive and interactive relationships) and to describe relationships as dialectical relationships (i.e., as relationships that are constitutive, interactive, and that lead to or involve developmental transformation).

Formal operational thinking, as described by Piaget, can be understood as efforts at comprehension that rely on the application of a model of a closed system of lawful relationships to the phenomenal world. In contrast, dialectical thinking can be understood as consisting of efforts at comprehension relying on the application of a model of dialectic to the phenomenal world. These latter efforts may be termed dialectical analyses, in contrast to formal analyses. What is suggested here is that dialectical thinking is an organized approach to analyzing and making sense of the world one experiences that differs fundamentally from formal analysis. Whereas the latter involves the effort to find fundamental fixed realities—basic elements and immutable laws—the former attempts to describe fundamental processes of change and the dynamic relationships through which this change occurs.

Dialectical analyses can be found in the history of a wide range of intellectual disciplines, representing the natural sciences (Provine, 1971; Feyerabend, 1975; Horz, Poltz, Parthey, Rosenhert, & Wessel, 1980), social sciences (Jay, 1973; Kilminster, 1979; Mandel, 1973) and humanities (Jameson, 1971; Adorno and Horkheimer, 1979). Each has provided the basis for recognizing and transcending limitations associated with earlier, more formalistic approaches (see Basseches, 1984, for examples). Dialectical approaches have been used to support political stances ranging from the very conservative (Hegel, 1965) to the revolutionary (Marx and Engels, 1955).

There are many examples of problems of young adult life which may be approached in relatively formalistic or relatively dialectical ways with differing outcomes. Consider, for example, the choice of a marriage partner. If one were to adopt a formalistic approach to analysis, one might start with the assumptions that "I am who I am" and that "There are one or more people out there who are 'right' for me." One might proceed to analyze one's personality traits and to try to logically deduce the traits a partner should have to be compatible. Courtship would then consist of evaluating potential partners to see if they have the desired traits and testing hypotheses about the traits required for compatibility. Notice that the formalistic approach begins with the assumption that people have fixed traits and that the goodness of a relationship is systematically determined by a matching of traits.

A dialectical approach might begin with the assumption that "My traits are not fixed" and that "The relationships that I enter will shape who I become as much as they are shaped by who I am and who my partner is." Here, courtship would involve entering relationships with potential partners, being open to being changed by relationships. Partners would then need to evaluate whether the relationship is evolving in ways which allow both of them to develop as individuals while it continues to develop as a relationship.

The alternatives of formal analysis and dialectical analysis may also be applied when a relationsip breaks up. If one adopts a formal approach, one might try to explain to oneself why the relationship ended by choosing among the following three interpretations.

    (a) "I was inadequate as a partner."
    (b) "My partner was inadequate as a partner."
    (c) "We weren't really right for each other, and we made a big mistake in choosing each other."

Adopting explanation (a) is likely to result in an increase in pain resulting from lowered self-esteem. Adopting explanation (b) is likely to result in a great deal of anger at the partner, which, among other things, will make it much harder for the couple to get back together in any sense. Adopting explanation (c) is likely to result in devaluing a great deal of what was valuable in the relationship for as long as it lasted, as well as result in possible hesitancy to make future commitments. One may say, "If I thought this person was right for me and I was wrong, it means I can't trust my own judgment."

In contrast, if one takes a dialectical approach to analyzing the breakup, one is likely to look for how experience both within and outside of the relationship has led the partners to grow in different directions, so much so that they would be hampered by remaining so tied to each other. The assumption is that a relationship can reach a point where it tends to interfere with the development of one or both of the partners rather than helping them to grow further and growing with them. This kind of analysis is likely to make it easier, rather than harder, to deal emotionally with the breakup. It also is likely to facilitate working together to strengthen or rebuild the relationship. If partners don't blame each other and don't treat the relationship as a mistake, but instead treat the occurrence as a natural function of human development, they are more likely to ask, "How does the relationship need to change in response to the changes it has brought about in us in order for it to continue?" If they do this, a developmental transformation of the relationship rather than its continued disintegration is more likely to occur.

A third example, that of the frustrated college students, opened this paper. In this example, the formal analysis (Mark's) assumed that problems in the college's procedures derived from an educational theory. This analysis led to the two choices of either rejecting the wisdom of one's teachers or discounting one's own perceptions as incorrect. The dialectical analysis (George's) interpreted the problems as reflecting tensions in the interrelationship of various aspects of the institution's functions and led to a recognition of problems facing teachers and students alike, as well as of potentials for the institution to be transformed.

In each example, a dialectical analysis does not preclude a formal analysis. We may believe that relationships change and that people change and still ask questions about what makes partners compatible and how individuals can learn to be better partners. We may trace problematic procedures at a college to fundamental contradictions among its functions and still inquire as to the educational impact of those procedures.

However, the capacity for dialectical analysis makes it possible both to see the limits and to see beyond the limits of the context in which we apply formal analysis. For example, in the matter of finding a marriage partner, one may hypothesize that one is a serious person and would have trouble getting along with someone who was not equally serious. But a dialectical perspective would prepare one for the possibility that in getting to know a very playful new friend one may reverse one's thinking about compatibility and find "I get along better with someone who can help me to laugh and play." One may even transform one's prior assumptions about oneself and find that "I am a fun-loving person, after all." In this case, one might then either (a) look back at one's prior seriousness as simply an emotional defense and understand the interpretation of oneself as serious as itself a useful product of the historical moment, or one might say, (b) "No, I really was a serious person then and now I am a fun-loving one." While (a) reflects a dialectical *epistemological* perspective on the evolution of self-knowledge over time through interaction, (b) reflects a dialectical *ontological* perspective on the evolution of personality through interaction.

As stated above, dialectical analyses of courtship, breakups, and frustrations of college do not preclude formal analyses. It is important to note that in each case that dialectical analyses provide alternatives to views of the problem which are destructive to self or others. For example, the "formalistic" approach to courtship, which attempts to evaluate the traits of potential partners, may be experienced by a potential partner as a barrier to emotional closeness as well as to the partner's influence. The "dialectical" approach, which anticipates the possibility of development resulting for interaction with partners, is, in contrast, likely to be experienced as a warm invitation to interact. In general, formal analyses which establish categories of analysis from the thinker's own perspective tend to remain relatively impermeable to the differing perspectives of others.* Dialectical thinking, in contrast, is actively oriented toward shifting categories of analysis and creating more inclusive categories, in response to the perspectives of others.

I do not want to present dialectical thinking as either an intellectual or psychological panacea. Dialectical analyses are not without costs. The willingness to question the permanence and intransigence of the boundary conditions of a problem, and to ask about situations which lie beyond those boundaries, characterizes each of the dialectical analyses cited above. In one case the boundaries were existing conceptions of one's own personality; in another, the assumption that educational practice follows purely from educational theory. In questioning these boundaries, we may be questioning precisely those points of reference which provide us with a sense of intellectual stability and coherence about our world.

To think dialectically, is, in a certain sense, to trade off a degree of intellectual security for a freedom from intellectually imposing limitations on oneself or other people. The open-mindedness which is thus gained is extremely important from the perspective of concern with cognitive development because it facilitates the joining in collective meaning-making efforts with others whose reasoning is shaped by very different worldviews or life-contexts. However, if our concern were only with individual psychological well-being, and not with cognitive development (as epistemic progress), we might not be so quick to advocate this tradeoff. It might well depend on the likelihood of the individual being able to organize his or her life in such a way as to avoid encountering events which shatter his or her particular sources of intellectual security.

There is also the problem that we face sources of limitations other than intellectual ones, and other sources of pain as well. In the example of the relationship breaking up, loss of the reassuring presence of someone one loves and whom one may have expected to spend one's life with is painful, usually excruciating, no matter how one thinks about it. Dialectical thinking cannot free one from that pain. However, the kind of formalistic analysis of the breakup presented earlier intellectually reinforces the pain. It adds to the pain of loss the self-punitive pain of failure or inadequate judgment or the divisive pain of blame and hatred. The dialectical analysis is more likely to allow one to experience the

---

*This problem is analogous to an oft-discussed problem of social research. When researchers deal with data by sorting subjects' responses into categories predetermined by the researchers, this excludes the possibility of the subjects contributing from their own perspectives to the definition of the problem and the shape of the results.

pain as loss and to mourn the loss. At the same time the pain of loss may be counterbalanced by an emotionally positive intellectual awareness of (a) order in the developmental process, (b) new discovery, and (c) the opening of new possibilities.

A parallel example in an academic discipline is provided in economics, where formalistic theories describe laws of economic behavior in capitalistic economies (Smith, 1937) while more dialectical theories locate the emergence and evolution of capitalistic economies within historical processes (Marx, 1967). If one is embedded in the midst of a capitalist economy, whether as a government economic advisor or as a young adult worker and/or consumer, it may seem far more worthwhile to spend one's time analyzing the laws of that economy formalistically, rather than analyzing how it got to be that way, how it maintains itself, and where it could be going dialectically. Granted, not being able to imagine what living under different laws of economic behavior would be like is a limitation; but needing to live among other people, all operating according to the current laws, poses a more serious limitation. Again, if we were arguing solely about individual welfare, the tradeoff between analyses which help one make predictions given boundary conditions that are unlikely to change in the near future and analyses which might help one to change or prepare for change in those conditions would be tough to evaluate. From the point of view of humanity, as an epistemic subject, involved in an ongoing pursuit of truth, the added power made possible by the capacity for dialectical analyses seems important to recognize. This paper claims, therefore, that dialectical thinking is an important phenomenon of young adult cognitive development. However, it also recognizes the importance of seriously addressing the empirical question, "Who has time for what kind of dialectical analyses when?"

To review, the following general characteristics of dialectical thinking have been cited above.

1. Dialectical thinking is thinking which looks for and recognizes instances of dialectic—developmental transformation occurring via constitutive and interactive relationships.
2. Dialectical thinking is philosophically rooted in a family of world-outlooks in which knowledge and existence are viewed as essentially dialectical processes and in which change, wholeness, and internal relations are emphasized.
3. Dialectical analyses draw attention to the limits of the contexts in which formal analyses are applicable.
4. As a result, dialectical analyses have a power to deal with relationships and transformations beyond the boundary conditions of a formal analysis, while still making use of the power of the formal analysis within those boundaries.
5. Dialectical approaches are more permeable than formalistic approaches by the perspectives of other people who may define a problem in fundamentally different ways.

DIALECTICAL SCHEMATA

In order to make the concept of dialectical thinking accessible to psychological research, the dialectical schemata (DS) framework was developed (Basseches, 1980). The framework breaks dialectical thinking down into twenty-four component *schemata*—specific types of moves-in-thought can then be readily identified in an individual's explanations, analyses, or arguments. Each of these moves in thought is in some way related to the idea of dialectic or the dialectical philosophical tradition, and each plays a somewhat different role in dialectical thinking.

There has been considerable variation within the dialectical tradition in both the aspects of dialectical thinking emphasized and the terminology employed. The DS framework draws on the work of many writers within the dialectical tradition including Engels (1940), Gould (1978), Hegel (1965), Kosok (1972), Marx (1967), Ollman (1971), Piaget (1952), and Unger (1975) in defining schemata. Although on the one hand, the DS framework was intended to leave out no important component of dialectical thinking, on the other hand an effort was made to avoid redundancy by abstracting commonalities from alternative formulations of what appeared to the author to be essentially similar ideas. The resulting DS framework is therefore a hybrid set of schemata names—some drawn from the terminologies established by different thinkers within the dialectical tradition and others representing the author's own abstractions. (For detailed explanation of the nature of each schema, the rules for coding each schema's manifestations in protocols, each schema's relationship to the other schemata and to dialectical thinking as a whole, and each schema's sources in branches of the dialectical tradition, see Basseches, 1979, or Basseches, 1984.)

The Dialectical Schemata are listed in Table 3.1, categorized according to whether they function primarily in *orienting* thought toward motion, forms, or relationships, or in *integrating* these three orientations. Motion-oriented schemata function to direct attention toward processes of change and to recognize dialectical qualities of these change processes. Form-oriented schemata function to direct attention toward wholes or contexts, and to conceptualize these wholes as forms or systems. Relationship-oriented schemata function to direct attention to relationships and to grasp the interactive and constitutive nature of these relationships. Finally, a fourth group of meta-formal schemata integrate the orientations toward motion, form, and relationships by describing relationships among forms and transformations through forms, as well as the process of form construction.

Table 3.2 provides a more differentiated accounting of the functions of the various schemata within dialectical thinking. The following description of the schemata is taken from Commons and Richards (1984b).

Schemata 1 and 4 function to preserve fluidity in thought. For example,

TABLE 3.1. Dialectical Schemata

A. Motion-Oriented Schemata
   1   Thesis-antithesis-synthesis movement in thought
   2   Affirmation of the primacy of motion
   3   Recognition and description of thesis-antithesis-synthesis movement
   4   Recognition of correlativity of a thing and its other
   5   Recognition of ongoing interaction as a source of movement
   6   Affirmation of the practical or active character of knowledge
   7   Avoidance or exposure of objectification, hypostatization, and reification
   8   Understanding events or situations as movements (of development) of a process

B. Form-Oriented Schemata
   9   Location of an element or phenomenon with the whole(s) of which it is a part
   10 Description of a whole (system) in structural, functional, or equilibrational terms
   11 Assumption of contextual relativism

C. Relationship-Oriented Schemata
   12 Assertion of the existence of relations, the limits of separation, and the value of relatedness
   13 Criticism of multiplicity, subjectivism, and pluralism
   14 Description of a two-way reciprocal relationship
   15 Assertion of internal relations

D. Metaformal Schemata
   16 Location (or description of the process of emergence) of contradictions or sources of disequilibrium within a system or between a system and external forces or elements which are antithetical to the system's structure
   17 Understanding the resolution of disequilibrium or contradiction in terms of a notion of transformation in development direction
   18 Relating value to (a) movement in development direction and/or (b) stability through developmental movement
   19 Evaluative comparison of systems
   20 Attention to problems of coordinating systems in relation
   21 Description of open self-transforming systems
   22 Description of qualitative change as a result of quantitative change within a form
   23 Criticism of formalism based on the interdependence of form and content
   24 Multiplication of perspectives as a concreteness-preserving approach to inclusiveness

Schema 1 involves a thesis-antithesis-synthesis movement within the subject's own thought. Such thought moves from reflection upon one idea to reflection upon something which is apart from, left out of, contrary to, or excluded from the first idea and then on to reflection upon a more inclusive idea which relates the original idea to that which was excluded from it.

Schemata 2, 6, 7, and 8 all function to direct the attention of the thinker to processes of change or to creative processes which allow for the possibility of change. For example, Schema 7 involves the avoidance or exposure of objectification, hypostatization, and reification. These moves counteract tendencies to describe complex processes as if they were static things. If one person were to talk about "a marriage" as if it were a thing, another person might employ Schema 7 in pointing out the processes of change which characterize marriage.

In Schemata 3 and 5 (and to some extent Schema 8) processes of change are described in ways that appeal to the idea of dialectic. For example, Schema 3 involves recognition and description of thesis-antithesis-synthesis movement. Here, *changes outside the thinker's own thought* are described as forming a pattern, wherein generation of an alternative to something then leads to the formation of a relationship between the thing and its alternative.

Schema 9 locates an element or phenomenon within the whole(s) of which

TABLE 3.2. Analysis of Functions of Dialectical Schemata

A. *Motion-oriented schemata*
  (i)   Preserve fluidity in thought—DS 1, 4
  (ii) Direct attention to actual or potential processes of change—DS 2, 6, 7, 8
  (iii) Describe movement as dialectical movement—DS 3, 5

B. *Form-oriented schemata*
  (i)   Direct attention to organized or patterned wholes (systems)—DS 9, 11
  (ii) Recognize and describe systems as systems—DS 10, 11

C. *Relationship-oriented schemata*
  (i)   Direct attention to relationships—DS 12, 13
  (ii) Describe relationships as constitutive and interactive, thereby relating them to the idea of dialectic—DS 14, 15

D. *Metaformal schemata*
  (i)   Direct attention to and describe the limits of stability (change potential) of forms or systems—DS 16
  (ii) Direct attention to and describe transformations (movements from one form to another)—DS 17, 21, 22
  (iii) Direct attention to and describe relationships among forms or systems—DS 19, 20, 24
  (iv) Direct attention to relationship of forms to process of form-construction—DS 18, 23

Source: Dialectical Schemata: A Framework from the Empirical Study of the Development of Dialectical Thinking" *Human Development*, No. 23: pg. 400–421, 1980. NJ: Abex Publishing Corp.

it is a part. It functions to direct the thinker's attention from the thinker's object of reflection to the larger whole(s) of which that object is a part. Schema 10 describes wholes in structural, functional, or equilibrational terms. Employing Schema 10 involves recognizing wholes as *organized* (i.e., as forms or systems). Schema 11 articulates the epistemological assumption of contextual relativism (Perry, 1970). The schema thus functions to direct the thinker's attention from ideas and values to the conceptual contexts of which those ideas and values are parts, and to the structural properties of those conceptual contexts.

Schemata 12 and 13 turn the thinker's attention to relationships. The former schema performs this role through assertion of the existence and value of relationships, and of the limits associated with maintaining separations. The latter schema performs this role through criticism of epistemological and metaethical perspectives founded on principles of separateness (viz., multiplicity, pluralism, and subjectivism).

In Schema 14, for description of two-way reciprocal relationships, the interactive aspect of relationships is brought out. Schema 15 which asserts the existence of *internal* relations brings out the constitutive aspect of the nature of relationships (by asserting that they are relationships which make the parties to the relationships what they are).

It is the inclusion of the metaformal schemata within the DS framework that most clearly reflects the metasystematic level of organization which I have attributed to dialectical thinking (Basseches, 1979, 1984). These schemata presuppose the explicit recognition of forms or systems (such as those which are implicit at the formal operations stage), since they refer to cognitive actions performed upon recognized forms and systems.

For example, Schema 16 involves locating contradictions or sources of disequilibrium within a system or between a system and external forces or elements which are antithetical to the system's structure. Such thought makes salient systems' limits of stability.

Schemata 17, 21, and 22 are those most clearly related to the process of transformation. For example, Schema 17 relies on the concept of "development" to conceptualize the transformations that occur when a system reaches its limits of stability.

Schemata 19, 20, and 24 relate systems or forms to each other. For example, when Schema 19 is employed, systems or forms are evaluatively compared to each other.

Finally, Schemata 18 and 23 both function to bring the process of form-construction into awareness. For example, Schema 18 asserts that facilitating the process of transformation in a developmental direction, in which more sophisticated forms are constructed or organized, is a source of value.

Although each of the schemata plays a functional role related to one of four categories as described above, the schemata are of quite different surface types. Some of the schemata describe steps in dialectical analyses of phenomena. For example, one might begin by locating a phenomenon in a context of which it is a part (Schema 9). Then, one might describe that context as a system and as obeying certain self-regulatory laws (Schema 10). Next, one might look for certain contradictions or tensions in the system and its relationship to external forces (Schema 16). After that, one might hypothesize how these contradictions might be resolved by a restructuring of the system in a more complex, differentiated, and integrated way (Schema 17). Often dialectical thinkers will use this potential for development as a basis for grounding practical suggestions and actions (Schema 18). Finally, after completing these steps in dialectical analysis, one could proceed to make one's analysis more inclusive by recapitulating the previous set of steps from one or more alternative perspectives (i.e., one could locate the same phenomenon in several different contexts and analyze each of those contexts dialectically (Schema 24).

Many of the dialectical schemata describe ways of introducing dialectical perspectives on existence and knowledge into argument and other processes of inquiry. While these schemata may seem to involve merely the statement of philosophical stances related to the dialectical tradition, these schemata do play a functional role because these stances have implications for how one conducts an inquiry. For example, the assertion that motion or fundamental change is a primary fact of the universe (Schema 2) is likely to lead to an inquiry into how certain lawful relationships which one might be studying have come into existence and what sorts of changes might lead those lawful relationships to hold no longer. Schemata 2, 6, 11, 12, 13, 15, 18, and 23 represent philosophical stances which have an impact on how cognitive inquiry proceeds.

Schemata 3, 4, 5, 14, 21, and 22 represent alternative languages for describing processes of dialectic—or alternative ways in which developmental transformation can occur via constitutive and interactive relationships. Schemata 7 and 8 describe ways of locating events and phenomena within dialectical processes. Since dialectics involves the analysis of the interrelationships of systems, simply viewing systems in relation to each other is a cognitive activity that may be organized by the notion of dialectic. Schemata 19 and 20 describe this sort of cognitive activity.

Finally, Schema 1 describes unselfconscious dialectical movement recognizable in the process of thinking itself. This is the kind of dialectical thinking emphasized by Riegel as well as Piaget (1952, 1974, 1980) in his descriptions of equilibration, contradictions and the *process* of cognitive development (as opposed to his descriptions of cognitive *structures)*. While this kind of movement occurs at every level of cognitive organization, dialectical thinking as a whole is a way of preserving dialectical movement within thought at a metasystematic level (in the context of the full use of formal operations).

Table 3.3 summarizes the types of dialectical schemata described above.

The DS framework provided an initial basis for making the notion of a dialectical level of cognitive organization operational. It made it possible to read any written materials or verbatim accounts of speeches, interviews, dialogues,

TABLE 3.3. Types of Dialectical Schemata

I.   Philosophical stances related to dialectical thinking: DS 2, 6, 11, 12, 13, 15, 18, 23
II. Steps in a dialectical analysis: DS 9, 10, 16, 17, 18, 24
III. Ways of describing dialectical processes: DS 3, 4, 5, 14, 21, 22
IV. Operations on systems: DS 19, 20
V.   Ways of relating particulars to processes: DS 7, 8
VI. Unselfconscious reflections of the dialectical nature of the thought process: DS 1

or meetings and note instances of the 24 elements of dialectical thinking listed above.

Interview protocols have been reliably coded for use of dialectical schemata (Basseches, 1979, 1980). An Index (I) designed to measure the number of schemata employed in a protocol and the clarity with which they were exhibited could be computed with an interrater reliability of $r = .91$ ($p < .005$). The probability of agreement on the presence of any given schema in a protocol was 76 percent ($p < .003$).

The dialectical schemata resemble Piagetian operations, in that both are hypothetical constructs presumed to regulate thought. Also, both perform this regulatory function in coordination with other schemata or operations.

However, there is a fundamental difference between the way in which Piagetian operations are coordinated with one another and the way in which dialectical schemata eventually become coordinated within the organization of dialectical thinking as a whole. Operations are organized into closed systems ("structures") of reversible operations in which the effects of any operation can be undone by the use of an inverse operation, and no operation or combination of operations yields a result external to the system as a whole. In contrast, the dialectical schemata are organized into a coherent whole by an underlying model of dialectic. Whereas a structure is a closed system, resistant to fundamental change, a dialectic is an ongoing process of developmental transformation. Thus, when dialectical schemata are applied in coordination, new thoughts are built upon old ones in nonreversible fashion, and unlike the case of reversible operations, the contents of thought are irrevocably changed. This means that dialectical schemata regulate a much more free, less conservative kind of movement in thought than Piagetian operations. Dialectical schemata refer to moves in thought free from the constraints associated with formal operations, while maintaining, in part, the order provided by formal operations.

Whereas formal operations and concrete operations describe how thought is structured and made to move within a closed system, the dialectical schemata describe how thought frees itself to transcend closed systems and thereby to create and comprehend change of a greater scope in itself and in the world. The examples of dialectical thinking thus far presented all involved challenging the boundary conditions of formal analyses and dealing with what lies beyond those boundaries.

DIALECTIC AS AN ORGANIZING PRINCIPLE

The organizing principle for formal operational thought is the structured whole or system. In contrast, the organizing principle for dialectical thinking is the dialectic. If we equate the notion of form in the definition of dialectic with that of structured whole or system we see how the concept of dialectic builds upon, but is more complex than, the concept of system. Dialectic refers to the developmental transformation of systems over time, via constitutive and interactive relationships.

Thus, whereas formal thinking is systematic, dialectical thinking is metasystematic. In formal operational thought, an underlying (closed) system, the INRC group, organizes a *logic of propositions* into a coherent whole. It enables the thinker to deal with various propositions and their necessary interrelationships systematically. It also makes possible the analysis of phenomena which can be effectively modeled as comprising closed systems. The closed system model is not adequate for problems requiring analysis of (a) multiple systems and their relationships to each other, nor (b) open systems which undergo radical transformation.

In contrast, in dialectical thinking, an underlying model of dialectic organizes a *logic of systems* into a coherent whole. It enables the thinker to deal with various systems and their relationships to each other over time dialectically. The model of dialectic does provide a basis for analysis of (a) multiple systems and their relationships to each other, as well as (b) open systems which undergo radical transformation.

DIALECTICAL THINKING AS A LEVEL OF EQUILIBRIUM

According to Piaget's strict definition of a structure (Piaget, 1970), a structure *must be* a closed system. Since a dialectic is a system which changes in fundamental and irreversible ways over time, as a result of dynamic relationships both within the system and between the system and its context (which may include other systems), a dialectic is clearly not a structure in the traditional Piagetian sense. Nor is thought organized by the concept of dialectic a Piagetian structure. Nevertheless, there is a form of equilibrium provided by dialectical cognitive organization. In fact, dialectical thinking allows the recognition of something as remaining constant amidst a far broader range of changes than formal reasoning can equilibrate. Let us explore the nature of that equilibrium.

The whole study of equilibration in genetic epistemology (Piaget, 1952, 1978) is based on the recognition of two properties of human cognition. First, there is a human need to impose stability on the reality that people experience. Cognitive schemata allow one to make sense of—to cognize and re-cognize— what without those structures would be nothing more than James' "blooming, buzzing, confusion." Secondly, there is a human process of applying and extending one's cognitive schemata by putting them into practice in the world (assimilation), which tends to result in changes (accommodation). Structures of equilibrium allow this process of extension and change to occur, while keeping something constant.

Consider the various structures of equilibrium that Piaget describes. The permanent-object concept allows one to recognize an object as constant, amidst continual change in its appearance resulting from the new perspectives from which it is viewed. Conservation of volume allows one to recognize the abstract concept of volume as remaining constant through the various transformations that occur in pouring a quantity of liquid from one receptacle to another. Propositional logic describes rules for keeping the truth values of simple propositions (p,q) constant, and for transforming them into determinate truth values of complex propositions as the simple propositions are recombined into complex propositions in various ways (e.g., $p \wedge q$; $p \vee q$; $\sim p \wedge q$; $q \rightarrow p$; etc.).

In dialectical thinking, what it is that remains recognizable across a range of changes is the historical process as an evolving whole. Any change at all, no matter how radical, can be equilibrated if it can be conceptualized as a moment in a dialectical process of evolution. New events are integrated within a dialectical conception of a process as later steps in the evolution of that process; old constructions are conserved—they remain part of the process of dialectic— although their historical role is reconstructed in the light of subsequent transformations.

For example, consider this dialectical analysis of sex roles. Systematic regularities have existed throughout history in male and female sex roles. In each era, the description of regularities in male and female sex roles has led to abstractions about how women's nature and temperament is on the whole different from men's. Now that certain changes in society have occurred (e.g., overpopulation), phenomena occur more regularly which are discrepant with traditional sex roles. The abstract models, as well as social norms and laws which are based upon and support those models, are viewed as no longer adequate. Contradictions or tensions have emerged in the system of sex-role regulated behavior including demands for political, social, and economic equality of the sexes. These contradictions will only be resolved as new, more developed conceptions of maleness and femaleness emerge which are consistent with a greater range of male and female activities and with equality between the sexes.

The basis of the equilibrium in this way of thinking are (1) the assumption that change is what is most fundamental; and (2) the ability to conceptualize changes as (a) emergences of contradictions within existing systems and (b) formations of new, more inclusive systems. The nature of maleness and femaleness is not viewed as fundamental—it is seen as likely to change through history. At any point in time, it may be useful to conceptualize the regularities in male and female roles, but these conceptualizations are meaningful as part of a historical process in which they will be challenged and transcended.

A closed-system model of sex-role behavior, which claims that such behavior derives from fundamental immutable laws of male and female temperament, must necessarily ignore or attempt to suppress what begin as anomalies and later become new patterns of behavior by males and females, if the equilibrium of the system is to be maintained* (i.e., if maleness is to continue to be recognized as maleness and femaleness is to continue to be recognized as femaleness). In contrast, a dialectical model can incorporate such anomalies and new patterns while maintaining equilibrium by recognizing them as developments in the continuing dialectic of the relations of the sexes.

I have argued elsewhere (Basseches, 1980, 1984) that dialectical thinking describes a postformal level of cognitive organization. This argument is based in part on the fact that dialectic as an organizing principle builds upon (and treats at a level of greater complexity by integrating with the dimension of change over time) the concept of system, which is the organizing principle of formal operations. The argument is also based in part on the greater equilibrating power (ability to maintain recognizable continuity in the midst of a broader range of change) of dialectical cognitive organization vis-à-vis formal operational organization. But it should be clear from the above example that my view that dialectical thinking is a necessary advance in equilibrium is also based on the general ontological assumption that people will be confronted with anomalous events which don't conform to prior closed-system laws.

In the natural sciences, this general ontological assumption amounts to the assumption that scientists will have to deal with scientific revolutions (Kuhn, 1970). In the life sciences and social sciences, it amounts to the assumption that the phenomena dealt with are highly susceptible to rapid and radical change, which scientists will need to comprehend. In day-to-day life, it amounts to the assumption that for making practical decisions, closed systems (including moral systems) that are constructed on the basis of limited data and from limited perspectives will be inadequate. Social life is complex and requires multiple perspective taking. People will be confronted with new data and new perspectives, and it is important that their cognitive structures leave them open to taking these new data and perspectives into account, accommodating to them, and dealing with them constructively. Confrontations, in science and in life, with phenomena that

---

*Note the arguments of the "Moral Majority" here.

demand recognition of multiple interacting systems and radical transformation of systems, will point out the limits of formal thinking and stimulate the construction of more dialectical forms of reasoning.

YOUNG ADULTS' USE OF DIALECTICAL SCHEMATA

Research on dialectical thinking in young adults has for the most part relied on the use of the dialectical schemata framework to analyze transcripts of tape-recorded, probed clinical interviews (Basseches, 1979, 1980, 1984). In this research, subjects were asked to formulate a conception of the nature of education, and then to explore with the interviewer the relevance of this conception to understanding their own educational experience and the educational institutions in which they had participated, as well as to generating ideas for improving these institutions.* The transcripts were then evaluated for dialectical thinking by noting the range of dialectical schemata employed and the clarity with which they were manifested. The research revealed apparent increases in the use of dialectical thinking with academic level, as well as with movement through those positions in Perry's (1970) scheme for intellectual and ethical development which represent adoption of more sophisticated epistemological assumptions.

In addition, research has begun exploring young adults' ability to comprehend and to paraphrase arguments containing dialectical schemata. In this research (Basseches, 1984; Olson, Basseches, and Richards, 1981), subjects are asked to read matched pairs of dialectical and nondialectical arguments on a variety of topics, paraphrasing each argument as they go, and discussing which of the two arguments they prefer and why, after they complete each pair. Results thus far have indicated significant increases in comprehension of dialectical schemata with academic level across groups of freshmen, seniors, and graduate students.

Just how much, and what types of dialectical thinking do young adults use? More research is necessary before this question can be answered for general populations. However, in one 1977 random sample of nine college seniors at a highly selective liberal arts college, two demonstrated the tendency to use a very broad range of dialectical schemata in highly coordinated fashion in interviews in which they were asked to discuss the nature of education. These two could be appropriately described as having achieved a dialectical level of equilibrium in their thought. For three other seniors, the narrow range, lack of frequency, and lack of clarity of expression of dialectical schemata in their interviews made it reasonable to infer the absence of an organized structure of dialectical think-

---

*Other topics for interview research on dialectical thinking have included the nature of work, (Slipitza as reported in Basseches, 1984) and the nature of psychotherapy (Bopp, as reported in Basseches, 1984).

ing. The remaining four seniors manifested partical but conspicuously incomplete coordination of dialectical schemata in their interviews. These subjects could be termed "transitional" dialectical thinkers. In contrast, among a random sample of nine freshmen at the same college in 1977, none demonstrated a dialectical level of equilibrium in their interviews. The interviews of three freshmen indicated transitional dialectical thinking while those of six freshmen indicated the absence of any organized dialectical structure. At the same time, among nine faculty members at the same college, six demonstrated a dialectical level of equilibrium, two indicated transitional dialectical thinking, and one indicated the absence of any organized dialectical structure.

These data are consistent with the claim that under the influence of high quality higher education, the young adult years are a time when development toward dialectical form of equilibrium in thought may occur. However, longitudinal research is needed to validate this claim, since the argument that advancement from freshmen to senior year and advancement from being a college senior to becoming a college faculty member is more likely to occur for individuals who already tend to employ dialectical schemata is also consistent with these data.

Among the transitional dialectical thinkers, three distinct patterns were detected in the schemata used and schemata absent. These three patterns, termed the "formalist" pattern, the "nonformalist" pattern, and the "value-relativist" pattern (described in detail in Basseches, 1979 and Basseches, 1984), may be seen as representing three alternative pathways to the development of dialectical thinking which different young adults may take. Each pattern provides some equilibrium to thought beyond the level provided by the use of formal operations. However, for each pattern, there are particular types of problems that the thinker is unable to handle, and confronting these problems leads to the manifestation of cognitive disequilibrium. For the formalist transitional thinkers, broad interdisciplinary questions are most difficult. Demonstrating both the power and limits of disciplinary modes of thought is relatively easy. For the nonformalist transitional thinkers, problems of choosing an analytic framework in which to organize and present the wide range of interrelated phenomena of which they are aware, are most difficult. Presenting critiques of the analyses of others is relatively easy. For the value-relativists, synthetically handling problems borne of differences among individuals' or groups' values is most difficult. Dealing with matters in which value issues don't arise or where there is widespread agreement on values is relatively easy.

If young adult transitional dialectical thinkers can avoid confronting the types of problems with which they have difficulty, their partial patterns of development of dialectical thinking may remain fairly stable. However, we can hypothesize that if they are confronted with the need to seriously wrestle with the sorts of problems which pose them difficulty, and if they are supported in this struggle, the dialectical form of equilibrium is likely to develop as a result. The data on adult faculty members suggest that for many, but not for all, the path to becoming an adult professional academic involves wrestling with problems that demand dialectical thinking.

ENVIRONMENTAL INFLUENCES

The importance of dialectical thinking to the achievement of cognitive equilibrium does not imply, then, that all young adults achieve this level of equilibrium. We may expect that just as all adults do not fully develop formal operations, so they may not all develop dialectical thinking. Whether individuals do develop dialectical thinking depends on both environmental factors and developmental characteristics of the person.

First of all, fully developed dialectical thinking presupposes something like what Piaget calls formal operations. The ability to organize the world into abstract consistent systematic patterns is a prerequisite to providing an account of how such patterns evolve and change. It is certainly possible to recognize the ontological and epistemological centrality of change, as well as the power of relationships, without organizing the world into systems. In fact, these recognitions may constitute preformal precursors of dialectical thinking. However, to do more than assert the importance of change and relationships—to actually describe the course of dialectical change over time—requires the ability to describe the temporary patterns of organization or systems which constitute moments in dialectical processes.

When adults systematize the world (a) using sets of fixed categories, and (b) holding to static ontological and epistemological assumptions often associated with formal thought, their maintenance of cognitive equilibrium depends on their power to seal themselves off from anomalous data and discrepant viewpoints. For example, with respect to the analysis of sex roles presented earlier, individuals may attempt (a) to force others to conform to their notions of sex-appropriate behavior, or (b) to isolate themselves from individuals whose behavior does not conform in order to maintain their systematic understandings of the nature of masculinity and feminity. These strategies are surely not optimal from the point of view of a concern with expanding human sociality, but they may succeed in the short term if the individuals employing them are powerful enough. However, if adults cannot seal themselves off from discrepant events, they are likely to experience frustrations and conflicts resulting from the limits of fixed categories of thought for addressing a changing reality.

When this happens, one of two things is likely to occur. Either the adults will reject formal operational thinking and resort to less logical forms of thought, or the adults will begin to reorganize their formal operations within the context of the more adequate organization of dialectical thinking. This has not yet been researched, but we may hypothesize that supportive circumstances and rich intellectual environments which provide opportunities for careful, critical reflection will facilitate the latter outcome.

Higher education appears to be a positive environment for promoting this kind of socio-cognitive development in young adults. But the positive effects of education could be expected to be limited insofar as the educational process is divorced from practical concerns. If one only studies the systematizations of science and philosophy as abstract objects rather than attempting to systematize the dynamic contradictory realities of life beyond the laboratory and classroom (students' own lives and those of others), the encounters with the discrepant may be avoided. On the other hand, if (as happens in much preprofessional education), practical problems are addressed but the definitions of the problems are taken uncritically from a single point of view, discrepancies may also be avoided (especially if the point of view is that of powerful elements of society—elements strong enough to impose the order of a static system on the lives of others).

Practical activity is the essence of work environments, but most jobs deny their occupants the opportunity to reflect intellectually upon the practical activity in which they are engaged. Work environments could have a much more positive influence on young adult socio-cognitive development if they were organized more democratically and organizational decisions were arrived at through discussion, reflection, and voting by all members of the work organization. The educational enrichment of work environments could make them even more likely to be positive influences on socio-cognitive development. Study groups which were designed to support members in reflecting upon, theorizing about, and researching areas of inquiry relevant to the organization's activity might stimulate individuals to reflect on that activity dialectically.

Perhaps the most powerful kind of environment for promoting young adult socio-cognitive development would be one which combined the intellectual rigor, explicit attention to cultivating the mind, and time to reflect characteristic of our best colleges and universities, with the diversity of participants, commitment of human energies, and practical challenges characteristic of our workplaces. Such environments do not yet exist, but there are trends in both the world of work and in higher education pointing in this direction.

Personal relationships are clearly characterized by the kind of dynamism and bringing together of different perspectives that are likely to challenge the limits of formal thought. But retreat from the contradictions of a relationship (and concomitant retreat from the relationship itself) may often inhibit cognitive development. In contrast, mutual emotional support and opportunities for intellectual reflection may make relationships powerful developmental contexts.

CONCLUSION

This discussion of environmental influences has been very speculative, because we still know so little about the prevalence, the rate of development, and the circumstances of development of dialectical thinking among adults. But what the proposed idea of dialectical thinking provides is a sense of the *direction* of adult cognitive development. It allows us to formulate research questions about the rate with which, and the circumstances under which, individuals develop in that direction.

The assertion that the achievement of dialectical thinking describes the direction of young adult cognitive development is a claim (a) that this achievement normally occurs after the achievement of formal operations, and (b) that this achievement is worthy of being called a "development" in the genetic epistemological sense of providing a more adequate way of understanding the universe than do formal operations alone. The earlier discussions of dialectic as a principle of organization and dialectical thinking from the equilibrium standpoint have addressed the second (b, above) part of this claim (see Basseches, 1979, 1984, for an elaboration of this claim). Results from empirical research (Basseches, 1980, 1984) have provided initial support for the first (a, above) part of the claim (viz., that there is a tendency for dialectical thinking to be achieved after formal operations).

Dialectical thinking is especially significant for cognitive development for two reasons. First of all, dialectical thinking enables one to embrace (rather than protect oneself from) contradictions between one's own reasoning and that of other people who have had very different experiences of the world from oneself. Such contradictions are viewed as moments of opportunity to build richer shared understandings within a comprehensible process of social and epistemic integration. The contradictions need not be taken as indicative of the invalidity of either party's reasoning or of a relativistic requirement to affirm points of view as separate-but-equal. Secondly, dialectical thinking also enables one to embrace (rather than deny) contradictions within the social world and within one's own thoughts and feelings. Understanding the self and the social world as constituted by a wide range of social relations, many of which are in tension with each other, leads one not to expect consistency. Here again, contradictions represent not the absence of coherent order, but rather developmental opportunities within the evolution of such order. The descriptions of stages of faith development, ego development, and moral development based on dialectical thinking (cited on p. 57) all reflect a readiness to fully embrace internal and external tensions.

In sum, the examples offered in this paper have illustrated the relevance of dialectical thinking to a range of problems which confront and intellectually challenge young adults. The data summarized are consistent with the claim that under the influence of effective higher education, increased use of dialectical schemata occurs during the young adult years. Nevertheless, even at a highly selective liberal arts college, less than 25 percent of the seniors interviewed demonstrated a dialectical form of equilibrium in their thought. This implies that while some young adults may achieve this form of throught while in college, for others college leaves them in a transition which will only be completed if they continue to confront particular types of problems under supportive conditions. Still others do not even develop transitional forms of partially dialectical reasoning while in college, so that their development is even more dependent on the sorts of problems with which adult life confronts them and the circumstances in which they confront these problems. More research, especially longitudinal research, is needed both to demonstrate that development toward dialectical thinking does occur in individuals during the young adult years, and to clarify the conditions under which it is more likely and less likely to occur, both during this period of life and thereafter.

4

Environmental Conditions for Discontinuities in the Development of Abstractions

Kurt W. Fischer and Sheryl L. Kenny

Cognitive development does not stop in early adolescence. To the contrary, evidence is growing that major cognitive-developmental advances take place during later adolescence and early adulthood. New, qualitatively different skills emerge in a wide range of domains, including logical reasoning, political thinking, moral judgment, and reflective judgment (Commons, Richards, and Armon, 1984; Kenny, 1983; Kitchener, 1983c).

The nature of these changes is far from clear, however. Along with the findings showing qualitative change, there are many other findings that seem to show no qualitative cognitive advances after adolescence (Flavell, 1970; Horn, 1976; Inhelder and Piaget, 1958; Neimark, 1975a). We will argue that these two sets of findings not only are both correct but also are fully compatible with each other: On the one hand, new levels of abilities emerge in late adolescence and early adulthood. On the other hand, most skill development during this period shows slow, gradual improvement and does not reflect the cognitive advances of the newly emerging levels. These apparently opposing sets of findings are not really in opposition, because people do not routinely function at their highest developmental level. Their level of performance varies systematically below the highest level as a function of environmental conditions such as practice and contextual support. Under certain environmental conditions, cognitive-developmental levels are strikingly evident; while under other conditions, they are nowhere to be seen.

COGNITIVE-DEVELOPMENTAL LEVELS AS DISCONTINUITIES

One of the central problems in cognitive-developmental research has been that the criteria for what constitutes a stage have been unclearly specified. Pi-

Preparation of this chapter was supported by grants from the Spencer Foundation and the Carnegie Corporation of New York. The statements made and views expressed are solely the responsibility of the authors. We would like to thank Daniel Bullock and Helen Hand for their contributions.

aget (1957) argued that the fundamental criterion for a stage is synchronous change across domains: The child's abilities in diverse domains should move nearly simultaneously into a new logical stage, such as concrete operations (Broughton, 1981). Yet research has shown overwhelmingly that such synchrony does not obtain (Fischer and Bullock, 1981; Flavell, 1971, 1982), as Piaget himself gradually acknowledged (for example, Piaget, 1941, 1972). With the failure of this straightforward criterion, investigators have fallen back on a loose, poorly articulated criterion: Some sort of qualitative change indicates a new stage or level. As a result, ways of detecting stages or levels have remained unclear. Indeed, if observers were to happen upon a genuine stage or level, how would they know they had found it?

One straightforward criterion for a cognitive-developmental level is a discontinuity or sudden alteration in the pattern of developmental change. The simplest form of discontinuity is a spurt in performance during a limited age period, as shown in Figure 4.1: A person shows a sudden improvement in performance during a relatively short time interval. To test for such a spurt, a number of methods are available, as outlined by Fischer, Pipp, and Bullock (1984); see also Globerson (in press). The fundamental requirements of all the methods are the use of a ruler and a clock. The ruler can be any scale that provides an approximately continuous measure of the ability hypothesized to change. The clock can be age or any other measure that can specify the length of the interval during which change takes place. A discontinuity is evident when a large change in performance occurs in a short time.

According to skill theory (Fischer, 1980), the emergence of a new cognitive-developmental level produces a cluster of such spurts in performance. Within some limited age period, spurts can be detected in a wide range of different domains. For example, one level hypothesized by skill theory typically appears between fourteen and sixteen years of age, as shown for three hypothetical domains in Figure 4.1. The spurts do not all occur at exactly the same age, nor do they take exactly the same form. Adolescents do not suddenly metamorphose on their fifteenth birthday. Instead, the change is only relatively rapid, occupying a small interval of time.

For such spurts to occur reliably, people must be performing at or near their optimal level the most complex skill that they can control. Complexity is defined in terms of a developmental scale of hierarchically ordered skill structures involving the coordination of sources of variation in behavior. For the cognitive levels that develop in adolescence and adulthood, the sources of variation are based in a structure called an abstraction, which typically specifies an intangible characteristic for coordinating some of the sources of variation in representations (concrete characteristics of people, objects, or events). Examples of abstractions include concepts such as justice, honesty, law, and responsibility, as well as arithmetic operations such as addition and division (Fischer, Hand, and Russell, 1984).

Environmental conditions determine when people perform at their optimal level. Only with practiced skills in familiar domains and with environmental support for high-level performance will most people perform at optimum and thereby show a spurt in performance with the emergence of a new level. Most of the time, people do not encounter such environmental circumstances, and so they do not usually show spurts in performance. Levels are therefore evident only under special environmental conditions. Most conditions are likely to produce slow, gradual, continuous improvements in performance, even when people are performing exactly the same tasks that show discontinuities under optimal conditions.

EVIDENCE FOR CONTINUOUS, GRADUAL CHANGE

The typical pattern of slow, gradual change is evident in most developmental and educational research. Study after study demonstrates that with age, children, adolescents, and young adults typically show small improvements in performance or no change at all (Brown, Bransfors, Ferrara, and Campione, 1983; Chi, 1978; Fischer and Silvern, in press; McCall, Meyers, Hartman, and Roche, 1983). However, it could be argued that many of these studies do not provide appropriate tests for stagelike change because they do not assess developmental sequences. Colby, Kohlberg, and their colleagues (1983) carried out a longitudinal study that does not suffer from these problems and so provides a particularly clear test of the hypothesis that most cognitive development is slow and gradual.

Kohlberg (1969) devised a structured interview comprising a series of moral dilemmas for assessing a six-stage sequence in the development of moral judgment. The stages were formulated within the Piagetian tradition to reflect changes in logical thinking about morality and were hypothesized to form what Piaget (1957) called "structured wholes." Consequently they should emerge in a stagelike manner, appearing relatively suddenly and permeating the child's moral thinking.

According to the optimal-level hypothesis from skill theory, on the other hand, performance on Kohlberg's interview should demonstrate slow, gradual continuous improvement over many years rather than abrupt stagelike emergence. The interview is administered in such a way that it does not encourage optimal performance: Each dilemma is given only once, subjects are never told what is a good answer, and no contextual support for high-level performance is provided.

Groups of normal boys were originally tested on Kohlberg's interview at ten, thirteen, or sixteen years of age, and they were retested on the same interview several times over the ensuing twenty years. Results showed that the stages did indeed form a developmental sequence, such that people consistently demonstrated later stages after they had first shown earlier ones. Because Kohlberg's interview was designed to detect true, Piaget-type stages and because the stages

FIGURE 4.1. Spurts in Three Hypothetical Behavioral Domains as a Result of the Emergence of a New Development Level

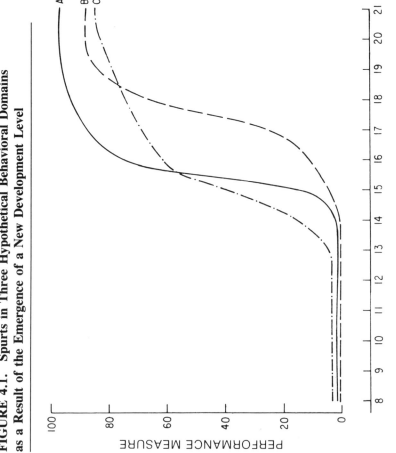

Source: Fischer, Pipp and Bullock (1984).

have been shown empirically to form a developmental sequence, the study provides a strong test of the two competing hypotheses: Will the stages show abrupt emergence, or will their development be slow and gradual because the subjects were tested under nonoptimal conditions? With the longitudinal design, it is possible to determine not only whether the group as a whole showed spurts or gradual change in moral stage but also whether individual subjects demonstrated such spurts.

We analyzed the published data (Colby et al., 1983) to test for spurts versus gradual change in performance. The results were clear. Movement from stage to stage was continuous—slow and gradual. There was no evidence at all for relatively sudden change from one stage to the next. The development of Stage 4 offered a particularly good case, because no Stage 4 reasoning was evident at the beginning of the study and virtually all subjects produced extensive Stage 4 reasoning by the end of the study. As shown in Figure 4.2, Stage 4 reasoning first appeared at approximately thirteen years of age, and the frequency of Stage 4 reasoning increased very slowly throughout the entire course of the study. Most subjects did not produce a preponderance of Stage 4 reasoning until they reached their thirties. The pattern was the same for individual subjects—a slow, gradual increase in Stage 4 reasoning over many years.

FIGURE 4.2.   The Development of Stage 4 Reasoning in Kohlberg's Longitudinal Study

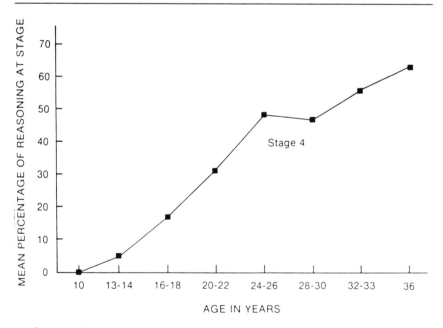

Source: Colby et al., 1983.

This study of Kohlberg's stages clearly demonstrated continuous change, not discontinuous, and the pattern of continuous change is typical of most other research. Nevertheless, a few studies do provide evidence of developmental spurts, during adolescence and early adulthood (for example, Martarano, 1977; O'Brien and Overton, 1982). We propose that the optimal-level hypothesis will predict how spurts appear and disappear as a function of environmental conditions and will thus explain the cases in which spurts have been found. To show how this explanation will operate, we first need to elaborate our skill-theory analysis.

BUILDING AND USING SKILLS: THE IMPORTANCE OF PRACTICE AND ENVIRONMENTAL SUPPORT

It takes work to build a skill. When a person develops a general capacity to build skills at a new developmental level, there is no automatic transformation of all skills to the new level. The human information-processing system follows what might be called a Calvinist principle: The person must actively construct every new skill. Skills do not emerge for free, without effort.

In general, at least two circumstances are necessary for a person to build a new skill. First, the environment must provide a context that induces and supports performance of the behaviors that constitute the skill. Second, the person must practice the skill until he or she has mastered it.

When stated so directly, the Calvinist principle about skill-building may seem sensible and obvious; yet it has not been included in the central principles of traditional cognitive-developmental theories such as Piaget's (1970). Once it is included, stagelike change can no longer be expected across all domains of behavior. Even if Piaget could magically touch the head of an eleven-year-old and instantaneously transform him or her to formal operations, the child would have to take time and effort to use the new capacity to build specific formal-operational skills. Only with time, then, would the new capacity become evident. And while the child was expending time and effort on building new skills in one domain, such as arithmetic, no skills would be built in other domains, such as morality. Consequently, even an instantaneous transformation of capacity would result in a gradual transformation of skills occurring during some interval of time. Relatively, this transformation would involve spurts in performance, but absolutely, it would still take time.

Furthermore, if the environment must induce and support the building of a new skill, then the levels of a person's skills will inevitably vary across domains. After a new capacity emerges, the environment will happen to induce the building of skills at the new level in certain domains and not in others. The person will experience the environmental contexts necessary for inducing the building of some skills, such as those for arithmetic reasoning, and not for the building of others, such as those for moral reasoning. It is physically impossible within a limited time period to encounter the contexts needed to induce all possible skills. Consequently, even if capacity were transformed instantaneously, the actual skills a person possesses would vary across domains.

According to skill theory, the environment not only induces the transformation of a skill to a new level but also affects the level of performance of a skill more directly. The environmental context provides varying degrees of support for high-level performance (Fischer and Bullock, 1984). A skill is not either present or absent, but it is internalized to a certain degree. The more it is internalized, the less environmental support is required for a person to perform it. Conversely, the less it is internalized, the more environmental support is required for performance. In Kohlberg's moral judgment interview, little support was provided for high-level performance: Subjects were not shown a good answer, nor given any other aids for high-level performance. They were not even allowed to work out an answer over a period of time and internalize it. Without environmental support or the opportunity to internalize a high-level skill, people do not typically function at or near optimum.

To find the discontinuities in performance predicted to appear with a new developmental level, then, skills must be assessed in the following manner. People must be tested (a) in familiar domains, where they have had the opportunity to construct high-level skills, (b) under environmental conditions that provide contextual support for high-level performance, and (c) with the opportunity to practice the tasks they must perform. In familiar domains, relatively short periods of practice will suffice, such as hours, days, or weeks. In unfamiliar domains, optimal performance will be possible only after long time periods for practice and instruction.

Traditionally, developmental and educational researchers have not assessed behavior under conditions for optimal performance (Feuerstein, 1979). As in Kohlberg's study, testing conditions have provided little contextual support for high-level performance, and there has been little opportunity for practice. Also in some cases, the domains tested have not been familiar. Inevitably, performance under such conditions will show slow, gradual, continuous change.

In a study in progress on the development of arithmetic skills, we have tested this interpretation by varying both degree of contextual support and opportunity for practice. Subjects were tested individually in two sessions, with two conditions in each session. In the first session, a series of arithmetic tasks was administered to them with no support or practice: They were shown each task for the first time, and they gave an immediate answer. Later in the same session, they were given each task again, but now environmental support was provided: The experimenter first showed them a sample good answer and allowed them time to read it over and ask questions about it. Then the sample answer was taken away, and they provided their own answer. At the end of this session, they were reminded that they would be tested on the same tasks in two weeks and that they should think about them during the interim. In the second session, the two conditions from the first session were repeated—first, assessment with no support, and then assessment with the support of first seeing a good answer.

Approximately eight subjects have been assessed in each grade between third grade and the sophomore year of college. (A few additional subjects must be tested for the study to be completed.) The tasks in the arithmetic study were designed to test several of the levels of abstract skills that are predicted by skill theory to develop during adolescence and early adulthood.

FOUR LEVELS OF ABSTRACT SKILLS

According to skill theory, abstractions first develop at about ten to twelve years of age, the period when formal operations are said to begin (Inhelder and Piaget, 1958). However, these first abstractions involve only the simplest level of abstract skills, and three additional levels develop over the next fifteen years, as shown in Table 4.1. These four levels of abstractions continue the hierarchical series of levels that starts in early infancy: The young infant first controls reflexes at successively more complex developmental levels, and the ultimate result is single sensorimotor actions. Next, the older infant builds successively more complex levels of actions, eventually producing single representations. The child in turn constructs more and more complex levels of representations, finally producing single abstractions. The cycle of successively more complex levels of abstractions is the focus of the present chapter.

Each level is defined in terms of a skill structure that is specified algebraically (Fischer, 1980). For Level 7, the structure is a single abstraction, which arises from the intercoordination of two or more representational systems. The simplest algebraic representation of the structure at each level is shown in Table 4.1. To avoid having to elaborate these structural definitions in this chapter, we will define the levels here in terms of one type of abstraction, the intangible category. Many instances of abstractions involve intangible categories and the relations between them, and they seem to have been investigated more than any other type, not only in our laboratory but in most research on cognitive development in adolescence and early adulthood. In describing the levels, we will focus on our arithmetic study as well as several other studies from the literature dealing with the following intangible categories: intention and responsibility (Fischer, Hand, and Russell, 1984; Hand and Fischer, 1981), political concepts (Adelson, 1972), moral concepts (Kohlberg, 1969; Rest, 1983), and reflective judgment about knowledge (Kitchener, 1983c).

In the arithmetic study, tasks were designed to assess each of the four levels of abstractions, although thus far we have collected data only for the first two levels. All the tasks involve using, defining, and relating the four basic arithmetic operations—addition, subtraction, multiplication, and division. For each task, the subject calculates a simple arithmetic problem or two, such as 7 + 3

= ?. Then he or she answers a general question about the operations used, such as "Explain what addition is, and show how the definition applies to this problem." In all cases, the problems dealt only with positive whole numbers. Each type of task was given in two different forms, one involving general verbal explanation without any visual props and one involving an explanation using the number line for positive whole numbers (a line along which the numbers are displayed at equal intervals).

In *Level 7 single abstractions*, which first appear as early as ten or eleven years of age, the child controls individual intangible categories, such as intention and responsibility, law, society, and justice. Children with single abstractions can coordinate two or more concrete instances to form an intangible category, but they cannot relate one intangible category to another. There were eight arithmetic tasks for assessing Level 7 skills. All tasks required providing a general definition of one of the four operations, as illustrated in Table 4.1, and showing how it applied to an arithmetic problem the child had calculated.

With *Level 8 abstract mappings*, emerging at about fourteen to sixteen years of age, adolescents relate one intangible category to another in a simple way. Examples include the relation of intention to responsibility, of liberal to conservative, and of one type of knowledge to another type. What is not possible at Level 8 is dealing simultaneously with several components or varieties of each intangible category, such as relating two types of intention to two types of responsibility. There were eight arithmetic tasks for assessing Level 8 skills, two each for the four following pairs of closely related operations: addition and subtraction, multiplication and division, multiplication and addition, and division and substraction. To pass each task, the person had to explain in general terms how the two operations in the pair relate to each other (how they are similar and different) and how that relation is evident in specific arithmetic problems, such as 7 + 3 = 10 and 10 − 3 = 7.

The findings from a number of studies support the emergence of the new capacities described by Levels 7 and 8, but there are not many studies relevant to Levels 9 and 10 (Fischer, Hand, and Russell, 1984; Kenny, 1983). Nevertheless, a few studies do suggest the emergence of the hypothesized capacities of Levels 9 and 10 in early adulthood (see Broughton, 1978; Commons et al., 1984; Jaques, Gibson, and Isaac, 1978; Kitchener, 1983c). Also, the theories of Case (1980) and Biggs and Collis (1982) predict levels of abstraction similar to those of skill theory. Because of the dearth of data, the description of the nature of these two levels and the ages associated with them should be considered tentative.

Level 9 abstract systems, developing initially at approximately twenty years of age, introduce more complex relations between intangible categories. The young adult can relate several components or varieties of one abstraction, such as intention, to several components or varieties of another, such as responsibility. For example, systems relating several types of intention to several types of responsibility seem to be common in the legal system, where intention and

TABLE 4.1. Four Developmental Levels of Abstract Skills

Level	Skill Structure	Examples from Arithmetic Study*
7 Systems of Representational Systems, which Are Single Abstractions		General Definitions of Arithmetic Operations and Application to Problem: "Addition is when you put together two numbers, and you end up with a bigger number. Like you put together the numbers 5 and 7, and you get the bigger number 12."
8 Abstract Mappings		General Relations or Two Closely Related Arithmetic Operations and Application Problems: "Addition and multiplication are similar operations. Both put numbers together to get a larger number, but the numbers are put together in different ways—by single numbers in addition and by groups of numbers in multiplication. Multiplication is really addition repeated a specific number of times. In 5 times 7, the first number 5, tells you how many times to do the second number, 7, so you have a group of five sevens. In addition, you take the single number 7 and put it together with another 7, and another, and another, and another."
9 Abstract Systems		General Relations of Two Distantly Related Operations: "Addition and division are opposite operations in two ways. Addition increases by single numbers, while division decreases by groups of numbers. The fact that one increases and the other decreases is one

way they are different, and the way they increase or decrease by single numbers or groups is the other way. Repeated addition can be used to express a division problem like $35 \div 5 = 7$. Five added seven times yields 35, so we know there are seven fives in 35."

10 Systems of Abstract Systems, which Are Single Principles*

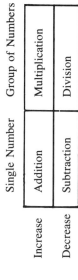

Principle Unifying the Four Arithmetic Operations: "Addition, subtraction, multiplication, and division are all operations, which means that they all transform numbers by either combining or separating them and doing so either in groups or one number at a time. There are relations between all possible pairs of operations. Some pairs are closely related, and others are more distantly related. . . . (Elaboration explaining the pairs, as diagramed in the table below, and applying them to concrete arithmetic problems, such as $5 + 7 = 12$, $12 - 7 = 5$, $5 \times 7 = 35$, and $35 \div 5 = 7$.)"

	Single Number	Group of Numbers
Increase	Addition	Multiplication
Decrease	Subtraction	Division

*The arithmetic concepts deal only with positive whole numbers.
Note: Script capital letters designate abstract sets. Subscripts designate differentiated components of the respective set. Long straight lines and arrows designate a relation between sets or systems. Brackets designate a single skill.

responsibility are two of the essential components for determining guilt and punishment. In arithmetic, one such system for relating several types of arithmetic operations involves the two pairs of distantly related operations: addition and division, and subtraction and multiplication. Each pair is related by variations in two distinct components—direction of change and type of unit (see Table 4.1). We devised a series of arithmetic tasks for assessing Level 9 skills based on these two distantly related pairs of operations.

The final reorganization, *Level 10 general principles*, involves the integration of two or more Level 9 abstract systems in terms of some general theory, ideology, or framework. A reasonable estimate is that this level first appears at approximately twenty-five years of age. Examples include an epistemological framework for coordinating variations in knowledge systems, such as the reflective-judgment framework outlined by Kitchener (1983c), and Darwin's principle of evolution by natural selection (Gruber, 1981). More modest principles also occur at Level 10, including the one integrating the relations among the four arithmetic operations: The four operations involve the possible combinations of the two different types of transformations of numbers implied by the components in the distantly related pairs assessed at Level 9: direction of change (increase or decrease) and type of unit (single numbers or groups of numbers), as outlined in Table 4.1.

EMPIRICAL CRITERIA FOR LEVELS

With the arithmetic tasks devised for testing the four levels of abstractions, it is possible to test the skill-theory analysis of the effects of environmental conditions on the pattern of developmental change. Under optimal conditions, performance on these tasks should demonstrate discontinuities upon the emergence of each new level. Under ordinary (nonoptimal) conditions, performance should demonstrate slow, gradual, continous improvement. This hypothesis specifies several empirical criteria for levels.

Spurt in Tasks for a Particular Level

The most obvious empirical criterion for the emergence of a new level is a spurt in optimal performance. In the arithmetic study, such a spurt occurred for both Level 7 and Level 8.

Between third and fifth grades, Level 7 performance under optimal conditions spurted from near zero to over 50 percent correct. Figure 4.3 shows the data for the two extreme conditions: no support or practice (the first condition in the first session) and both support and practice (the second condition in the second session). The latter, the optimal condition, produced the spurt in performance, while the former, the nonoptimal, ordinary condition, produced slow,

FIGURE 4.3. Development of Level 7 Arithmetic Skills under Ordinary and Optimal Conditions

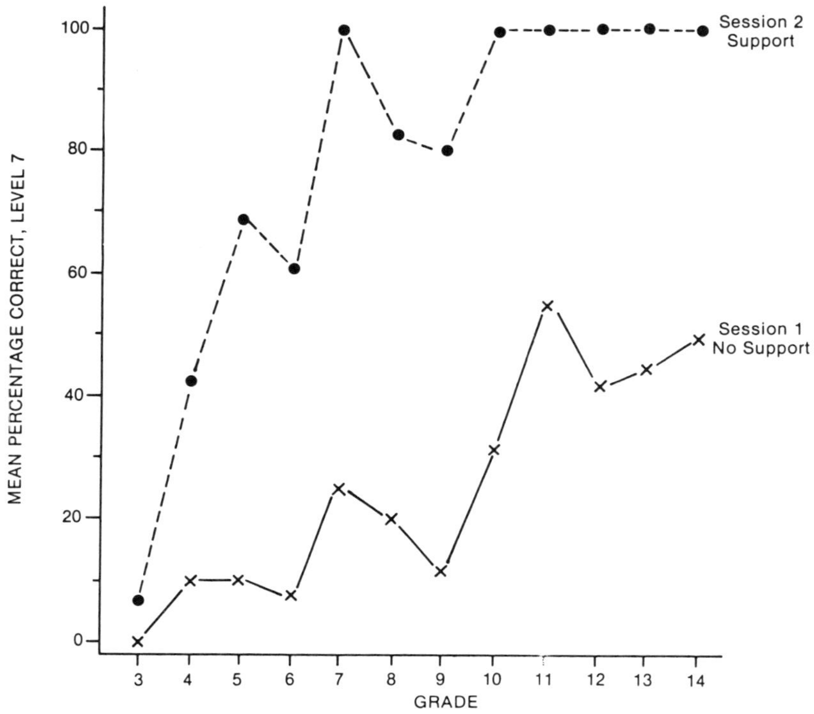

Source: Fischer, Pipp and Bullock, 1984.

gradual improvement on the same tasks. (We call the nonoptimal condition "ordinary" because most standard cognitive and educational research seems to employ that type of testing condition.) Under each condition, children performed eight tasks assessing Level 7 skills, but two of the tasks dealt with division, which is not taught until late in elementary school. Consequently, only the six tasks for addition, subtraction, and multiplication are included in the analysis for Level 7.

Between ninth and tenth grades, Level 8 performance under optimal conditions spurted from near zero to over 80 percent correct. To illustrate the change from gradual, continuous increase to abrupt spurt across environmental conditions, Figure 4.4 includes all four conditions, ranging from ordinary to optimal conditions. For every condition, each subject performed eight tasks assessing Level 8 skills, as described earlier.

For both levels, the spurt was closely tied to age and grade: Level 7 was marked by a spurt that occurred for all subjects between third and fifth grades (approximately nine and eleven years of age), and Level 8 by a spurt for all subjects between ninth and tenth grades (approximately fifteen and sixteen years).

To meet the criterion for a discontinuity, however, such a close tie to age and grade is not necessary. All that is required is that every subject show a spurt in the tasks for a given level at some point; different people can demonstrate the spurt at different ages. To test for such a spurt, the researcher can use either a longitudinal or a cross-sectional design: The fundamental pattern of data predicted is that under optimal conditions most subjects will either fail all or most of the tasks at a given level or pass all or most of them. In a cross-sectional design, this pattern will produce a bimodal distribution of scores for each level. In a longitudinal design, it will produce not only the bimodal distribution but also a relatively abrupt change at some age for each subject from failing most tasks to passing most of them (Fischer, Pipp, and Bullock, 1984).

The spurt criterion applies to performance in a single domain, such as the understanding of arithmetic operations. When tested across domains, people's optimal performance will demonstrate a cluster of spurts in a given age region, as shown in Figure 4.1 for Level 8. According to skill theory, every person will produce the spurts, although they will occur only for optimal performance in familiar domains (Fischer and Pipp, 1984). It is possible that all normal people will show the cluster of spurts within the same age region, such as thirteen to sixteen years for Level 8, or there may be substantial variation across people. If there is substantial variation, however, what will vary is (a) the exact time interval for the cluster of spurts and (b) the specific domains that show spurts. Across these variations, there will be a universal phenomenon, the cluster of spurts itself. That is, every individual will show such a cluster for each level at some limited age interval. For example, one person might spurt to Level 8 at thirteen to fifteen years, and another might do so at eighteen to twenty years.

FIGURE 4.4.   Development of Level 8 Arithmetic Skills under Four Conditions

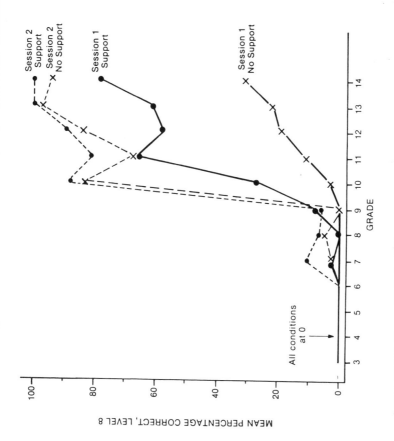

Source: Fischer, Pipp and Bullock, 1984.

Note that the cluster of spurts is predicted only for optimal performance in familiar domains. Spurts will not occur consistently for ordinary, nonoptimal performance, nor for performance in unfamiliar domains. Except for optimal performance, the norm for development is slow, gradual change, with discontinuities occurring only under limited circumstances.

Spurt on Emergence of the Next Level

The data from the arithmetic study allow a partial test of the cluster hypothesis. Different tasks were used to assess each level, and the tasks for one level can in some cases be used to test not only for a spurt at that level but also for one at the succeeding level. When two such spurts occur, they should cluster within an age region.

For example, with the spurt in optimal performance upon the emergence of a given level, such as Level 7 in Figure 4.3, performance may not reach 100 percent. In that case, the opportunity still exists for substantial improvement in performance, and so a second spurt can be predicted upon emergence of the next level. When Level 8 emerges, performance on the Level 7 tasks will spurt again as the new capacity produces consolidation and differentiation of the Level 7 skills. The findings in Figure 4.3 support the second-spurt hypothesis. After the initial spurt in Level 7 performance, performance leveled off at 50 to 60 percent correct. Level 7 performance then showed a second spurt beginning at thirteen years. Performance reached 100 percent by age sixteen, the age at which the spurt in Level 8 tasks occurred (Figure 4.4). According to these results, the age region for the two spurts indexing the emergence of Level 8 was thirteen to sixteen years.

For performance on Level 8 tasks, a similar second spurt can be predicted at approximately eighteen to twenty years, when Level 9 emerges. The data in Figure 4.4 suggest such a spurt, although performance in the optimal condition was already so high that the magnitude of the increase is necessarily small.

In general, then, the arithmetic study supports the skill-theory hypothesis that development shows spurts in optimal performance with the emergence of each new cognitive level while showing gradual, continuous change in performance under ordinary, nonoptimal conditions. Further tests of the hypothesis seem warranted by these initial encouraging results.

In addition to investigating the effects of different testing conditions on the form of developmental change, researchers also need to assess the relation of change across domains. According to our hypothesis, optimal conditions will produce a cluster of discontinuities in familiar domains, but in unfamiliar domains performance will not show discontinuities until the individual has had a lengthy period of time to become familiar with the domain. Also, the spurt emphasized in the arithmetic study is a simple first-order discontinuity. More complex discontinuities should also occur, such as second-order discontinuities involving an abrupt change in the relation between performance in different domains. There are also straightforward empirical criteria for detecting these second-order discontinuities, based on measures of the relation between performance in different domains (Fischer, Pipp, and Bullock, 1984; McCall, Eichorn, and Hogarty, 1977).

ADULT FUNCTIONING BELOW OPTIMAL LEVEL

Developmental research suggests that adolescents and young adults do not typically function at their optimal level. In the arithmetic study, for example, the ordinary testing conditions generally produced performance far below optimum. This conclusion is not limited to the arithmetic study but is supported by a vast array of other research, especially that involving Inhelder and Piaget's (1958) tasks for assessing formal operations and other tasks designed to assess sophisticated thinking (Martarano, 1977; Neimark, 1975a; Piaget, 1972). In general, adolescents and adults seem to show a large gap between their optimal level and the level at which they usually function. That is, their functional level in most situations seems to be far below their optimal level.

We would like to propose that this gap reflects more than a global, general tendency to function below optimum: The likelihood that adolescents and adults will function at optimum varies as a function of their level within the abstract tier. As people become capable of higher levels of abstraction, there is an increase in both the size of the gap and the probability that a gap will occur in any specific context. That is, at the lower abstract levels, it is easier for people to behave at optimum, but as they attain higher levels, it becomes harder to behave at optimum. Only under special conditions is a person's functional level the same as his or her optimal level. The gap between functional level under ordinary conditions and optimal level grows as the person's optimal level increases. Another way of saying the same thing is that at higher levels, support and practice become more necessary for the occurrence of high-level functioning (Fischer, Pipp, and Bullock, 1984; Hand, 1981).

The arithmetic study generally supports this gap hypothesis. The gap between functional level in the ordinary condition and optimal level was generally smaller for Level 7 than for Level 8. However, interpretation of this pattern is complicated by the small sample size and the differences between the percentage of tasks passed under the optimal condition for the two levels.

In a study of development of the concepts of intention and responsibility, Hand and Fischer (1981) provided another test of the gap hypothesis. They predicted and assessed a developmental sequence for the abstract concepts of intention and responsibility. Adolescent subjects were tested initially in a structured (high-support) condition: For every predicted step, the experimenter demonstrated a story about intention, responsibility, or the relation between them, and then the subjects told the story back and explained it. In addition, after this condition, subjects took part in a low-support, spontaneous condition, in which they made up two stories of their own about intention and responsibility.

According to the gap hypothesis, the size of the gap for performance in the structured and spontaneous conditions should differ for different levels. Level 7 is the first level of the abstract tier and therefore the easiest of all the levels of abstraction. Even in a low-support condition, adolescents should be able to demonstrate this level with relative ease, and therefore many of them should evidence a small gap. Level 8 marks a major increase in difficulty level, because it involves relations between abstractions. Consequently, the size of the gap between structured and spontaneous conditions should grow substantially at Level 8. (Note that this hypothesis predicts a second-order discontinuity, in which the relation between performance in the two conditions shifts abruptly between Levels 7 and 8).

The results strongly supported this hypothesis. There was a close match between structured and spontaneous performances for most subjects at Level 7 but a gap for most at Level 8. Among subjects whose highest step in the structured condition was at Level 7, 80 percent showed the same highest step in the spontaneous condition. Among subjects whose highest step in the structured condition was at Level 8, none showed the same highest step in the spontaneous condition. That is, all the subjects whose optimal level was 8 showed a lower functional level, while most of those whose optimal level was 7 showed the same functional level.

Of course, these results do not provide the last word on the gap hypothesis. In any single study, the results can be subject to other interpretations. For example, the pattern could result from the particular tasks or the specific content area, so that a change in tasks or content would drastically alter the findings. Only a series of studies with different tasks in different domains can definitively test the gap hypothesis. Nevertheless, our research to date does suggest that the hypothesis is promising.

Also, some support for the hypothesis comes from the fact that it helps to explain earlier findings on formal operations. Earlier studies indicate that many adolescents and adults can readily pass a few of the easiest of Piaget's formal-operations tasks, but they fail the rest of them (Martarano, 1977; Neimark, 1975a). Most of the tasks that they fail seem to require levels of abstraction beyond Level 7 (Fischer, 1980). Adults, it seems, routinely function at the lowest levels of abstraction. Only under special circumstances do they demonstrate abstractions at the highest levels.

CONCLUSION: EDUCATIONAL IMPLICATIONS

Both data and theory indicate that cognitive development does not end with early adolescence but continues into adulthood. New capacities develop that allow the individual to relate abstractions in increasingly complex ways. These capacities are hypothesized to develop through four successive levels—single abstractions, abstract mappings, abstract systems, and principles integrating abstract systems.

The development of these capacities has powerful implications for education, as well as any other enterprise involving adolescents or young adults. Apparently, there are certain kinds of concepts and relations between concepts that will pose great difficulty for students who have not yet reached the highest developmental levels. Of course, intelligent individuals will be able to learn parts of these concepts and so to mimic high-level functioning, but only at the highest levels will students be able to master such concepts in a straightforward manner.

When people develop a new optimal level, what changes is the most complex skill they can construct and control. Their general cognitive functioning does not change abruptly, because to function at the new level they must actually build specific skills at that level. The building of such skills takes time and effort. Even when students have the capacity to function at a certain level, they cannot be expected to do so easily or automatically. They need time to construct the needed skills and environmental support to stimulate and guide the construction.

The environment plays an important role in supporting not only the construction of skills but also their use after they have been constructed. The construction of an optimal-level skill in a specific domain is insufficient to lead to functioning at that level in that domain. A gap seems to exist between people's optimal level and the level at which they ordinarily function, and the gap seems to grow larger at the highest levels. Although environmental support is required for optimal functioning at any developmental level, it seems to be especially important at the highest levels of abstraction. One of the most important roles of educational institutions may well be to provide the support that is necessary for functioning at high level of abstraction.

Indeed, people may be almost incapable of routinely using high-level skills without supportive environments like those provided by educational institutions such as high schools and colleges. At lower cognitive levels, the ordinary environment seems to provide infants and children with the support they need for functioning near optimum. At the highest levels, the ordinary environment will no longer suffice. Socially constructed environments designed to facilitate abstract thinking seem to be essential (Fischer and Bullock, 1984; Rest, 1981).

5

The Reflective Judgment Model: Characteristics, Evidence, and Measurement

Karen S. Kitchener

The Reflective Judgment model describes the development of assumptions about knowledge or forms of epistemic cognition. Epistemic cognition has been defined as the cognitive "processes an individual invokes to monitor the epistemic nature of problems and the truth value of alternative solutions" (Kitchener, 1983a, p. 225). It includes the individual's assumptions about what can be known and what cannot (e.g., our knowledge of some things is ultimately uncertain), how we can know (e.g., by observing what exists; via authority), and how certain we can be in knowing (e.g., absolutely, probabilistically). Following from each form of knowing is an understanding of how beliefs may be justified in light of the characteristics of the knowing process. Different assumptions about knowledge imply different limits to the cognitive strategies which are accessible to the individual for identifying and choosing between the forms of solutions appropriate for different problem types.

Churchman (1971) was one of the first to note that problems differ in the ways they are knowable and in the decision-making procedure required to solve them. For example, a problem in mathematics, e.g., $2 + 2 = 4$, in base 10, and the problem of nuclear waste differ both in terms of the completeness with which they can be described and in the certainty with which a solution can be identified as true and correct (Wood, 1983). Churchman names this first problem type a "puzzle" and suggests that puzzles are of limited interest in either measuring or in describing the problem solving required in the daily decision making of adults. For one thing, "real world" (Neisser, 1976) problems such as pollution, nuclear energy, poverty, or alcoholism can rarely be constructed as puzzles since one of the biggest difficulties is to determine when and whether a solution has occurred. Churchman labels this second kind of problem as an "ill-structured" or "wicked" problem.

Wood (1983) uses statistical decision theory to describe the problem-solving structure of puzzles and ill-structured problems. He suggests that ill-structured problems result when one of the following are unknown or not known with any degree of confidence by the decision maker: acts open to the decision maker (A), the states of nature (S), potential outcomes (O), and the utility of the possible outcomes (U). By contrast, in puzzles, these variables are known with certainty or a specifiable degree of certainty. For example, in a simple deductive problem, all sets of A, S, O, and U are known and there is a procedure for determining the outcome. Similarly, inductive problems, in which the relationship between A and S is probabilistic but known with a specifiable degree of certainty and the rules of inference are agreed upon, are also forms of puzzles.

Thus when it was stated in the opening paragraph that the Reflective Judgment model describes the development of different forms of epistemic cognition, the implication is that some sets of assumptions about knowledge allow individuals to differentiate between puzzles and ill-structured problems and some do not. For example, if individuals assume that all knowledge is absolute and known by someone, then they cannot allow for unknowns in the problem structure. They assume all problems are reducible to puzzles, i.e., they would assume that A, S, O, and U were known with certainty. The task of decision makers would be to merely apply the correct algorithm. As I have said elsewhere, "As long as individuals assume that a single, correct answer exists for all problems, they cannot consider the possibility that no answer may ever be recognized as universally correct for some problems" (Kitchener, 1983a, p. 226). It should also be noted that such assumptions preclude the possibility that the decision maker needs to generate a solution. By contrast, an individual with the above assumptions, could quite adequately handle puzzle type problems, assuming he/she has the necessary skills to do so.

The Reflective Judgment model describes a sequence of forms of knowledge. At the initial stage, beliefs are characterized by the view that knowledge can be had with absolute certainty via direct experience of the world. Such a view assumes that all problems are of the puzzle variety. In some subjects, assumptions evolve through a sequence of seven stages (Table 5.1) to a form of knowing which can differentiate between puzzles and ill-structured problems. These subjects recognize that while the answer to puzzles can be known with certainty, in the case of ill-structured problems knowledge must be constructed. At this highest stage, knowledge is understood as a reasonable conjecture about the world or a reasonable solution to the problem at hand. In the case of scientific problems, knowledge is constructed via the process of inquiry but in the case of other kinds of ill-structured problems, a viewpoint may need to be constructed based on a higher order integration or synthesis of different perspectives. In this sense, forms of knowing which develop later in the sequence are better since they allow more differentiated responses to problem types and require new ways to integrate diverse perspectives into a solution.

It should be noted that treating an ill-structured problem as a puzzle does

TABLE 5.1. Reflective Judgment Stages

	What Can We Know?	How Certain Can We Know?	Through What Process Can We Know?	How May Beliefs Be Justified?	Differentiation/ Integration
1	Reality	Absolutely certain	By direct observation	Beliefs are a direct reflection of reality. No need to justify them.	Single category belief system. "What I believe is . . ."
2	True reality and false claims.	Absolutely certain and certain but not immediately available.	By direct observation and via what authorities say is true.	Direct observation or via authorities.	Two category belief system; knowledge is true but some claims are false.
3	True reality, false claims, uncertainty.	Absolutely certain about some things; temporarily uncertain about others.	Via authorities in some areas; through our own biases when knowledge is uncertain.	Via authorities in some areas; via what feels right in the moment where knowledge is uncertain.	Three category belief system; knowledge is true, some claims are false, and others are uncertain.
4	While there is a reality, it can never be known. Knowledge	No certainty because of situational variables (e.g., time).	Via our own and others' biases, data, and logic.	Via idiosyncratic evaluations of evidence and unevaluated beliefs.	Uncertain-knowledge becomes further differentiated into types

is individually idiosyncratic.				of uncertainty and becomes overriding category, i.e., ultimately uncertain.
5 Personal interpretations of individual realities.	No certainty except via personal perspectives within a specific context.	Via evidence and rules of inquiry appropriate for the context.	By rules of inquiry for a particular context.	Greater differentiation within domains. Evidence integrated within specific domains.
6 Reality assumed. Evaluated personal interpretations.	Some personal certainty about beliefs based on evaluations of evidence on different sides of the question.	Via personal assessment of arguments and data, via evaluated opinions of experts.	Via generalized rules of inquiry, personal evaluations that apply across contexts, evaluated views of experts.	Evidence and opinion can be integrated across as well as within different domains. Greater differentiation.
7 Reality is never "given." Facts and assumptions may be constructed into evaluated knowledge claims about reality.	Certainty that some knowledge claims are better or more complete than others although they are open to re-evaluation.	Via process of critical inquiry or synthesis.	As more or less reasonable conjectures about reality or the world based on an integration and evaluation of data, evidence, and/or opinion.	Viewpoint constructed by abstracting or synthesizing across as well as within different domains.

not guarantee a poor solution nor does treating an ill-structured problem for what it is guarantee a better one. In other words, it is not necessarily the case that epistemic assumptions which develop later lead to better problem solutions. The probability that they will lead to more adequate solutions is, however, greater because they more fully allow several perspectives to be brought to bear on the problem. As a consequence, existing data and opinion will be integrated more completely in the solution.

MEASURING REFLECTIVE JUDGEMENT

Reflective Judgment stage is assessed with the Reflective Judgment Interview (RJI) (King, 1978; Kitchener, 1978). In the interview, subjects are individually presented with four ill-structured problems, called dilemmas, drawn from the domains of physical science, social science, history, and biology. Each offers the subject two alternative conceptions of a problem. An example follows:

> Some people believe that news stories represent unbiased, objective reporting of news events. Others say that there is no such thing as unbiased, objective reporting and that even in reporting the facts, the news reporters project their own interpretation into what they write.

The task for the subjects, during the interview, is to explain and defend their judgment about the issue and in what way they know their belief to be true. Subjects' responses on these issues are elicited through six semistructured probe questions, i.e., can you say you know for sure your position is correct or true? If individuals do not have a judgment about the issue, six parallel probe questions are used to elicit their rationale for not taking a point of view and how this is related to their assumptions about knowing. Further, interviewers ask subjects for elaborations of ideas and explanations of word use, e.g., what do you mean by "probably true"? While such probing does not guarantee that a subject will use the highest stage of thinking of which he/she is capable, as Kohlberg and Armon (1984) seem to suggest, it does clarify the nature of assumptions currently being used and encourages subjects to take the interview seriously.

Responses to probe questions are scored by stage, using the Reflective Judgment scoring rules jointly developed by King (1978) and Kitchener (1978). Criteria for scoring include assumptions about knowledge, use of evidence, certainty of knowledge, and nature of justification. Scoring is usually done by two certified raters.* Three scores are assigned independently to a subject's response

---

*A certification procedure has been established for both interviewers and raters in order to increase the comparability of data gathered by different researchers. Permission to use the copy written RJI interview is dependent on using certified raters and interviewers. For more information, contact the author at the School of Education, University of Denver, Denver, Colorado 80208, or Dr. Patricia King, Education Building #318, Bowling Green State University, Bowling Green, Ohio 43403.

to a dilemma by each rater using a procedure derived from Perry (1970). The first score represents the dominant stage used. The second score represents the subdominant stage. A third score is given if there is evidence of a third stage. A third score has been used in scoring responses to less than 1 percent of the dilemmas. If no third stage is apparent in the response, the third score is used to weight the dominant stage, e.g., dominant stage 3, subdominant stage 2 is scored "323."

Mean scores for subjects are derived by averaging stage scores across all dilemmas and both raters, i.e., 4 dilemmas × 2 raters × 3 scores per dilemma by rater = 24 scores, and have been used for group comparison purposes. In addition, longitudinal change has been examined in several ways including stages with losses and stages with gains (Kitchener, 1978) and changes in rounded mean score (King, Kitchener, Davison, Parker and Wood, 1983.)

The RJI was designed to meet several criteria. First, as already noted, each dilemma was designed as an ill-structured problem. Second, ill-structured problems were chosen from the intellectual domain in order to differentiate assumptions about knowledge from moral judgments or ego/identity issues. This differentiation was based on the assumption that development was not necessarily even across areas. Third, dilemmas were written about content with which subjects in the United States would be familiar, so that knowledge of content would not unduly influence stage scores. Fourth, the reading level was designed so that most subjects with more than a junior high school education could comprehend the dilemmas. Since the interviewer reads the dilemma out loud while the subject reads his/her copy silently, comprehension may not be a problem with younger subjects. To date, the interview has been used successfully with over 900 subjects, ranging between 16 (Kitchener and King, 1981) and 55 years (Glatfelter, 1982); with undergraduate and graduate college students (Brabeck, 1983; Hayes, 1981; Mines, 1980; Schmidt, 1983; Shoff, 1979; Strange and King, 1981; Welfel, 1982); with nonstudent adults (Glatfelter, 1982; King et al., 1983; Lawson, 1980; Schmidt, 1983); and with German university students (Kitchener and Wood, 1984). A project is currently underway at the University of Denver using the interview with junior high subjects. (This data is also reviewed in King and Kitchener, 1984.)

Fifth, in order to evaluate the generalizability of Reflective Judgment stage scores across similar problems, four content areas are sampled. The subject's mean score represents the best general indicator of how that individual will reason in similar contexts. In addition, as Rest (1979a) suggests, such sampling also minimizes idiosyncratic subject-situation interaction, e.g., attention during the interview. Sixth, the interview and scoring are standardized to minimize the influence of the specific testing situation on score. An interviewer and rater certification procedure has been established to reduce the variability of both across different researchers. Furthermore, scoring rules have remained essentially unchanged since 1977.

The psychometric properties of the RJI have been reviewed elsewhere

(Mines, 1982). In general, interrater reliability has been moderate to high, depending on the heterogeneity of the sample tested and interrater agreement for first round ratings has consistently ranged between 70 percent and 80 percent. Raters occasionally make errors due to fatigue, so a procedure has been established to blindly re-rate all dilemmas for which the raters' scores are more than one stage discrepant. These second round agreement rates have been between 90 percent and 98 percent. Cronbach's alpha, an estimate of the extent to which the dilemmas are measuring the same construct, has ranged from .63 (Strange and King, 1981) to .96 (Kitchener and King, 1981).

TO WHAT EXTENT IS THE REFLECTIVE JUDGMENT MODEL A STAGE MODEL

Because of the criticism (Brainerd, 1978; Fischer, 1980; Flavell, 1971, 1977, 1982) and skepticism about the usefulness of stage concepts in developmental research, the use of the term stage in this research needs to be explained and defined. Basically, the term stage is maintained because the concept better fits the data and the model than do terms like period, phase, or level (von Glaserfeld and Kelley, 1982) or simple sequence (Flavell, 1982). On the other hand, the data do not fit some of the characteristics that have been identified with the classical or simple stage model.

Flavell (1971, 1977) argues that the characteristics of a stage model include organized structures of qualitatively different forms of thinking, which appear in an invariant sequence; abruptly and concurrently. Piaget (1970) argued additionally that higher stages are hierarchical integrations of the structural components of lower stages. Flavell and others (Rest, 1979a) have already noted that this simple characterization of stage fits neither the data on the Piagetian stage model nor the Kohlbergian one.

What then does the term stage mean in the Reflective Judgment model? To begin with the least controversial claim, it appears that individual thinking about knowledge is structured. Flavell (1971) has suggested that as a minimum, this means that two or more elements are interrelated. In addition, it usually implies that these organizations are relatively stable and form the basis of apparently unrelated acts. In this regard, it has already been noted that assumptions about the nature of knowledge, how one comes to know, and how one justifies beliefs in light of these assumptions, appear to be connected in an interrelated network as subjects reason about ill-structured problems in the intellectual domain.

The connections appear to be logical ones although the logic is probably not apparent to most subjects. Rather, it is implicit in the structure of the belief system. For example, if an individual has only a single category with which to classify knowledge, e.g., true and observable, then it is not only illogical but impossible for the individual to justify his/her beliefs by reference to the probability of one view of a phenomenon over another. The structure appears to underlie some superficially unrelated beliefs, including the validity of authorities' claims, the way beliefs can be justified as better or worse, and understanding of bias and interpretations. For example, an individual might suggest that authorities' views just represent their own biases, that no view is better than any other of an issue, and that everybody has the right to his own opinion. What seems to be at the basis of this belief system is the assumption that knowledge is ultimately subjective, i.e., it is unknown and there is no rational way to understand; therefore authorities' claims to know are just their own subjective bias, etc.

The structuring does not appear to be as extensive in terms of its horizontal generalizability as Piaget had in mind by the term "structure d'ensemble." First, the structuring does not appear to be an all or nothing matter. A better analogy is a loosely related network of assumptions, some of which are more closely associated than are others. While epistemological assumptions may change, the implications for related beliefs may not be understood immediately nor generalized to all content areas at the same time. Thus development does not appear to be abrupt nor show total synchrony.

Interdilemma correlations are one indicator of the similarity of scores across dilemmas which differ in content. These correlations have been moderate to high in most Reflective Judgment studies, usually ranging between .65 and .92, depending on the raters and the heterogeneity of the sample. (See Mines, 1982 for a recent review.)

Hayes (1981) designed a study to measure whether familiarity with content would significantly affect Reflective Judgment scores. Using two ill-structured problems from education and two standard dilemmas with teacher trainees, he found a small range of scores across dilemmas. Although students scored significantly lower on one of the standard dilemmas (Egyptian pyramids), the amount of difference between it and the other dilemmas only ranged between .20 and .30 of a stage. While he concluded that content made some difference in Reflective Judgment scores, the differences were quite small.

Hayes' study and interdilemma correlations support the claim that epistemic assumptions become structured networks of beliefs. On the other hand, both are based on subjects' mean scores on a dilemma and may mask individual variability across content areas. The clearest indicator of intersubject variability is the range of scores across all dilemmas.

The scores of most individuals who are tested on ill-structured problems covering content from physical science, social science, history, biological science, and religion show strong modal tendencies with a distribution of scores ranging across three stages or less. Specifically, Kitchener and King (1981) reported that 58 percent of their subjects' scores fell in their modal stage. They and others (King et al., 1983) report that about two-thirds of their subjects' scores spanned three stages or less and only a few subjects (between 5 percent and 8 percent) had scores spanning more than four stages. Some of the variability in this latter group may be attributable to measurement error. In other words, evaluating the range and modal tendencies of subjects' scores further supports the claim that the components of the Reflective Judgment stages form structural networks.

The stability of structure over time is relatively difficult to access since it involves following an individual and retesting him/her periodically over an extended period, and such methodologies are subject to the usual criticisms associated with repeated testings. As a consequence, data on this issue comes from a variety of sources. First, Sakalys (1982) reported no significant difference in RJI scores over a three-month period for two groups of senior nursing students. The first group was enrolled in a course on research methodology and the second group served as controls. Test-retest reliability was .83 and .71 respectively for the two groups. Both the pre- and postdata and the test-retest reliability support the stability of RJI scores over this short time span. This claim is further supported by the failure to find change in the experimental group who were explicitly taught rules of scientific inquiry. If higher stages in the Reflective Judgment model merely reflect the learning of new rules of knowledge, the experimental group should have shown greater changes in RJI scores than the control.

In addition, longitudinal studies of high school and college students show only small positive changes in Reflective Judgment scores over a one to three year period (Brabeck and Wood, 1983; King et al., 1983; Schmidt, 1983). Changes of about one-half of a stage over a two-year to three-year period are reported for the majority of subjects. (See King and Kitchener, 1984 for a summary of the data.) On the other hand, King et al. (1983) and Schmidt (1983) report that the scores of between 25 percent and 40 percent of their college and/or graduate students did not change in two- to three-year periods. By contrast, Welfel and Davison reported 92 percent of their subjects showed upward change after four years and Kitchener, King, and Wood (1984) report that 100 percent of their samples of high school and college students reported gains after six years. In other words, these data suggest that for most people, Reflective Judgment scores remain stable over short periods of time and that for some individuals thinking styles remain stable for up to three years and possibly longer. On the other hand, over longer periods of time, change does occur and in a direction that is theoretically consistent with the model.

Another criterion of stage models is the claim that there are qualitative differences in the forms of thinking although quantitative differences may also be present (Flavell, 1971). Several authors have noted that whether changes appear qualitative or quantitative depends on the level of analysis (Flavell, 1977; Werner, 1957). On a macrolevel, changes in assumptions about knowledge, described in the Reflective Judgment model, clearly have qualitative components. The assumption that knowledge is absolutely knowable is qualitatively different from and carries different implications than the assumption that knowledge is relative to time and place or that knowledge is constructed via rational inquiry. These differences have been recognized historically in philosophy. Further, as has already been suggested, these differences are important in structuring how an individual approaches and justifies solutions to ill-structured problems. This does not mean, however, that quantitative changes are not also present. As can be observed in Table 5.1, one of the major changes that is present in the shifts between stages one, two, and three is quantitative, i.e., the number of categories the individual has available to classify types of knowledge increases. While such quantitative changes are not as clearly identified in stages four through seven, they are implicit in the Reflective Judgment scoring rules (King, 1978; Kitchener, 1978) as individuals appear able to process more complex information.

Another major criterion of stage models is that the different forms of thinking form a sequence that is invariant across individuals. Invariance is also a claim that is difficult to confirm or disconfirm since time between measurements, as well as measurement error, does not allow the researcher to trace all changes in the individual thinking or track them with absolute accuracy. Data support the claim, however, that in general, Reflective Judgment stages change in the direction and sequence specified by the model.

The first set of data that bears on this claim is cross-sectional. Ten studies have compared the Reflective Judgment scores of subjects who differed in educational level, but whose age was controlled within educational level (e.g., sixteen-year-old high school juniors). As would be predicted, scores have increased significantly for traditionally aged students, by grade level in all (Glatfelter, 1982; Hayes, 1981; King and Parker, 1978; Kitchener and King, 1981; Lawson, 1980; Mines, 1980; Schmidt, 1983; Strange and King, 1981; Welfel, 1982) but one sample (Brabeck, 1983). (See King and Kitchener, 1984 for a complete report of this data.)

Longitudinal data on traditionally aged students have supported the overall findings of the cross-sectional studies. Group mean scores have increased significantly for all groups tested at one to four year intervals, even when controlling for subjects who did not participate in retesting. (See also King and Kitchener, 1984 and Brabeck, in press, for a more complete review of these findings.) In general, high school students' mean scores have ranged between Stages 2 and 3.5. For college students, they have ranged between 3.0 and 4.5 and for advanced graduate students, they have ranged between 4.5 and 6.5. As has already been noted, upward changes of about one-half a stage have been observed over two to four year periods in college students.

Davison's (1979) test of sequentiality in development, which is based on a unidimensional, qualitative unfolding model has also been used to evaluate the sequentiality of the Reflective Judgment stages. His test preserves the concept of qualitatively different and ordered stages, but does not assume synchrony or abruptness in the appearance of the stages; nor does it assume that the stage values satisfy a metric. The model has been used to evaluate the ordering of stages two through seven on subjects both from the United States (Davison, 1979;

King et al., 1983) and West Germany (Kitchener and Wood, 1984). In all cases, the results of Davison's test support the claim that Reflective Judgment stages emerge in the order predicted by the model and do so, as well if not better, than do the stages of other developmental models (Davison, King, Kitchener, and Parker, 1980).

In other words, the data support the claim that epistemic assumptions develop in a structured network and in a sequence of qualitatively different stages. The last characteristic of stage models, hierarchical integration, is not one that is easily subject to empirical tests, although Rest (1973) has used a Guttman scale of a cumulative sequence of comprehension to evaluate the hierarchical relationship of Kohlberg's moral judgment stages. Such a test has not been used on the Reflective Judgment stages. From a theoretical perspective, Kohlberg and Armon (1984) have argued that it is necessary to show that later stages not only replace earlier ones but transform them. Such an argument for each stage of the Reflective Judgment model is beyond the scope of this paper. However, it can be noted that more than one philosopher (Hiley, 1979; Lakatos, 1978; Popper, 1963) has argued that dogmatism and skepticism are logically prior to and integrated in critical rationality. Such analyses certainly lend support to the claim that lower stages are hierarchically integrated in higher ones in the Reflective Judgment model.

It should be noted that complex stage models offer less diagnostic precision than do simple ones (Flavell, 1977). One cannot say that a subject or a subject's reasoning is "in" a particular stage. This does not make the qualitative distinctions of the model useless, however, because probabilistic statements can be made about what general style of reasoning an individual will use when faced with a specific type of problem and this may be useful in designing educational and clinical interventions. This is particularly true of the Reflective Judgment stages, since each stage describes a narrower band of cognitive assumptions which apply to a more circumscribed set of problems than do Piaget's stages. In addition, the assumptions of adjacent stages in the model are not as discrepant as are the assumptions that are two stage discrepant. For example, if a subject scores as dominant stage four, subdominant five, we can conclude that he/she will see knowledge as ultimately uncertain since this is a characteristic of both stages. Further, in most cases, he/she is probably skeptical about the ability of people to know anything via reason, but in some cases his/her view is closer to a true relativism. Such information allows a greater diagnostic clarity about reasoning errors than, for example, do intelligence test scores.

Reflective Judgment scores do not, however, provide us with all the information that might be necessary in understanding how an individual reasons about "wicked" problems. After reviewing hundreds of Reflective Judgment protocols, it has become apparent to me that there are subtle, within-stage differences that the model doesn't capture. We know almost nothing about these differences nor whether they represent different degrees of familiarity with content, facility with logical reasoning, or personality differences. This is an important area for further research.

HOW DOES DEVELOPMENT IN REFLECTIVE JUDGMENT RELATE TO OTHER ASPECTS OF INTELLECTUAL DEVELOPMENT?

The Reflective Judgment model does not claim to describe all aspects of intellectual development in adulthood. There is evidence, for example, from the study of human abilities (Horn, 1982) that the skills underlying what we commonly think of as intelligence continue to develop at least through the young adult years as people gain new information and additional experience at tasks. Thus, it is important to ask, "What else is developing and how does it relate to changing assumptions about knowledge and justification?"

Generally, data from the intelligence testing tradition suggest that most people become better puzzle solvers in the young and early-middle adult years (Bayley, 1970; Honzik and McFarlane, 1973; Horn, 1982). While some, e.g., Wechsler (1958), might disagree that intelligence tests measure puzzle solving, in general, the items on these tests evaluate the amount of information available to the individual and how the information is related either deductively or inductively in well-structured problems. For example, analogies are frequently used to measure intellectual abilities, e.g., Terman's Concept Mastery Test (1973), Horn's crystallized intelligence (1982). They are inductive problems in which the answer can be specified with a high degree of certainty. Even problems used to measure judgment (Horn, 1982) can be included in the puzzle category, since the parameters of the problem are specified and therefore known.

In other words, many of the abilities underlying puzzle solving continue to develop in the young adult years. On the other hand, not all young adults show evidence of using the highest Reflective Judgment stages. Thus it is conceivable that some adults become exceptionally able puzzle solvers, but never move beyond assuming that there is a single absolute way to know the world. For these individuals, all ill-structured problems must be treated as puzzles. Therefore, by a set of preconceived assumptions, all unknowns in a problem (e.g., the acts open to the decision maker, possible states of nature) are specified and the problem is reduced to one that can be handled via deductive or inductive inference.

On the other hand, the skills basic to puzzle solving may be necessary but not sufficient for high levels of Reflective Judgment. If this is so, there should be a moderate and positive correlation between measures of intellectual ability and Reflective Judgment. The studies (Glatfelter, 1982; King, Kitchener, Davison, Parker, and Wood, 1983; Kitchener and King, 1981; Lawson, 1980; Schmidt, 1983; Welfel, 1982) that have looked most closely at the relationship between Reflective Judgment and intellectual ability have used a measure of verbal reasoning, Terman's (1973) Concept Mastery Test (CMT), since the ability to reason inductively about verbal problems appears closely related to the skills necessary to reason about ill-structured problems in an interview setting.

Correlations between the CMT and RJI have been low to moderate (range = .14 to .55) with college aged samples, while they have been low to high with graduate samples (range = .22 to .78). The high positive correlation between Reflective Judgment and verbal ability of .78 was found in Kitchener and King's graduate sample. In a second testing of these same subjects, it dropped to .61 and in a third testing it dropped to .55 (King and Kitchener, 1984). In general, the results of these studies support the claim that Reflective Judgment and verbal ability are related but are not identical constructs. On the other hand, in four studies (Kitchener and King, 1981; Glatfelter, 1982; Lawson, 1980; Schmidt, 1983) of cross-sectional samples differences between the Reflective Judgment scores of one or more groups could be statistically accounted for by differences in verbal ability.

The longitudinal relationship between the two measures provides a stricter test of the hypothesis that verbal ability can account for differences in Reflective Judgment scores. With longitudinal data, subjects act as their own control, thus the failure to find differences in Reflective Judgment score between different groups at two points of time when controlling for verbal ability cannot be attributed to cohort differences. In fact, in the three longitudinal studies that have measured both Reflective Judgment and verbal ability (King et al., 1983; Schmidt, 1983; Welfel and Davison, 1983), differences in Reflective Judgment score over time could not be statistically accounted for by changes in verbal ability. These data support the claim that Reflective Judgment is related to but not the same construct as verbal ability.

The second construct from which Reflective Judgment must be differentiated is formal operations (Inhelder and Piaget, 1958). This is particularly true since Inhelder and Piaget appear to think it involves more than puzzle solving. They suggest that it underlies adolescents' ability to engage in the construction of theories, systems, and ideologies which are predominantly philosophical tasks and which often involve epistemic assumptions (Kitchener and Kitchener, 1981). I have argued elsewhere (Kitchener and Kitchener, 1981), however, that formal operations is reducible to a deductive-inductive model, and that these processes are inadequate to account for the epistemic assumptions which allow individuals to compare competing conceptions of a problem. It appears that the development of epistemic assumptions is not superimposed upon the development of formal operations, i.e., in the sense of being postformal. Rather, formal operations and the development of epistemic assumptions reflect two different but important interrelated aspects of intellectual development, neither one accounting fully for the development of the other, nor for what is broadly meant by intellectual development.

King (1978) empirically investigated the relationship between Reflective

Judgment and formal operations using the chemicals and the pendulum tasks (Inhelder and Piaget, 1958). Despite the fact that 91 percent of her sample scored as fully formal on either one or both tasks, significant differences were found between high school, college, and graduate students on Reflective Judgment scores. The correlations between the two Piagetian tasks and Reflective Judgment scores were essentially zero (.0002 and .017, respectively) and nonsignificant. While the low correlations can be accounted for, in part, by the limited range of scores on the Piagetian tasks, King concluded that the differences she observed between groups in RJI scores could not be attributed to differences in formal operations.

The third construct, which could potentially compete with Reflective Judgment, is critical thinking. Brabeck (1983) points out that, in addition to sharing the domain of intellectual problem solving, they share similar "attitudes" toward it, since both critical thinking and higher Reflective Judgment stages theoretically presuppose an awareness of and willingness to consider alternative conceptions of a problem. Brabeck notes, however, that deductive and inductive logical skills are seen as the core of problem solving, in the critical thinking tradition. The differences between this conception and the Reflective Judgment model need not be repeated here. Studies investigating the relationship between Reflective Judgment and critical thinking have found, in general, that high critical thinking scores taken globally or by specific subtests, e.g., interpretation, cannot account for high RJI stage scores (Brabeck, 1983; Mines, 1980).

CURRENT PROBLEMS AND FUTURE DIRECTIONS

At this time, the first phase of Reflective Judgment research is coming to a close. The initial conception of the model has proven useful in investigating an aspect of adult problem solving that has been ignored by most other schools of thinking about intellectual problem solving. To reiterate an earlier point, epistemic assumptions provide individuals with a framework through which they monitor the nature of problems and the way in which the solutions are knowable. In particular, they are critical in distinguishing ill-structured problems and puzzles and in identifying appropriate models of justification for each.

The model has stood up well to various tests of sequentiality and structure. The fact that subjects' responses vary slightly over different tasks is not unduly troublesome for the model since it doesn't postulate that a total synchrony or concurrence ought to occur. While changes in core assumptions may converge, experience with new content areas may be required before the individual can understand similarities and differences in the structure of problems and the knowability of solutions in different areas.

Fischer's (Fischer, 1980; Fischer and Pipp, 1984) concept of optimal level is useful, in conceptualizing this process. Fischer and Pipp define optimal level as the most complex type of skills that an individual can control. They note that optimal performance is strongly influenced by environmental factors. In addition, although optimal level describes the highest level at which an individual can function, the person retains the ability to use lower order skills and concepts. Because of fatigue, lack of familiarity about the particular issue, etc., the individual may not use the highest level skill he/she can control.

This differential level of functioning is particularly apparent in assessing Stages 6 and 7 in the Reflective Judgment model. Some individuals reason at Stage 7 on one or two dilemmas but use Stage 6 reasoning on others. Occasionally, subjects will spontaneously comment on the discrepancy of their own thinking across dilemmas, noting that they aren't familiar enough with the content or haven't immersed themselves enough in the issue to make the more generalizable judgments that are required for Stage 7 rating. Thus, the differences in stage usage across dilemmas may partially be accounted for by personal or environmental variables and the influence they have on optimal performance.

While the model has held up reasonably well under the first set of studies examining sequentiality and structuring, other theoretical and empirical problems exist. (1) No adequate explanation exists for why or how change occurs between stages. It has been suggested, elsewhere, that the sequence is a logical one but that environmental factors play an essential role in motivating development (Kitchener, 1983b). Experiences with knowing particularly about ill-structured problems seem critical (Kitchener and King, 1981). However, these processes are imprecisely defined. It was originally assumed that these experiences were most closely associated with an educational setting and they probably are. However, data on nontraditional students, e.g., twenty-two-year-old college freshmen, suggest that development does not uniformly occur in such settings (See King and Kitchener, 1984, for a review). Retrospectively, questioning individuals about the life events that have led them to change (Schmidt, 1983; Welfel and Davison, 1983) has shed little light on the issue. (2) While the RJI has been a useful methodological approach to identify differences in epistemic assumptions, it is difficult and time consuming to use and score. Rater training is tedious, particularly because stage concepts have been difficult to articulate clearly and objectively and the unit of analysis has not been defined precisely. Consequently, scores reflect a global assessment of any individual's response to a dilemma. For these reasons, further clarification of the measurement process is needed. An objectively scored measure of Reflective Judgment would also be useful and is under construction (King, 1983). (3) While mean scores have been useful as an index to measure group change and as a "best" estimate of how the individual will reason on similar "ill-structured" problems, they may not be the most meaningful scores for other purposes. For example, if a score was being used to develop educational interventions, an optimal stage score might be a better indicator of the highest set of assumptions the individual could use. Specific dilemma scores might also help identify content areas to which core assumptions had not yet generalized. Further, mean scores may provide an overly pessimistic estimate of the assumptions that a particular group, e.g., college seniors, is capable of understanding.

As Rest (1979a) has noted, mapping a developmental sequence and its structural components is only the first step in a research program. This is clearly the case for Reflective Judgment research; however, some questions are more critical to address than others. First, the validity of model needs to be addressed directly. In particular the question: Do the assumptions identified by Reflective Judgment stages generalize to problem solving outside the laboratory setting? If so, the manner in which they influence how people process information about real-world, ill-structured problems needs direct empirical investigation. Second, the issue of how change between Reflective Judgment stages occurs is as critical to identify. My hypothesis is that at a microlevel, change is quite idiosyncratic. This certainly appears to be the case in moral judgment research. (See Rest in this volume.) Third, after having rated hundreds of interviews, it is apparent to me that there are important individual differences in how stage assumptions are constructed and expressed. It may be that these are individual differences which are related to stage acquisition as Magaña (1982) found in her research on moral development or they are content differences which are embedded in the dilemmas as Colby and Kohlberg (in press) have found in their work on moral judgment rating rules.

After six years of research, we can say the Reflective Judgment model describes a structural sequence of assumptions about knowledge which can be measured with reasonable accuracy and reliability. On a microlevel, the next task is to identify whether the stages can be more precisely distinguished by identifying content differences on stage acquisition and/or subcomponent skills. On a macrolevel, the next task is to investigate the question, do the stage differences make a real difference in how adults understand and operate in the world around them?

6

Moral Development in Young Adults

James R. Rest

What is moral development in young adults? That is, what are the major psychological processes involved in moral behavior that improve in adequacy? What experiences and events influence moral development in young adulthood? In particular, what influence does college attendance have on moral development? These are the major questions that are addressed in this chapter. In discussing them I will describe existing lines of research and where the gaps exist in current research.

THE MAJOR COMPONENTS OF MORAL DEVELOPMENT

In the tradition of Piaget and Kohlberg, the cognitive development approach focuses on moral judgment; that is, how people conceptualize what is morally right, fair, and just. While I think that moral judgment is very important and crucial in moral development (indeed, most of the research on moral development in young adulthood pertains to moral judgment development, and almost all of my own research is on moral judgment), nevertheless it is a mistake to represent *all* of moral development in terms of only moral judgment. Other psychological processes are involved in the production of moral behavior, and these other components must be recognized. It is a mistake to view morality as involving a single process (e.g., moral reasoning, empathy, altruistic motivation).

Support for this research came in part from NIMH grants #RO3MH38031 and #RO1-MH38656, and from the University of Minnesota Computer Center. Portions are adapted from Rest, J. R. "Morality." In P. Mussen (ed.), *Handbook of Child Psychology,* 4th ed., Vol. III, New York: Wiley, 1983.

Rather, the psychology of morality should be viewed as involving an ensemble of processes. Although these processes may interact with each other, they cannot be reduced to a single variable. I propose that we consider four major processes as the components involved in the production of a moral act, as follows: (1) interpreting the situation in terms of how people's welfare is affected by possible actions of the subject; (2) figuring out what the ideally moral course of action would be; (3) deciding what one actually intends to do; and (4) executing and implementing what one intends to do. All these processes are necessary to the performance of a moral act. It follows then that development in being moral involves becoming more proficient in each component process.

Let us consider in more detail each of the components.

Component 1. Component 1, interpreting the situation, involves imagining the possible courses of action in a situation and tracing out the consequences of action in terms of how they affect the welfare of all the parties involved.

Four findings from psychological research stand out in regard to Component 1. The first finding is that many people have great difficulty in interpreting even relatively simple situations. Research on bystander reactions to emergencies shows this. For instance, research by Staub (1978) shows that helping behavior is related to the ambiguity of the situation: when his subjects are not clear about what's happening, they don't volunteer to help as much. A second finding is that striking individual differences exist among people in their sensitivity to the needs and welfare of others. For instance, this is shown in social psychological research by Schwartz (1977) on a variable he described as "Awareness of Consequences." A third finding is that the ability to make inferences about the needs and wants of others—and about how one's actions would affect others—is a developmental phenomenon. People get better with age in being able to make inferences about others. The vast emerging field of "Social Cognition" is relevant here and documents this point (Selman, 1980; Shantz, 1983). A fourth finding is that a social situation can arouse strong feelings even before extensive cognition encoding. Feelings can be activated before one fully understands a situation (Zajonc, 1980). For instance, Hoffman (1977) has emphasized the role of empathy in morality and views the arousal of empathy as a primary response which need not be mediated by complex cognitive operations. The point is that aroused affects are part of what needs to be interpreted in a situation, and therefore are part of Component 1 processing.

Recently, at the University of Minnesota, research has begun on how well students in the health sciences detect moral issues in their professional settings (how well these students carry out Component 1 processes in job-related situations). In dentistry (Bebeau, Rest, and Yamoor, 1983; Yamoor, Bebeau, and Rest, 1983) and in counseling psychology (Volker, 1984), tape-recorded dramatizations of transactions between respective professionals and patients were prepared. The transactions are ones professionals are likely to encounter on the job and which contain a moral problem (such as inferior work by a previous dentist, suspicion of child abuse, etc.). Students in the respective professional training programs were asked to comment on these tapes and their responses were scored for their moral sensitivity. In general, Bebeau, Rest, and Yamoor (1983) and Volker (1984) found that young adults in professional studies were quite good at identifying aspects of technique important to their profession, but did not always hear the moral issue.

Component 2. Whereas the function of Component 1 processes is to identify possible courses of action and their consequences, the function of Component 2 is to identify which course of action is the *moral* action (or the one best satisfying moral ideals). Cognitive developmental research—notably that influenced by Piaget (1932) and Kohlberg (1969)—is primarily dealing with Component 2 processes. For me, the most important theoretical contributions of the cognitive developmental approach are (1) that development is characterized in terms of a person's progressive understanding of the purpose, function, and nature of social cooperation, instead of characterizing development in terms of learning more social rules, or being more willing to sacrifice oneself. (2) The lasting effects of social experience are portrayed in terms of increased understanding of the rationale for establishing cooperative arrangements, particularly on how each of the participants in the cooperative system are reciprocating the burdens and benefits of that system. Therefore, the general long term impact of particular social experiences is characterized in terms of basic concepts of justice (or "schemes of cooperation"). At first, children become aware of fairly simple schemes of cooperation, involving only a few people who know each other through face to face encounters, and who reciprocate in concrete, short-term exchanges. Gradually they become aware of more complicated schemes of cooperation, involving long-term, society-wide networks, institutionalized role systems, divisions of labor, and law-making and law-enforcement systems (see Rest, 1979a, for discussion). The various schemes of cooperation (or "justice structures") are called "stages" of moral reasoning, each characterized in terms of its distinctive notion of justice—that is, progressive awareness of the possibilities and requirements for arranging cooperation among successively wider circles of participants. Each stage is viewed as an underlying *general* framework of assumptions about how people ought to act towards each other. (3) There are a finite number of basic "schemes of cooperation." These can be identified and are essentially like Kohlberg's descriptions of six stages. Furthermore, the stages comprise an ordered sequence such that the latter stages are elaborated from the earlier. (4) When a person is faced with a particular new social situation and is trying to figure out what would be the moral course of action, the person calls from Long Term Memory those general knowledge structures in order to aid in identifying the most important considerations, in order to prioritize the conflicting claims of various people, and in order to judge which course of action best fulfills one's ideal of justice. And so a moral judgment for a particular situation involves assimilating the situation to general social knowledge represented by the "stages" of moral judgment. Research on the six-stage model of moral judgment along the general lines proposed by Kohlberg has been one of the most productive and significant research enterprises in social-personality development (see my review of the field, Rest, 1983). I will come back to further discuss this research as it relates to young adulthood in the next section.

Component 3. Component 3 involves deciding what one actually intends to do by selecting among competing values. Typically, a person is aware of a number of possible outcomes of different courses of action each representing different values and activating different motives. It is not unusual for nonmoral values to be so strong and attractive that a person chooses a course of action that preempts or compromises the moral ideal. For instance, Damon (1977) asked young children how ten candy bars *ought* to be distributed for a fair distribution of rewards, explaining why they thought a particular distribution *ought* to be followed. However, when these same children *actually* were given the ten candy bars to distribute, they deviated from their espoused schemes of fair distribution, and instead each gave himself a disproportionate number of candy bars. Thus the children's espoused moral ideals were compromised by other motives, in this case, by desire for those tasty candy bars.

Given that a person is aware of various possible courses of action in a situation, each leading to a different kind of outcome or goal, why then would a person ever choose the moral alternative, especially if it involves sacrificing some personal interest or enduring some hardship? What motivates moral behavior? A large number of answers to this question have been proposed. I'll briefly list some of the moral motivation (see Rest, 1983, for more complete discussion):

1. People behave morally because evolution has bred altruism into our genetic inheritance (e.g., Wilson, 1975).
2. "Conscience makes cowards of us all"—that is, shame, guilt, conditioned negative affect, fear of God motivates morality (e.g., Aronfreed, 1968; Eysenck, 1976).
3. There is no special motivation to be moral; people just respond to reinforcement and/or modeling opportunities and "learn" social behavior (Bandura, 1977; Goldiamond, 1968).
4. Social understanding of how cooperation functions and one's own stake in making it work lead to moral motivation (e.g., Dewey, 1959; Piaget, 1932).
5. Moral motivation is derived from a sense of awe and self-subjugation to something greater than the self—identification with a crusade, dedication to one's country or collective, reverence for the sacred (e.g., Durkheim, 1961; Erikson, 1958).
6. Empathy is the basis for altruistic motivation (e.g., Hoffman, 1977).
7. The experience of living in just and caring communities can lead to moral commitment (e.g., Kohlberg, 1980; Rawls, 1971).
8. Concern for self-integrity and one's identity as a moral agent is what motivates moral action (Blasi, 1980).

These eight theories about moral motivation indicate the diversity of views on the issue. None of these views is supported by very complete or compelling research evidence at this point. Erikson (1958, 1969) is the only writer in this set of writers who focuses especially on youth and young adults, however, his research is in the form of description of clinical case histories. Clearly, an enormous amount of work needs to be done on this component.

Component 4. As popular widsom advises, good intentions are often a long way from good deeds. Component 4, executing and implementing a plan of action, involves figuring out the sequence of concrete actions, working around impediments and unexpected difficulties, overcoming fatigue and frustrations, resisting distractions and other allurements, and keeping sight of the eventual goal. Perseverence, resoluteness, competence, and "character" are virtues of Component 4. Psychologists sometimes refer to these processes as involving "ego strength" of "self-regulation skills." A biblical term for failure in Component 4 processes is "weakness of the flesh." However, firm resolve, perseverance, iron will, strong character, ego strength, and so on can be used for ill or good. Ego strength comes in handy to rob a bank, prepare for a marathon, rehearse for a piano concert, or carry out genocide.

In one study of Stage 4 "Law and Order" subjects on Kohlberg's measure, those with high "ego strength" cheated less than Stage 4 subjects with low ego strength. Presumably the former had "the strength of their convictions," whereas the latter had convictions but didn't act on them (Krebs, 1967). Various other lines of research also suggest that a certain inner strength, an ability to mobilize oneself to action, is a factor in moral behavior. D. E. Barrett and M. R. Yarrow (1977) found that social assertiveness was an important component in children's "prosocial" behavior. Perry London (1970) interviewed people who were involved in saving persecuted Jews in Nazi Germany and was struck by their adventurousness as well as their caring (presumably an attribute somewhat related to Component 4).

Some recent research on self-regulation processes has described techniques for improving or altering self-regulation. One technique involves the "cognitive transformation" of the goal object. Mischel and Mischel (1976, p. 94) state:

> By knowing the relevant rules of cognitive transformation and utilizing them during self-control effects, individuals may be able to attain considerable self-mastery in pursuit of their goals, even in the face of strong countervailing situational pressures.

Staub (1979, p. 134) adds, "what a person thinks about in the course of helping another person may well determine the persistence of his helpfulness."

In summary, if one is to understand and describe moral development at any age, one must attend to all four components. I believe that sufficient research exists to make a strong case that each of these components represents important and distinct determinants of moral action. However, most of the research on moral development (particularly on Components 1, 3, and 4) has been done with children as subjects, not young adults, and much effort deserves to be devoted there. On Component 2, the component including moral judgment research, a substantial body of research now exists on young adults, and it is to this research that we now turn.

MORAL JUDGMENT DEVELOPMENT IN YOUNG ADULTS

This review of moral judgment research focuses on studies using the Defining Issues Test (DIT), which is a multiple choice test based on Kohlberg's characterization of six stages but developed at Minnesota (see Rest, 1979a). Although Kohlberg's own interview method for measuring moral judgment is better known, few studies using his interview have attended to moral judgment development beyond adolescence. In the few Kohlbergian studies that have attended to moral judgment development beyond adolescence, not much development seems to be taking place and most subjects seem to plateau after reaching Stage 4. For instance, in a recent reanalysis of 20 year longitudinal data scored according to the most recent Standard Scoring Guide, there are *no* adults who are solidly at the principled morality level (Stages 5 and 6) only 7 percent of the subjects attain even a recordable trace of Stage 5 thinking (see Colby, Kohlberg, Gibbs, and Lieberman, 1983). The lack of growth after adolescence and the rarity of higher thinking may be due, in part, to the stringent criteria for scoring the higher stages. To be credited with higher stage thinking on Kohlberg's test, subjects must provide highly articulate and detailed explanation. On the other hand, the DIT is a recognition task which places much less emphasis on verbal articulation. The DIT shows much more variance in scores among adolescents and adults, and since this variance is patterned in ways congruent with theoretical expectations about the moral judgment construct, the DIT appears to be much more sensitive to higher level development and to development beyond adolescence. Furthermore, the data base on the DIT is far more extensive than for any other measure of moral judgment: Over 500 studies have been completed on the DIT, whereas only a few exist on Haan's (1978), Murphy and Gilligan's (1980), or Gibbs and Widamon's (1982).

The DIT is based on the premise that people at various stages of development interpret moral dilemmas differently and the particular ways that they define the issues give indication of what basic schemes (or stages) they are using. Subjects are presented with a moral dilemma and with various statements defining issues which represent the perspectives of different stages. For instance, one story is the Heinz story (involving whether a husband should steal a drug to save his dying wife if he can get the drug no other way). Subjects are asked to consider such issues as, "whether a community's laws are going to be upheld," and "Isn't it only natural for a loving husband to care so much for his wife that he'd steal?" The subject is asked to read each issue and indicate on a 5-point scale how important each issue is in making a decision about what ought to be done in the dilemma. Subjects are also asked to rank the four most important issues. Based on which items a subject rates and ranks, scores for each of the stages can be derived. Most research using the DIT has used the "P" score—that is, the relative importance given to items keyed at Stages 5 and 6 ("Principled" items). (See Rest, 1979a for details on test design and validity and reliability information.)

From samples of subjects collected by many researchers across the country, we are able to look for the association of moral judgment (the P score) with age, as well as with education, socioeconomic status, sex, geographical region, and religious and political affiliation. Table 6.1 presents the average scores of several samples.

Notice that there is a definite age-education trend: The students in junior high (the youngest group that can take the DIT) have low scores, the college students have medium scores, and the graduate students have high scores. In some studies, age and education account for almost 50 percent of the variance in scores (Rest, 1979a). Notice also that the moral philosophy/political science graduate students have the highest scores—this makes some intuitive sense if we regard moral

TABLE 6.1. Selected Groups in Moral Judgment Development*

Average P-Index	Group
18.9	Institutionalized delinquent boys, average age = 16.1
21.9	Average junior high student
23.5	Prison inmates
28.2	Adults with senior high education
31.8	Average senior high school student
40.0	Average of adults in general
41.6	Navy enlisted men
42.3	Average college student
46.4	Staff nurses
46.8	College volunteers for community service project
49.5	Practicing medical physicians
50.2	Medical students
52.2	Advanced law students
59.8	Seminarians in liberal Protestant seminary
65.2	Moral philosophy and political science doctoral students

*DIT scores are expressed here in terms of the P-Index which represents the relative importance that a subject gives to "principled" considerations in making a moral decision—in other words, the degree to which a subject takes a philosophical perspective in deciding what ought to be done in a moral dilemma. The score is determined by the percentage of Stage 5 and 6 items that a subject ranks as more important than items at lower stages.

philosophers as experts on moral reasoning (or at least people who are very interested in moral thinking and spend a large amount of time engaged in it). Notice that the average college student is about 22 points below the moral philosophy students; and that the average junior high student is about 21 points below the college student. This suggests that the average college student is about as far away from thinking like a moral philosopher as the junior high student is away from the college student.

In several studies of adults, the correlations of DIT scores with education are higher than for age: Coder (1975) found a negative correlation with age ($r=-.10$) and a positive correlation with education ($r=.25$); Crowder (1976) found correlations of $-.05$ and $.25$ respectively; G. Rest (1977) found a correlation of .45 with education; and Dortzbach (1975) found a negative correlation with age and a positive correlation with education. The cross-sectional data suggest that, generally, a person's moral judgment score increases while he or she is in formal schooling, and after a person ends formal education, the moral judgment score levels off. For instance, a group of adults who are fifty or sixty years old with only a high school education have DIT scores similar to current high school students; adults who have college educations and who are fifty to sixty years old have scores similar to current college students (Rest, 1979a). Of all the demographic variables examined, formal education (number of years in school) is the most powerful and the most consistent correlate of moral judgment. There is definite development in moral judgment beyond adolescence but it seems to be strongly linked to formal education.

STUDIES OF EDUCATIONAL INTERVENTIONS

Several educational programs at the college level have been specifically designed to enhance moral judgment development (reviewed in Lawrence, 1977 and Rest, 1979a). These programs ranged in duration from two weeks to six months, and hence were considerably shorter than the time interval used in the longitudinal studies. Of the eight programs in higher education, several reported a significant pre-post gain in the experimental group, but the studies did not report sufficiently on comparisons with gains in control groups; therefore gains cannot unequivocally be attributed to the intervention, per se, in all cases. Even so, gains were small (whether due to the intervention or not) and in no case did an intervention turn college students into a group scoring like moral philosophy graduates on the DIT. In examining these studies, the most striking trend is how *little* movement one does get on DIT scores over short periods of time, even in interventions specifically emphasizing moral reasoning. Therefore, the impact of higher education upon moral judgment development does not seem to be particularly mediated through specific moral education courses, although the data indicate some of these special programs do have significant immediate effects.

Furthermore, whatever gains in moral judgment do come from higher education experiences, they are not simply a matter of picking up a few ideas and technical verbalisms from moral philosophy. If moral judgment was simply a matter of being taught some specific phrases or verbal conventions, then gains on short term interventions should be much more dramatic than they are. How education has its impact upon moral judgment development will be discussed below.

LONGITUDINAL STUDIES OF CHANGE

The problem with the cross-sectional studies is that age and education are confounded with many variables since different groups of subjects are compared. The virtue of a longitudinal study is that we can trace the course of development of particular groups of subjects over time. In one longitudinal study begun in 1972 (Rest, Cooper, Coder, Masanz, and Anderson, 1974; Rest, 1975) samples of subjects were followed every two years beginning as high school seniors. In the years after high school graduation, the youth embarked on different career pathways—some continuing their education in college, some not. Data are available on fifty-six subjects at a point four years after high school graduation, and for thirty-six subjects followed up six years after high school graduation.

Figure 6.1 shows the course of development in P-score for the two groups over six years after high school, with the college group ($n=23$) becoming increasingly different from the noncollege group ($n=13$). Two way analysis of variance was computed on P-scores of subjects grouped by education (college/noncollege) and time of testing (four times: high school, two years after, four years after, six years after). There was a main effect for education $F(1,34)=5.41$, $p=.026$ and a main effect for time of testing $F(3,31)=8.73$, $p=.000$, and an interaction effect of education with time $F=3.09$, $p=.03$. The significant interaction indicates that the course of development is significantly different for college group than for the noncollege group.

This trend of increasing divergence of the college group from the noncollege group was indicated also in a sample of fifty-six subjects who had complete data for three testings over a span of four years. In high school, the P score of the college group ($n=38$, mean$=34.8$) was not significantly different from the noncollege group ($n=18$, mean$=29.3$): $t=1.43$, $p=.16$. However the difference became greater *two* years beyond high school (44.4 versus 35.1) and was significant even after controlling for high school scores by ANACOVA: $F=9.2$, $p=.004$.

A more differentiated way of representing education than the simple dichotomy of college/noncollege is to create a variable reflecting number of years of college education, ranging from 0 to 6. Then multiple regression analysis can be conducted, predicting to a subject's P-score in the last testing, six years after high school. As predictor variables, first the P-score in high school is en-

FIGURE 6.1. Moral Development P-Scores

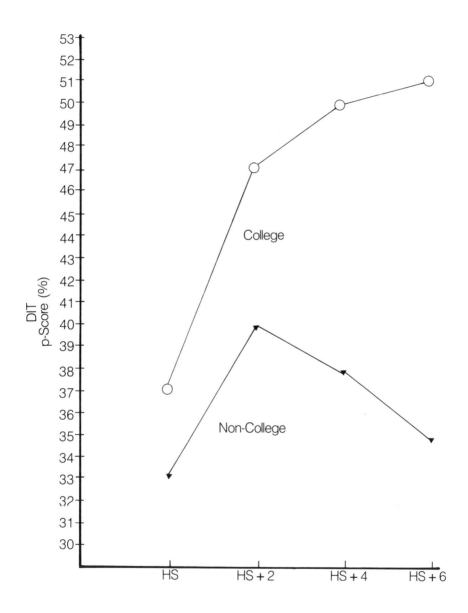

tered to control for initial differences; and second, the number of years of college education is entered. We find that college significantly increases the predictability to P-scores at the last testing (F to enter or remove $=7.4$, $p=.01$), adding 14 percent to the accountable variance above and beyond that accounted for by initial high school scores. And so again, by a different method of analysis, formal education is significantly associated with development in moral judgment.

Moreover, the correlation of education (ultimate number of years in college) with the P-score increased systematically over time; in high school, the correlation was .15; two years later, it was .36; four years later, .37; and six years later, .44. The correlations increase as the college group becomes increasingly divergent from the noncollege group. The pattern that we find is that the college group continues to increase in P-score and the noncollege group does not. This pattern is corroborated in a number of ways. Other indices of the DIT were also analyzed by 2-way ANOVA, ANACOVA, and multiple regression, both on data from the $n=56$ sample (three testings) and $n=36$ sample (four testings). Other indices of the DIT also show significantly different pathways for college and noncollege students.

These longitudinal data clearly indicate a relationship of moral judgment development with formal education, collaborating the cross-sectional data. The course of development of college-bound subjects is different from noncollege subjects. With college, scores continue to rise whereas without college, scores plateau.

Six other longitudinal studies of college students have shown significant increases in the DIT P scores (Broadhurst, 1980; Kaseman, 1980; Kitchener, King, Davison, Parker and Wood, 1984; Mentkowski and Strait, 1983; Sheehan, Husted, and Candler, 1981; Whiteley, 1982). One other longitudinal found an increase but not statistically significant difference over a two year span (McGeorge, 1977).

Although the empirical trend is clear, the theoretical significance of the relation between moral judgment and formal education, however, is not completely clear because several cause-effect explanations are possible. At least five different interpretations can be advanced:

1. *"Socialization" into the college milieu.* According to this interpretation, college students gain in moral judgment as they adopt the preferred mode of moral argumentation on campus. Students are reinforced for talking like college professors and are reinforced for certain socio-moral attitudes, just as other "collegiate" behaviors are acquired in that particular milieu (particular preferences in dress, politics, music, entertainment, etc.). The progressive increase in moral judgment scores, therefore, would reflect the cumulative impact of college socialization. Nonstudents, of course, who are not exposed to these socialization influences do not prefer to talk like college professors and do not show the increase in moral judgment scores.

One possible problem with this explanation is that when college students did leave the college milieu, their scores did not revert, but actually continued to increase slightly. Nineteen subjects who had graduated from college by Time 4 (high school plus 6 years) went from a P-score of 43 to 46, and so the milieu effect had not reversed itself after they left the college milieu. Moreover, construing the DIT P=score as reflecting a *stylistic preference* (as if high P-scores were an option for anyone who merely preferred to talk like a college professor) does not take account of previous findings that only subjects with high Moral Comprehension scores (a measure of the capacity to understand the concepts of higher stages) tend to have high DIT scores (cf. Rest, 1979a). In other words, increasing DIT scores reflect an increasing capacity to comprehend higher level thinking—it is not simply a matter of stylistic preference. Furthermore, in experimental studies, subjects who were given incentives to increase their moral judgment scores could not do so (cf. Rest, 1979a). Therefore the relation of moral judgment to formal education is not likely to be due to a milieu effect which simply "socializes" preferences for particular verbalization styles.

2. *Particular skilll or knowledge learning.* A second interpretation that does take account of the relation of moral judgment to moral comprehension might portray the impact of college as the learning of particular verbal skills, or particular contents of moral philosophy. Just as one goes to school to learn long division or the names of the American presidents, so also one might learn in school how to make moral arguments at a Principled level. In this interpretation, the increasing DIT scores of college students reflect an increase in cognitive ability, but the cognitive ability is viewed as a delimited skill or particular knowledge content. In contrast cognitive developmentalists want to claim that moral judgment reflects a pervasive, fundamental perspective on society and human relationships that underlies one's understanding of the social world.

One problem with a "narrow skill" interpretation is that educational intervention studies indicate that gains in moral judgment are slow and difficult to produce. Educational programs concentrating on moral problem solving and running for three to five months only improve students' DIT score typically by 3 to 8 points for the group, and such educational programs never raise the scores of college students to the scores of moral philosophy doctoral students (see Ch. 7 in Rest, 1979a). If moral judgment primarily reflects a narrowly delimited verbal skill or particular knowledge content, why then is it so difficult to teach, and why do not college students who take a moral education course quickly attain scores like moral philosophy doctoral students? Moreover, the "narrow skill" interpretation requires that the particular skill (or knowledge content) be identified and described, and to date this has not been done. Furthermore, there is difficulty in locating in what part of the college curriculum the particular skill or knowledge is taught: Students in the humanities show about the same amount of gain in DIT P-scores as students in the sciences or business. While moral philosophy or moral education courses might account for *some* of the gain for some subject, nevertheless the four year college gain is about twice the gain from specific moral education courses, and not all students take a moral education course. Therefore, explaining the increase in moral judgment scores of college students as due to specific skill or knowledge learning is also problematic.

3. *Learning a general perspective on society and human relationships.* A third interpretation is that at college there is a general socio-moral perspective, a general way of orienting to moral issues that emphasizes Principled moral thinking. Attendance at college and involvement in college activities slowly imbues students with this general perspective. This interpretation is somewhat akin to the notion that law school teaches a student to "think like a lawyer," or that science education teaches a student to "think like a scientist." In each case, attaining a general perspective is not reducible to learning sets of facts nor to learning a set of specific skills, but constitutes a framework of assumptions, and guiding principles for approaching a problem domain. Presumably the student has to be actively engaged in constructing for him/herself this general perspective. This implies having a way of operating upon information and organizing it, not just data storage or skill learning. Despite the emphasis upon the student as active learner, nevertheless Interpretation 3 implies that a general, socio-moral perspective exists prior to and independently of the student coming to college, and that the impact of college experience is to influence the student to attain this perspective. This kind of influence seems to be what some proponents of a college liberal education have in mind when they talk about the "broadening" and "liberating" effect of college.

One problem with this interpretation is in the diffuseness of the notion, "general perspective." What is a "general perspective"? Furthermore, how does a student find out about this "general perspective"? Is it through assigned readings, formal lectures, extracurricular activities, faculty models, the college newspaper, conversations over coffee at the student union, or what? (This question is further discussed in the next section.) At the present time, while I am aware of no evidence that contradicts Interpretation 3, neither am I aware of specific corroboration of this interpretation. Because of its diffuseness, it may be difficult to substantiate. We would need to have evidence that a general socio-moral perspective exists in colleges, that somehow the college experience influences students to attain this perspective, and that people outside of college are not so influenced, by and large.

4. *General intellectual stimulation.* In contrast to Interpretation 3, this interpretation does not assume that there is a general socio-moral perspective in colleges, but only assumes that the college experience encourages and supports intellectual activity. The college milieu prizes incisive, inventive, elegant, and complex thinking. There is a delight and encouragement in intellectual activity for its own sake. Intellectual advance in all domains is fostered, and this includes advance in moral thinking even if it does not directly foster any moral ideology in particular.

Interpretation 4 requires fewer assumptions about the deliberate influences of college (college only encourages intellectual activity), but it requires stronger assumptions than the previous interpretations about the inevitability of Principled moral thinking, given only nondirected encouragement for intellectual activity. According to the interpretation, given nondirective encouragement to think, Principled moral thinking increases. Why should this be so? The claim that Principled moral thinking is a natural outgrowth of more primitive forms of moral thinking is based on several assumptions about the fundamental character of living in social groups, about how humans attempt to understand and organize cooperation, about certain inadequacies and flaws in more primitive thinking (Stages 1 to 4). It assumes that Principled moral thinking (Stages 5 and 6) is seen by thoughtful, cognitively advanced people as presenting the best kinds of solutions to approaching moral issues. An extended discussion of the lines of thinking is given in chapter 2, Rest, 1979a, but it must be admitted that the matter is highly controversial among both psychologists and philosophers.

A slight variation of the "general intellectual stimulation" explanation is to characterize the college experience as affording special opportunities for encountering heterogeneous social attitudes and ideologies. The clash of different social ideas with one's own provides an especially stimulating environment for moral judgment because it prompts one to reexamine one's assumptions and rethink the implications and logical tightness of one's own view. Some support for the special effect of heterogeneous social attitudes comes from studies by Edwards (1978) and Maqsud (1977) who found that students attending culturally diverse schools were more advanced in moral judgment than students attending culturally homogeneous schools.

5. *Preselection effect.* Interpretation 5 does not attribute to college any special influence or any special impact on moral judgment. It explains the gains of college students as due to the special characteristics of the people who choose to attend college. College students are predisposed to seek intellectual stimulation, are motivated to develop their cognitive capacities, and find pleasure in working on complex problems. Wherever these people would be, they would show developmental increases. It so happens that a disproportionate number of them attend college, and so college attendance is associated with gains in moral judgment. But this effect is due to the special characteristics of the subjects themselves and their self-selection into college, not due to college itself. The fact that some subjects who do not continue in college attain very high DIT score indicates that college is not absolutely necessary for moral judgment advance (Thoma and Davison, in press). However it is also true that the cross-sectional data generally suggest that moral judgment scores usually plateau after leaving college (Rest, 1979a). Therefore, as with the other interpretations (especially 3 and 4), there is not decisive evidence one way or the other.

The clear empirical association of moral judgment development with college attendance along with the indecisiveness of the interpretation of that effect is warrant for extensive research on this phenomenon. The data from subjects' retrospective accounts of the influence on their thinking suggests that different life experiences may influence different people. Therefore detailed, intensive descriptions of life experiences of heterogeneous subjects along with longitudinal data on their moral judgment development are needed to proceed further.

CAUSES AND CONDITIONS THAT FACILITATE DEVELOPMENT

In an attempt to explain why formal education is so consistently and powerfully associated with moral judgment development, several studies have been aimed at elucidating the causes and conditions of moral judgment development. In one recent study, subjects were asked to speculate about what life events or experiences had influenced their moral thinking. In four lines on a questionnaire, subjects wrote about a variety of experiences which were coded into the eighteen categories of Table 6.2. The categories are very close to the wording used by the subjects themselves, and while the boundaries between categories may not be very sharp, any response that fell between categories was coded in both. This information was analyzed in terms of whether a particular category was cited by the subject or not. Hence for every category, subjects were grouped as citing the influence (the "yes group") and not citing the influence (the "no group").

Note that this "life experience" information is the subject's own theory in retrospect about what had an effect on his/her thinking. These data have unknown correspondence with a subject's actual experiences. For instance, only three subjects cited "travel" and we do not know if only these three subjects did any substantial travel, whether others traveled but did not get anything out of it (regarding moral thinking), or whether they were really influenced by travel but did not think to mention it. The disadvantage of this kind of data is that it depends upon the subject's theory about what influences his/her thinking (which some research suggests can be very erroneous—see Nisbett and Wilson, 1977). On the other hand, subjective data like this may be valuable because it can indicate subjective impact rather than just record an outward event. That is, even if many subjects did travel, we are only interested in those for whom the experience was provocative and stimulating. Many people may be exposed to some objective event but only some of them may be stimulated to reformulate their thinking from it. If a particular experience is stimulating in this way, and causes reflection, this may be what we want to know, not just outward exposure.

Table 6.2 lists the categories of experiences cited by fifty-nine subjects, first grouping them into "positive" influence (top half of the table) and "negative" influence (bottom half of the table). If those subjects citing the experience gained more in P-score over three testings than the subjects not citing the experience, then the experience was classified as a "positive" experience. If, on the other hand, those subjects citing the experience showed less gain in P-score longitu-

TABLE 6.2. Comparison of P-Scores of Subjects Who Attribute Change to Various Life Experiences

Type of Life Experience	Number of Subjects Citing This Influence		Time 1	Time 2	Time 3
Positive					
1. Formal instruction	16	YES	29.1	41.4	44.5
or study		NO	34.9	42.8	46.5
2. Spending more time	8	YES	34.6	48.8	53.6
contemplating issues		NO	33.1	41.5	44.8
3. Religious experiences	4	YES	16.7	35.0	40.0
and/or instruction		NO	34.5	43.0	46.4
4. Travel	3	YES	31.1	53.9	58.9
		NO	33.4	41.9	45.3
5. Direct involvement in	3	YES	31.1	44.5	55.0
community/world		NO	33.4	41.9	45.5
political affairs					
6. Particular time of personal	1	YES	23.3	35.0	46.7
stress as a turning point		NO	33.5	42.6	46.7
Negative					
7. New social contacts,	28	YES	31.9	41.7	39.4
an expanding social world		NO	28.8	43.1	51.9
8. New "real world"	22	YES	38.3	38.5	45.5
responsibilities—marriage, job,		NO	30.3	44.8	46.3
managing money, children					
9. Current issues and	19	YES	35.1	42.9	46.5
events		NO	32.4	42.3	45.7
10. Reading	13	YES	29.2	38.9	41.3
		NO	34.4	43.5	47.3
11. "Making decisions	11	YES	42.1	45.8	45.5
on my own"		NO	31.3	41.7	46.1
12. Living away from home	11	YES	42.0	50.0	52.1
		NO	31.3	40.7	44.6
13. Maturation, "getting older,"	5	YES	24.3	34.0	29.0
sense of "growing up"		NO	34.1	43.2	47.6
14. Experiencing or witnessing	5	YES	35.3	45.7	39.0
personal tragedy		NO	33.1	42.2	46.6
15. Specific influential	3	YES	37.8	42.2	41.7
people		NO	33.0	42.5	46.2
16. Making decisions	3	YES	35.0	34.5	40.0
for the future		NO	33.2	42.9	46.3
17. "Change in lifestyle"	2	YES	38.3	39.2	47.5
		NO	33.1	42.6	45.9
18. No change in thinking	6	No change	31.7	41.4	45.7
		Others	33.5	42.6	46.0

dinally than subjects not citing it, then the experience was classified as a "negative" experience. The gains for each group for each experience are shown, in the last three columns of Table 6.2 indicating average P-scores for the three testings (high school, high school plus two years, plus four years). For each experience category, the "yes" group cited that experience, and all other subjects are grouped into the "no" group. Thus for each experience category by comparing the longitudinal changes of the "yes" group with the "no" group, the relative impact of that experience is shown.

The middle column shows the number of subjects who cited a particular experience category as influencing their moral thinking. For instance, out of fifty-nine subjects, sixteen said that "Formal instruction or study" (Category 1) had influenced their moral thinking (but forty-three subjects did not cite this an influencing experience). Perhaps the most striking finding to come out of Table 6.2 is that no particular experience is cited as influential by a majority of subjects. And, of course, developmental theory does not guarantee us that one particular type of life event is the single cause of development in moral judgment. It is possible for different events to have different effects for different people. If people's retrospective theories about what influences them are accurate, it would seem that development has many causes, not just a single common cause.

Of all the categories of experience cited by the subjects, "New social contacts, an expanding social world" (Category 7) was most frequently cited, however comparing the longitudinal trends of the "yes group" (i.e., subjects who cited this as an influence) with the "no group" shows that subjects *not* citing this influence actually showed more gain over the three testings. Perhaps this explanation of development is a hackneyed explanation, invoked by the less reflective and perceptive subjects whose theories of change are no more sophisticated than their moral thinking. On the other hand, only one subject mentioned that change was due to "a particular time of personal stress" (Category 6), which is a little surprising because almost all cognitive development theories of change (e.g., Turiel, 1969) have stressed "disequilibrium" and "cognitive conflict" as the essential conditions for development. Six subjects were of the opinion that their moral thinking had not changed (Category 18), but it turned out that their moral judgment scores went up as much as the subjects who thought they had changed. Category 1, "Formal instruction or study" was of special interest for its link to education. If education is associated with greater gains, then it might seem that the gainers should cite "formal education." But those citing it showed only a little more gain than those not citing it. Category 2, "Spending more time contemplating issues," was one of the few categories in which subjects citing it showed a greater rate of increase than subjects not citing it. The emphasis here on reflection and reworking one's thought is consistent with developmental theory. Perhaps *reflection* rather than *reading* or *taking courses* is more crucial. Category 13 might be a reason that the less imaginative subjects preferred—those not citing it did much better. Category 12, "living away from home," was cited

· by subjects who were relatively more advanced in high school and who retained a comparable advantage, although they did not increase at a faster rate than those not citing this influence. Category 5, "direct involvement," was only cited by three subjects (and differs from Category 9 in that it is active participation as opposed to passive reading); the pattern of gain for those citing it showed a higher rate of increase. Similarly "travel," Category 4 was endorsed only by a few subjects, but those who cited it had a higher rate of gain.

Statistical analyses were not run on the data in Table 6.2 because of lopsided and small cells, the undramatic change differences, and so many multiple analyses are likely to turn up spurious significant results. Nevertheless, these data suggest that the causes of development are likely to be multiple and the different life experiences are likely to affect different people in different ways.

A number of other correlational studies have attempted to find clues about what life experiences prompt or facilitate moral judgment development. Several researchers have contrasted students with different college majors. It would seem feasible that history and sociology majors would have higher moral judgment scores than agriculture and chemistry majors. Yet the results from several studies are inconclusive (Bransford, 1973; Dispoto, 1974; Gallia, 1976; McGeorge, 1977; Schomberg, 1975). Biggs, Schomberg, and Brown (1977) found slight relationships in college freshmen between moral judgment and degree of familiarity with book titles, authors, painters, artists, and people in the news. Rest (1979b) examined type of college (large research university versus small liberal arts college), and found no difference. Type of residence (living at home with parents versus living away from home) was significantly associated with moral judgment; however, the residence effect was due to college students leaving home and noncollege students staying home, and so the effect is really due to the education effect. Volker (1980) devised a checklist of experiences (including discussing controversial moral issues with others, new responsibilities for taking care of others, new life decisions, and new life styles, etc.). He asked subjects both to indicate whether a particular experience had happened and also whether the subject thought the experience had influenced the subject's moral thinking. While no single experience was consistently and powerfully associated with high or low DIT scores, the results suggest that different experiences have influential effects on different subjects.

Building on this previous research on causes and conditions, two studies are currently in progress. Our approach is to use longitudinal data on moral judgment spanning five to ten years and also to intensively interview subjects about what has been going on in their lives and what they make of these experiences. Our approach has several features: (1) we do not assume that there is one single common cause of development in young adulthood; (2) we do not depend on a single item or single event as the basis for attributing development to a particular experience (as in the case in the previous studies), but with extensive interviewing, look for recurrent and pervasive patterns of life experiences; (3) we do not rely on the subject's own theory of his/her development, but seek extended descriptions of life events in a number of categories we asked and then the researchers look for an association or the experience with change in moral judgment; (4) we attend both to the objective occurrence of some external influence and also to the subject's subjective reaction to the event—in other words, an "experience" is coded in both objective (external) and subjective (internal) terms. Since analyses are still underway, I cannot yet report on the outcome of these studies. However, throughout all of this research, we have been impressed with the multiple and varied events that seem to influence moral judgment development, and with the importance of the subject's own subjective reaction and processing of the event in addition to the basic fact of whether or not a particular event occurred.

MORAL JUDGMENT AND BEHAVIOR

About thirty studies using the DIT have correlated moral judgment with various measures of behavior. The studies have employed a variety of measures of behavior: these include naturalistic measures (e.g., delinquency, anti-social school behavior, conscientious objection to the military, clinical performance ratings of doctors, voting in a presidential election); also included are experimentally controlled measures of behavior (e.g., cheating, promise-keeping, distribution of rewards, conformity, "whistle blowing," mock jury trial verdicts); and also included are studies of advocacy behavior—that is, expressing an attitude or point of view—(e.g., positions taken on controversial public policy issues, attitudes of teachers toward disciplinary episodes, attitudes toward political candidates, nurses' views about health issues, attitudes toward the environment). The consistently positive and statistically significant correlations between DIT scores and these various measures of behavior attest to the definite link between moral judgment and behavior—in short, moral judgment does seem to play a role in the way subjects lead their lives in important, real-life situations (see Rest, 1983 for a review).

The aim of our current research is to clarify the nature of the linkage of moral judgment to behavior, to understand better the specific role that moral judgment plays in regulating behavior. This brings us back to the first part of this chapter concerning the four-component model. The four-component model depicts the moral judgment variable as the second step in an ensemble of inner process leading to the production of moral behavior. Moral judgment research deals with how subjects define which course of action is morally right in a situation. The other components act (and interact) in concert with the moral judgment process in producing behavior. Accordingly, our general long term strategy is to develop measures of each of the four components, so that together we can hopefully improve our predictability to behavior. I have already mentioned some of our progress in developing measures for Component 1 with regard to moral problems in the job settings of health professionals. Our next step is to develop measures of Component 2 which will replace the DIT by creating assessment tools that are more specifically attuned to the dilemmas of health professionals and more fine-grained representation of the judgment process. Afterwards, we hope someone will figure out how to measure Components 3 and 4 in the health professional setting. Then it will remain to model how all these various processes interact to result in moral behavior.

Having a four-component model entails that moral development (in this wider sense) must be tracked along several types of cognitive-affective processes. It entails a much more complicated research enterprise than single variable theories of morality. It entails much more complicated educational intervention strategies as well, if development means building adequate functioning in all four major components. Research on Component 2 perhaps has more of a head start than research on the other components. However, to clarify its role in behavior, research on the other components must progress. Hopefully this more complicated picture of moral development will lead to more accurate and powerful models.

7

Which Way Is Up?
A Developmental Question

Howard E. Gruber

ABSTRACT

Any interactionist developmental theory must be responsive to historical change. Assertions about universal patterns of psychological growth must be examined both for their pertinence and correctness in the light of this criterion. Even claims that progress and dialogue are universals of social-cognitive development may be Platonic and ahistorical.

Developmental progress, when it does occur, instead of being unilinear, can occur along many developmental lines. One person's progress is another's stagnation. This makes the whole concept of progress much more difficult and subtle than is usually realized.

Conventional developmental research is oriented toward supposed species-typical norms, rather than toward understanding historically emergent diversity and maximal realization of human potential along varied lines. Research that would focus on such diversity and maximization cannot employ the traditional paradigms of experimental-developmental psychology. Alternatives are discussed, especially the case study approach.

What can be learned from intensive case studies of creative work that might be relevant to understanding ordinary development? The Evolving Systems Approach to creative work describes a set of loosely coupled subsystems—organizations of knowledge, of purpose, and of affect. Each is continually evolving, more or less independently, and yet each contributes to the "internal milieu" in which the others evolve. The approach is both phenomenological and constructivist. Some suggestions can be drawn from all this connecting the study of creativity with the study of ordinary lives.

The author warmly thanks Doris B. Wallace for helpful discussions while writing this paper, and for comments on the manuscript.

Finally, fulfilling the agenda of placing developmental theory in historical perspective, I examine the relation of adolescent and young adult development with the world's most pressing issue, the danger of self-extinction of our own species. Developmental issues are thus placed in an appropriate ecological perspective, the individual's experience of his own environment as one that may or may not permit his continued personal growth.

Developmental Theory and the Idea of Progress

The idea of progress is implicit in almost all developmental thought. But it is not often examined very closely by developmental psychologists. It contains many puzzles, of which I will mention only a few.

Thomas Kuhn (1962) argued that, although there is a sort of progress in actualizing the potentialities of a paradigm, when a paradigm shift occurs we cannot speak of progress. The identification of problems changes, criteria of solution change, and almost everything else. When a revolution has occurred, we can say that the intellectual situation is different, but there is no communication possible across the historical barrier that separates the old from the new paradigms. Hence there is no scientifically valid means by which these incommensurables can evaluate each other.

And yet, if we step outside the framework of pure science and look at that whole endeavor from the perspective of the practical control of nature, it seems reasonably clear that there has been directional change, progress of a sort that can be in good part attributed to the alliance of science and technology. Human longevity has increased dramatically, bridges can be built much longer, and the world circumnavigated more quickly—in about ninety minutes if we include travel by satellite.

Still, matters are not so simple. The doubter would agree with all of the above but might add: Increased longevity has meant a threatening population explosion; better roads and bridges have facilitated the worldwide pollution caused by automotive travel; and satellite technology is the same as is required for delivery of the nuclear weapons that may destroy all life on earth. So stepping outside science for an external criterion of progress produces an ambiguous result. *Only* if a profoundly new equilibrium can be found between technological prowess and social control will our descendants be able to look back in admiration on our "progress."

At the level of individual development matters are not much clearer. Newton may have been alluding to a kind of within-paradigm progress when he said, "If I have seen further it is because I stood on the shoulders of giants."* A col-

---

*For interesting discussions of this famous remark of Newton's see Merton, R.K. *On the Shoulders of Giants*. New York: Free Press, 1965; and Christianson, G.E. *In the Presence of the Creator: Isaac Newton and His Times*. New York: Free Press, 1984.

lege physics student today standing on Newton's shoulders can see further still: His individual knowledge has progressed beyond Newton's. But it is not so easy to say whether or not this constitutes individual progress. Even an ''A'' student may not actually have a more powerful mind than Newton's! But, if we say that, are we admitting that the mastery of powerful ideas does not make a mind powerful?

A further dilemma arises in evaluating individual intellectual development. Suppose the very process of cognitive growth leads the individual further away from the humane values needed to control the technical fruits of thought. Would we happily call that progress? Instead, we protect ourselves from this dilemma by conceptually separating issues: We make a sharp distinction between cognitive and moral development. In other words, we absolve the individual of responsibility for his work. In thus exalting the intellect we emasculate the person. Such postures have led to deep crises in psychology about the relation between values and cognition, about the adaptive nature of thought.

So the progress we can speak of with some confidence has led to a widening gulf between technological power and human values, and between the sum of human knowledge and the individual human intellect. *Only* if we accept the single-valued idea of power, both intellectual and technological, can we speak with any certainty of criteria for progress and use comfortably the vocabulary of ''higher'' education, ''advanced'' stages of development.

In thinking about these dilemmas I once wrote a poem for my nine year old daughter.

Upoem

''Which way is Up?'' seems an odd sort of query.
''Toward the sky,'' says one famous theory.
''Over your head,'' runs another idea.
The difference between them is not always clear.
But if you lie down you may have to choose:
Is Up away from the earth, or away from your shoes?

Do we really know which way is Up?

Special Problems in Extending Developmental Theory to Adult Development

Existing developmental theory is framed around the idea of cognitive and affective universals. Although there are serious problems, this works well enough in dealing with child development. The intrauterine environment is remarkably stable; and within each society, a reasonably stable environment is provided for every child, especially in the form of developmental tasks which must be mastered one way or another. But as maturity approaches, the individual is required to differentiate himself from this stable environment, build his and her own nest, find a suitable terrain, carve out an ecological niche: In an exogamous world, everyone must adapt to meet the new conditions imposed by moving to the next village.

The idea of universal developmental progress toward a number of broad species-specific attainments depends either on a *non*interactionist theoretical position (i.e., hereditary dispositions) or on an interactionist position with the assumption of a stable environment. If we reject the noninteractionist position, which almost all developmentalists certainly do, then the conditions of a rapidly changing world impose on us the theoretical task of reconsidering our theories in the light of the world in which development actually takes place.

These problems are severe enough when we consider individuals who stay fairly close to their societal norms. They become almost overwhelming when we extend our scope to consider extraordinary individuals. For then we see another facet of most developmental research: It is centered on the *typical* performance rather than the *optimal* development of those studied. If we are seriously interested in how developmental innovations come about, we need to know how the extraordinary individual develops and functions. To be sure, since we remain interested in the whole species, we need also to be interested in the diffusion of novelty. Most likely, invention and diffusion are quite different processes, but up to now we have no knowledge of how they interact in psychological development, because the question has hardly been raised. While this problem is important even in child development, it becomes acute in understanding young adult development in a changing world, one requiring new adaptations for survival.

Alternative Approaches to Unilinear Universalism

Alternatives to the fixation on the universal and the typical have been proposed and do guide some research. In addition to contributions in this volume, I will mention a few. David Feldman's (1980) seminal book, *Beyond Universals in Cognitive Development*, sets out the claim that psychologists must attend to the two-way relation between the unique and the universal, each setting the stage for the other. Howard Gardner's (1983) recent *Frames of Mind: The Theory of Multiple Intelligences* takes a less radical stance, since he only proposes about seven major types of intelligence, each with its distinct neurological substrate and each with its particular requirements for optimal development.

Relatively minor modifications of conventional research designs can sometimes produce dramatic effects on level of performance achieved. Harlow's pioneering work on learning sets remains an important example of a change in our conception of cognitive capacity produced by a change in experimental design. Elsewhere (Gruber, 1982), I have summarized more recent efforts in the same direction by Ericsson, Chase and Faloon (1980), Kuhn and Ho (1980), and Spelke, Hirst and Neisser (1976). These all involve massive amounts of well thought out training. But even as simple a change as allowing a child or adolescent to perform a formal operations task (e.g., the bending rods test or the idea of isolation of variables) *twice*, with an interval of one week but no intervening instruction, can produce a sizable shift in performance (Stone and Day, 1978).

In their seminal work, *Plans and the Structure of Behavior,* Miller, Galanter, and Pribam (1960) called the attention of a wide audience of cognitive psychologists to the facts of mnemonic processing. Half a century of experimental research on memory, with meaningless materials and subjects hamstrung by cramping experimental procedures, had produced a picture of human memory as slow, limited, and laborious (e.g., ten trials to learn a list of ten items). Once the subject is invited to use his memory imaginatively, it is hard to find the limits of this capacity (e.g., one trial to learn a list of 1,000 items). The authors concluded, "Let us imagine that this hooking operation is available and that it is as cheap and easy as it would have to be to support the discursive human intellect. What do we do with it? Given that we can nail two boards together, how do we build a house?" (p. 138).

Since 1960 when those words appeared, there have been hundreds of experiments on mnemonic processing, in the main confirming the same line of thought. We know a lot more about memory, but we still know little about the psychology of building a house, mainly because we as a discipline have not looked. Yet, if we are interested in adult cognitive development, should our main concern not be with the way in which part-processes are integrated into larger functional units with productive consequences?

Are there any knowable ultimate limits on human performance? Psychologists might have a look at the history of athletic records. Between 1864 and 1981, the world's record for the mile run declined steadily from 4:56 seconds (Charles Lawes) to 3:47.33 seconds (Sebastian Coe). No doubt, at each stage there was intense debate as to whether the record, or some other standard, could ever be broken. When I was a boy, Glenn Cunningham was a heroic figure, but he never ran a four-minute mile, and we very much doubted whether any human ever would.

The plain fact is that psychologists do not understand cognitive processes well enough to know anything at all about human limitations. By the same token, we are ignorant of the meaning of any progressive change we observe: is it a small increment with untold progress still lying before us? Or is it near the ultimate of what we can expect—for that individual, that age group, that type, the species?

As applied to adolescent and young adult development, this ignorance of process has led to a theoretical situation in which it is fair to argue any of the following positions about formal operations: (1) they are attained by all normal adults and represent the final stage of cognitive development; (2) they are attained by only some adults and represent the final stage of cognitive development; (3) there are stages beyond formal operations, such as dialectical operations; (4) the whole concept of unilinear stagewise development is questionable.

In Geneva, one important reaction to this crisis of understanding has been to set aside study of developmental progress for the time being in favor of a more process-oriented approach. Thus, in Inhelder's "Strategies Group" very small numbers of subjects, often adults, are studied very intensely in problem-solving situations. Cybernetic and dialectical ideas are being blended with Piagetian structuralism. Although they work with unselected subjects (that is, not individuals selected for extraordinary attainments), the style of their work comes very close to the "evolving systems approach" that has guided my work and my collaborators'. The key points of similarity are first that one goes deeply enough into a problem to really understand the structure of the situation confronting the subject; second, that one works intensively enough with the subject over long enough periods to watch a cognitive process unfolding, a struggle going on; third, that the analysis of results does not focus on the number or time of solutions, but on the changing configuration of the ongoing set of processes.

A key difference is that the focus of attention in the "strategies group"— as in most problem solving research—is on the activities of subjects working for an hour or so on a single task provided by the experimenter, and chosen to be *unlike* the things the subject has previously mastered. For all its virtues, this kind of work cannot possibly tell us how the young adult becomes a person confronting situations that engage his or her whole spirit and energies, who can orchestrate multiple activities in a workable life, and synthesize larger wholes to make coherent products.

To be sure, many adults do not have a full opportunity for such a self-actualizing pattern of existence. Alienated and infantilized by oppressive conditions of life, they would not be good subjects for studying the "upper" limits of human potential. That is why, difficult as it may be, it is important for us to keep as our benchmark, well-developed people doing creative work.

WHY WE NEED TO STUDY CREATIVE WORK

Perhaps we need and will eventually be able to elaborate a new kind of stage-oriented developmental psychology, one in which development moves in a number of alternative directions. This idea of multi-directional development fits in with the theory of homeorhesis proposed by Waddington (1957), the geneticist-embryologist: there are strong environmental forces maintaining the individual in one course of development. But if a strong enough deviating force is introduced he may be pushed over into another valley, or creode, of the "epigenetic landscape," and follow quite a different path. Michael Armstrong's (1980) book, *Closely Observed Children*, is one example of the kind of attention to the individual subject that we would have to give in our research to detect and study such developmental differences.

Piaget (1971) was interested in Waddington's ideas and cited them often. But he was too preoccupied with elaborating a model of "logical determinism" (see Gruber and Vonèche, 1977) and applying it to human cognitive development to pursue the possibility of divergent development implicit in Waddington's ideas. Instead, he exploited the ideas of homeorhesis and creode to explain the universal features of cognitive development that interested him. In my opinion this was a good strategy for guiding Piaget in his chosen work, sketching out the main lines of intellectual development and pioneering the search for models of thought. But we will never get very far beyond Piaget simply by extending his approach to one or two more stages. Instead we must understand the process of change. This requires a focus on the individual. And this methodological decision leads us in turn to look at creative individuals, for it is in them that we see the processes of change and innovation clearly displayed in adult development.

The idea of multiple developmental pathways meshes well with Darwin's fundamental metaphor and underlying model, his image of the "irregularly branching tree of nature" (Gruber, 1978). Each evolutionary branching point results from an unrepeatable encounter between organism and environment, unrepeatable because neither will ever be the same again. The general fact of evolutionary divergence is not happenstance but a necessary consequence of combining natural selection and the branching model. In human history as we have known it thus far, the same sort of idea applies with even greater force to the continuous production of cultural diversity.

Thus one reason for studying creative individuals stems directly from our interest in understanding the behavior of our species as a whole. Extraordinary individuals pioneer, innovate. They create an environment in which their contemporaries and descendants can emulate or reject what has been put before them. The processes of choice and reproduction are distinct from the processes of production of novelty. Together, they form a whole in which continuing adaptation can be understood.

It is sometimes argued that the child, too, is creative, constantly constructing his own intelligence. In a sense, this is true. But there are at least two profound differences between child development and creative work. First, child development moves the individual *toward* pre-existing norms; this point bears not only on the result but on the process of intellectual growth, as evidenced in the recent literature on imitation and modelling. Clearly, creative work moves the individual away from such norms.

Second, creative work is characterized by long term goals consciously pursued by a subject well aware of his unusual relation with the world. In 1831, age 22, just before setting out on the *Beagle* voyage, Darwin's creative aspirations were so vague and unexpressed that his father expressed the fear that it would be "disreputable to [his] character as a Clergyman hereafter." Dr. Robert

Darwin was reassured by Charles' uncle, Josiah Wedgwood, who wrote to him that "the pursuit of Natural History, though certainly not professional, is very suitable to a clergyman." The idea that he would return home to find a "quiet country parsonage" remained with Darwin for some time. It was in the work he did on the five-year voyage that Darwin reshaped his goals.*

SCRIBBLES IN THE ATTIC

There is a practical reason for centering much of our discussion on the growth of thought of creative people. They leave better traces. Every child produces many, many drawings and other creative acts. In a fortunate enough family these may make their way to the attic, there to lie for a generation or so, and then to be discarded with a sigh on moving day. But if in the meanwhile the child has become Picasso, his childhood leavings will be spared and treasured. They are there for us to study.

There is another facet to the matter of tracks. In our work on the creative process we have seen over and over that the making and leaving of tracks—preliminary sketches, countless revisions, early notebooks, variations on a theme, and so on—is part and parcel of the process itself. This is a kind of activity characteristic of people doing creative work. Wittingly or not, they create the conditions under which we can study their development.

Finally, of course, the creative person does not merely make one work and then stop. His intention is to lead a creative life, to make a series of works, an oeuvre. Sometimes, it is the cumulative impact of his work that we feel; in other cases that accumulation provides the setting for the one masterpiece that marks the person off for all to see.

Where the traces exist, there is nothing to stop us from applying the same methods to the study of less extraordinary people. It may even turn out that as a field of scientific inquiry, ordinary people are more intriguing than extraordinary ones. In any event, as psychologists we hardly have the luxury of such choices. In the long run we are responsible for understanding the interplay between stable adaptations and innovations, the spectrum from the universal to the unique.

---

*The story of Darwin's appointment to the *Beagle* is recounted in *The Life and Letters of Charles Darwin,* edited by his son Francis Darwin, 3 vols. London: John Murray, 1888, see especially vol. 1, chapter 5. The quotations I have given, together with Darwin's early entries in the *Beagle Diary,* make clear that although he intended to go into the clergy, natural history formed an important part of his plans. Within that vast domain his plans were entirely vague.

SOME POSSIBLE MODELS OF INDIVIDUALIZATION IN DEVELOPMENT

By now it may seem to the reader as though I am slipping from my earlier agnostic position about developmental progress into a more hopeful, some might even say, prayerful attitude toward creativity. Of course I am. I hope, however, that what is gained from the discussion thus far is a more questioning attitude toward the idea of *unilinear* developmental progress through a single set of stages. Possible models of development include the following:

- *Linear model with alternative pathways* to each developmental way station. It should be noted that the precise nature of each point of arrival would vary somewhat, depending on the pathways taken.
- *Radial model*, in which a number of developmental lines move out from a common center. The common center might be construed as some basic set of achievements which provide the point of departure for later differentiation along a number of lines, such as Gardner's frames of mind.
- *Irregularly branching model.* Even granting some common set of achievements as a base line, subsequent departures from it may be quite haphazard, depending on innumerable organism-environment interactions in an irreversibly evolving historical context.

The models are not necessarily mutually exclusive. Historically, they may have been developed as alternatives to each other. But each may capture certain parts of a developmental cycle.

Figure 7.1 shows one possible way of exploiting the merits of all four models that have been discussed here. The strict linear model is reasonably close to the major developmental theories that make no theoretical effort to represent individuation. It is probably a good representation of prenatal development; obviously, some would argue for its pertinence much later on. The linear model with alternative pathways is similar to an idea recently expressed by Fischer and Bullock (1984); the radial model, depicting the emergence of cognitive types, corresponds moderately well to Gardner's (1983) recent proposal, although he did not locate the appearance of his proposed types somewhere in a developmental sequence. The irregularly branching model is, of course, a representation of my own leitmotif about the uniqueness of each person. Stringing the four together in this way and referring to them as phases is meant to suggest that each may capture a part of a complex picture of increasing differentiation and individuation.

This picture is historically bounded in two ways. First, it is based on psychological knowledge and reflection as of now. Perhaps, for example, if we looked more closely at infant or even fetal development, we would not be tempted to apply the unilinear model at all. For the time being, however, it should be admitted that there are some marvelous regularities in prenatal human growth.

FIGURE 7.1. A Hybrid Developmental Model

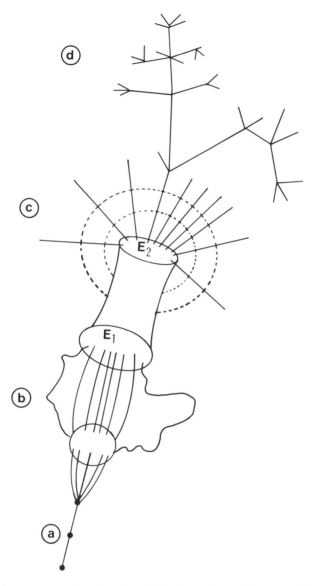

Phase *a*: precise stages in embryonic development, repeated by every individual. Phase *b*: developmental way stations with multiple pathways from one to another, and some variability at each point of arrival. Phase *c*: radiation of types from some common, shared point of departure. Phase *d*: irregular branching as individualization continues. The ellipses E₁ and E₂ are really the same phase, with separated projections of it for pictorial convenience in showing differentiated inputs and radiating outputs.

Second, the d-phase of irregular branching and almost unbounded individuation in at least some aspects of development, can probably only occur under certain societal conditions. We can imagine societies or communities so cramped that only very narrowly constrained channels become actualized.

In any event, every model of development that emphasizes the divergent variability of human development must also build in some constraints. People who are quite different must be able to understand each other, cooperate, marry, teach each other, and so on. Artist and scientist can draw from each other without being alike. The artist-poet William Blake had Newton in mind when he wrote the lines

> To see a World in a Grain of Sand
> And a Heaven in Wild Flower,
> Hold Infinity in the palm of your hand
> And eternity in an hour.*

He caught something about Newton, whom he saw as the rationalist extraordinary, whom in some moods Blake exalted and in others detested as the arch enemy. That they could have shared their experience of the universe is shown in Newton's own remark, and its likeness to Blake's lines:

> I do not know what I may appear to the world; but to myself I seem to have been only like a boy, playing on the sea shore, and diverting myself, in now and then finding a smoother pebble or a prettier shell than ordinary, whilst the great ocean of truth lay all undiscovered before me.†

Frank Manuel has suggested that this remark by Newton, made in his old age, may have been false modesty rather than authentic humility in front of nature. But I think it penetrates deeply into our questioning about human progress. "Boy" or not, Newton suggests that we can make only finite progress, but the "ocean of truth" is infinite. Making such progress as we can depends on carving out a finite universe of action, thought, and discourse within which to work. Doing creative work requires both a sense of mastery of what we can do and a sense of awe of what we cannot. Blake and Newton were a century apart, and one spoke the language of mathematics while the other detested it. But on the marriage of mastery and awe they could agree.

---

*These are the first four lines of William Blake's poem, "Auguries of Innocence."

†Quoted in many places. I take it from Manuel, Frank E., *A Portrait of Isaac Newton*. Washington, D.C.: New Republic Books, 1979.

THE CURRENT STATE OF CREATIVITY RESEARCH

Let us for a while at least presuppose (1) that the study of human creative work could in principle illuminate our discussions of the "upper" levels of development and (2) that there is sufficient connection between creative work and ordinary human functioning that the study of each could illuminate the other. I say "could" deliberately, for I believe that in our present state of knowledge we would be doing very well if we could understand even a single person doing creative work. In what follows, I first very briefly sketch the "evolving systems approach" to creative work, and then survey a number of contradictions and gaps in our present understanding.

THE EVOLVING SYSTEMS APPROACH*

The evolving systems approach to creative work grew out of my reconstruction of Darwin's thought processes during the period in which he was searching for and elaborating the theory of evolution through natural selection. Darwin was in his twenties. The focus of attention was the period in 1837–39, just after the *Beagle* voyage, a period in which he kept marvelous notebooks that have been preserved and permit such a reconstruction. But in order to understand that period it was necessary to examine earlier documents from the five-year *Beagle* voyage. As matters turned out, Darwin's work on the theory of evolution could not be separated from his thinking about the connections between humans and other animals. In the middle of his work on evolution, in July 1838, before he had hit upon the idea of natural selection in a clear way, he opened a new set of notebooks, on "man, mind, and materialism."

This work eventuated, twenty years later, in the *Origin of Species* (1859) and twelve years later still, the *Descent of Man* (1871) and *Expression of Emotion in Man and Animals* (1872). The double delay resulted from the combination of strictly scientific problems on major scientific distraction, and Darwin's fear of ridicule and persecution for his heretical ideas.

The study of Darwin's notebooks provided a clear occasion for the formulation of an approach toward understanding:

---

*My most complete presentation of this approach is the chapter, "And the Bush Was Not Consumed: The Evolving Systems Approach to Creativity." In S. Modgil and C. Modgil (eds.), *Toward a Theory of Psychological Development*. Windsor, England: NFER Publishers, 1980. It is given a much fuller statement in a collective volume: D.B. Wallace and H.E. Gruber (eds.), *Creative People at Work: Twelve Cognitive Case Studies*. In preparation.

1. The evolving organization of knowledge; the growth of a theoretical structure for synthesizing a very wide range of biological and geological knowledge and thought.
2. The emergence of an organization of purpose; the continuing development and modification of Darwin's scientific enterprises, their interplay, and their role in regulating his life work.
3. The organization of affect; the early growth of his cathexis with nature, the role of values and emotion in governing his work and his relations with others—scientists, other intellectuals, pigeon keepers, family members, etc.

This study formed the basis for my book, *Darwin on Man: a Psychological Study of Scientific Creativity* (1981), and from that book emerged the evolving systems approach. We say "approach" only because the word "theory" seems a little pretentious for the present state of our understanding. In this approach, we try as much as possible to avoid the term "creativity" because that suggests a trait or possession that the person might have in some fixed and even measurable amount—an idea of which we are profoundly sceptical. Instead, we try to speak of "creative work," a process or ensemble of processes that we can study as it occurs over extended periods of time. The basic idea is that the person doing creative work (sometimes abbreviated to "creative person") comprises three loosely coupled subsystems, organizations of knowledge, purpose, and affect. It is important to stress that they are loosely coupled: that they evolve somewhat independently, but always in interaction with each other, each in a sort of "internal milieu" provided by the rest of the whole system. This kind of interaction is not unlike the loose coupling of the organism and its extenal environment necessary for any plausible conception of adaptive behavior.

I have been writing "we" because the evolving systems approach is by now elaborated as the product of some ten doctoral dissertations and other collaborations. Although in our work thus far we have concentrated on individual creative work, we are mindful of the social context in which such work goes on—both the general social context and the social organization of the work itself. Unfortunately, there has been very little serious study of the process of collaboration. Much of the sociologically oriented research that might have gone in that direction has instead been concerned to deny the reality of individual creative work. One might as well deny the reality of the individual organism because it exists in a milieu, mates with others, and rears its young. There should be absolutely no conflict between an interest in individual creative work and an interest in the social nature of all thought. As studies of scientific collaboration appear, this will surely be the result.

In the evolving systems approach as we conceive it, it is not necessary to suppose that we are looking for some set of traits shared by all people doing creative work, or by some subset, such as artists or scientists, or cubists or particle physicists. We choose a creative person to study because he or she has done or is doing something unique. Consequently, a parsimonious starting point is to assume that if the person does something unique it is because he or she is unique. Creative work is almost by definition difficult, and success improbable: Correspondingly, it requires vigor, boldness and persistence. *But these may come about in many ways.* A sick person may be vigorous in work by carefully husbanding energies. Darwin was bold in his study for many years, but circumspect in his relations with the world. Persistence can be expressed by unremitting toil, or by sporadic returns to a nagging problem.

To be sure, also, the creative person doing something very special may have developed some very special abilities. But we need not assume, without examination, that these abilities pre-existed and made the work possible. Applying the idea of "determination from above" (Wertheimer, 1945)—now sometimes called "top-down processing"—to this relationship, it may well be that the person works to perfect certain skills because those skills are needed for his or her chosen tasks. Leonardo drew a thousand hands and *then* painted the *Last Supper* with its marvelous hands. The Nobel prize winning chemist, Robert Woodward, was noted for his seemingly miraculous ability to visualize chemical structures: He spent *thousands* of hours making structural drawings of molecules that his colleagues thought could be well enough represented by chemical equations. No wonder they later marveled at his aesthetic, intuitive feel for structure (Woodward, in preparation).

THE PLACE OF UNIQUE PHENOMENA IN SCIENTIFIC THOUGHT

Of course, *every* human being is unique. Of the creative person it might be said that he or she becomes unique in more and more interesting ways by persevering at interesting work.

This state of affairs leaves us with a difficult problem. How will we make a *science* of the study of creative people, if each object in the domain, i.e., each creative person, is unique? Does science not necessarily aim at universals and general principles?

Yes and yes but. If each person in our collection is unique, we can still hope to arrive at some general principles that help us to understand each such unique configuration. For example, suppose it be the case that a person doing creative work must have some strategies or heuristics for identifying unusual ideas, recording them, and elaborating them. We might call this a "deviation amplifying system" (Maruyama, 1963). There are probably thousands of ways of doing this, and an indefinitely large number of combinations of these. We could develop in ourselves a set of skills of studying such configurations without ever having to assume that any two are alike. This attitude is similar to the idea of the evolution of new species. We cannot predict which phenotypic variations will occur, only that they must obey certain constraints and satisfy certain functions; our hypotheses are not disappointed if yet another unique species is discovered.

Instead, our comparative anatomists, geneticists, etc. set to work to try to understand this new configuration in the living world.

You may ask, in wondering if we should devote all this energy to studying creative people: Suppose we go along with your next step, that this is not only interesting in its own right, but that understanding innovation is important for understanding the environments in which everyone lives. Can we take the next step and also say that learning about extraordinary people will help us to understand ordinary people? If we cannot generalize from one creative person to another, how in the world can we generalize from a collection of them to the person in the streets?

No, we cannot legitimately make inductive generalizations of this sort. But what we learn about creative people may teach us *where to look* to understand more ordinary lives. For example, the idea of network of enterprise became evident in the study of creative lives; it is readily extended to other lives; in my current research I am beginning to look into the origins of such networks in children. To take another example, the idea of an "ensemble of metaphors"—an interacting group, rather than a single ruling metaphor—become important in studying Darwin's life; it has now been readily applied to other creative lives; and it could readily be extended to more ordinary people. In fact, a cognitive anthropologist, Naomi Quinn, has been applying a similar approach to people's representations of the state of marriage (personal communication).

The evolving systems approach helps us to understand the frequent failures of proposed measures of ability both formal and informal. This problem was foreshadowed in Francis Galton's pioneering *Inquiries Into Human Faculty* (1883). Hardly any idea is more deeply rooted in the folklore of creativity than the belief that strong visual imagery is an important asset. Yet the majority of scientists in Galton's famous "breakfast table" questionnaire claimed that visual imagery was unknown to them. Galton was astonished and concluded "They had a mental deficiency of which they were unaware."

For a while, from 1950–70 there burgeoned a psychometrics of creativity, and an arsenal of tests now exists. But the yield of validity studies has been close to zero. Getzels and Csikszentmihalyi's (1976) important book, *The Creative Vision,* reports a follow-up study of art students. It was indeed possible for the authors to tease out of their many observations some correlations between an early sample performance and later success in the art world. But results of quasi-standardized tests of creativity yielded little. Barron and Harrington (1981), in a recent review concluded that there was no evidence for the validity of existing tests of creativity. Except for the highly questionable practice of validating one test against another, few such validity efforts have been made, and those have failed.

I think the problem may reside in applying the whole logic of psychometrics to the issue of creative work. In order to measure an ability, the psychometrician must find some variable on which it is reasonable to test a fairly large population. If any validation studies are done at all, the prediction is made that some special population will score higher than the rest. But in the case of creative people, each one may become excellent at something no one else has even thought of or cared about. Yet, by the time a creative person has won his or her struggle to bring that "variable" to others' attention, it would no longer be a good measure of creativity. Today, for example, with powerful computer graphics techniques available, Robert Woodward's long nights of reconstructing molecules by painstaking drawings would not avail him much. Today's creative chemist must do something else that has not been dreamed of yet, and which therefore cannot be an item in the psychometrician's battery.

In other words, the evolving systems approach does *not* lead us to reject the idea that creative people have special abilities. I argue only that the attempt to freeze the profile of the creative person in a battery of tests displays a complete and disastrous lack of historical perspective. A good antidote to this ailment is *Born Under Saturn: The Character and Conduct of Artists, a Documented History from Antiquity to the French Revolution* (Wittkower and Wittkower, 1963). In this penetrating survey by two distinguished art historians, the authors conclude that their evidence "militates most strongly against the existence of a timeless constitutional type of artist" (p. 293). Perkins (1981) makes a similar point.

A second and closely related difficulty in the psychometric approach to creativity is the loose attitude toward criterion levels. Studies of the gifted sometimes use a criterion level of the upper one percent of the population. This leads to moderate correlations showing that the gifted, so identified, lead quite successful lives, stay married, are healthy and well adjusted. Such claims may well be justified, but they have little or nothing to do with an adequate description of highly creative people.

We should not really be surprised at the failure of attempts to measure creativity. The creative person does something unique because he or she is unique, and is so in unexpected ways. Obsessed by her subject she comes to know more about it than anyone else and more important, to know it in a different way. Köhler has given a good account of the changes in the psychological field that come about as a result of such non-pathological, creative obsessions. Keller, in her recent biography of the great geneticist, Barbara McClintock, has shown how one life exhibits a quality of "strangeness"—not mere superiority in what others also do well, but excellence in something as yet unthought of—in McClintock's case, *A Feeling for the Organism* which is the title of Keller's (1983) book. Keller's central point is that most geneticists had been interested in certain abstractions that they hoped to test and elaborate without much regard to the particular organism being studied. Unlike her seniors and contemporaries, McClintock immersed herself in the life of one organism and came to know corn genetics at a level of intimacy down to the individual, unheard of by her colleagues. Her strange approach made it possible for her to discover fundamental aspects of genetic patterning that had gone unnoticed.

THE ORGANIZATION OF PURPOSE

In addition to these unique aspects of the organization of knowledge, the creative person works out a special, highly personal organization of purpose, expressed in his or her network of enterprise. Although this can take many forms, it may be that each part must operate in a context that both nourishes it and disequilibrates it, so that progress here creates a problem there, and the person is "never at rest," which is the title of Westfall's (1980a) biography of Newton.

Each creative person probably also constructs a unique organization of affect. But here psychologists know the least. Freud wrote somewhere that before the problem of the creative artist psychoanalysis must "lay down its arms" (See Jones, vol. 3, chapter 15, 1957). Psychologists have no powerful theory of those positive emotions that must play a powerful role in organizing creative work—such as joy in nature, passion for truth, outrage at injustice. Although Kurt Lewin and his group made a promising start in the study of "level of aspiration," little or nothing has been done to extend this concept to the study of creative lives. From my work thus far, nothing could be more obvious than that people like Darwin believe that they are doing something that has never been done before, that they want to do something new, and that they suffer knowingly the anxieties of life in the vanguard. Indeed, they *must* have some grasp of where they stand in relation to their fellows, for this knowledge is an important guide to creative work. Moreover, nothing is more powerful than the sense of personal identity, and *my* purposes are a part of *my* identity, not of yours! Darwin would have been dumbfounded and disturbed to wake up one morning and find that he had just taken a step that was a part of the network of enterprise of his contemporary, Faraday! The individual's activities must be mapped onto his own organization of purpose, and the constant renewal of this mapping forms an essential part of the creative person's identity.

RECENT GROWTH IN INTEREST AND UNDERSTANDING OF SCIENTIFIC THOUGHT

Whatever we might mean by "upper" levels of development, it is bound to include scientific thought. We probably now know much more about scientific thinking than about other domains (a disparity that remains to be discussed). In several quarters, knowledge of scientific and quasi-scientific thought is being vigorously pursued: history and philosophy of science, genetic epistemology, psychology of science, and sociology of science are some of the disciplinary rubrics employed, along with Big Brother, cognitive science. The "psychology of science" enjoys an uneasy relation with the booming field of "cognitive science." Its subject matter is far too complex to satisfy the thirst for simplification and formalization exhibited by the latter. Yet the two exist side by side and give each other useful hints.

This very connection between cognitive science and the psychology of science brings out new gaps in our knowledge. As yet, there is no way of linking the clearly stated heuristics, algorithms, and production systems of artificial intelligence to the vague intuitions and strange cathexes that guide creative work. True, the *General Problem Solver* (Newell, Shaw and Simon, 1962) over twenty years ago could prove a theorem from *Principia Mathematica* but it took Bertrand Russell to conceive of the task of making that work, to invest it with his peculiar intensity, and to find the necessary collaborator (Whitehead and Russell, 1925–27).

There is nothing yet either in artificial intelligence *or* in more conventional cognitive psychology that can deal, for example, with Newton's lifelong preoccupation with alchemy. I am not advancing the by now tired argument that artificial intelligence will ''never'' simulate this or that cherished feature of human intelligence. One might as well say that psychology will ''never'' understand creative work. In this quest, both disciplines are simply tools.

Newton's life is instructive in other ways that pertain to our present discussion. For years, the comfortable belief was prevalent that as a young man he did all his properly cognitive work, enjoyed his ''annus mirabilis,'' and after that simply filled in and perfected a scheme he had already grasped. Then, well past his prime, he took up arcane subjects. We now know this picture to be almost entirely false.

His miraculous year was really two years, age 23–24. He did indeed sketch out a lifework for himself and produce many important insights. The multifaceted work of that period is an excellent example of the emergence of a network of enterprise—a set of lifetime tasks that guide the person's work over many decades. At the same time, as Westfall (1980b) has shown he was very far from mastery of the problems he had set himself, or solutions. If we are willing to chop up creative work into parts, such as thinking of good questions and thinking of good answers, we may say that most of the job was already ''done'' by young Newton. But no serious historian of science any longer entertains that view. Newton, too, needed his lifetime of creative effort.

Even more troubling for the purist in cognitive science is the role of arcane subjects in Newton's life. We know now that these interests were *not* consequent upon a late middle-aged weakening of his intellectual powers but emerged very early and remained with him to the end. Although there was almost certainly some hoped-for connection between his more conventional scientific thought and his alchemical ideas, he also distinguished between them. He had some clear and effective sense of which part of his thinking formed a coherent whole that belonged in his *Principia,* and which parts to withhold from the world. This complicates the problem for psychologists who are interested in the whole person, in the integrated working of a number of parts or loosely coupled subsystems. Thinkers like Newton are often guided by broad points of view that do not fit easily into the currently available cognitive story. To add only one brief example, Niels Bohr, a giant of quantum physics, was struck by William James' idea of the stream of thought. He gave newcomers to his laboratory a Danish novel to read, an early example of stream-of-consciousness writing, in which the main character, going up the stairs meets himself coming down. Bohr thought that would help his collaborators to do good physics! (Gruber & Vonèche, 1976).

The life of Newton brings out other important features of creative work—the role of self-criticism, level of aspiration, and social interaction. He has been painted as a lonely man, and indeed he was. Wordsworth's lines about him give the picture:

Newton with his prism and silent face
The marble index of a mind for ever
Voyaging through strange seas of thought alone.*

But in some ways this is an exaggerated picture. Even Newton, that most secretive and private of men, knew how much his work would mean. And for all his secrecy, his work was connected to the world's work, and he had ways of letting the world know this, before he published *Principia.* How else account for the famous conversation between Robert Hooke, Christopher Wren, and Edmund Halley. They discussed the possibility of proving that gravitational attraction (an idea already having some currency) varied inversely with the square of the distance. As none of them saw a way of proving it, Halley went up to Cambridge to visit Newton. He asked Newton for the shape of the curve of planetary orbits if gravity varied inversely with the square of the distance. Newton answered immediately: an ellipse. He had already calculated it and could provide Halley with the proof—except that he had lost it in his study! Not long after, he sent Halley not one but two proofs. A strange man, but not out of contact with the world.

In this essay, I have stressed the many areas of our ignorance about creative work, especially how to understand the process as a whole. But none of this is intended as a cry of despair. Even though we do not yet quite have our paradigm, we are making a sort of within-paradigm progress. We have a tolerable if very rough sketch of the evolving systems approach that must guide the study of creative work. We have won a certain degree of acceptance for the intensive study of the single case as a useful method in scientific research. This point should be qualified by the admission, or complaint, that it is still very hard to get financial support for this kind of research.

There remains a steady if relatively low interest in understanding the whole person as the necessary scene of creative work. It must be admitted, however, that "personology" is not a very popular sub-discipline of scientific psychology. On the empirical side, Carlson's (1970) complaint—"Where is the Person in Personality Research?''—could be written today. On the theoretical side, the idea

---

*Wordsworth, William. *The Prelude,* Book III, lines 60-63.

of the creative person as an evolving system—loosely coupled organizations of knowledge, purpose and affect—represents a programme rather than an achievement. Actual theoretical models capable of accounting for the creative work of any single person are still far out of reach, and efforts in that direction—including my own—remain primitive.

Scientists and intellectuals working under many different banners do now form a loose federation, or "invisible college" interested in most of the questions I have raised here. Philosophy of science, history of science, genetic epistemology, dialectical psychology, cognitive psychology, cognitive science, psychology of science, psychohistory, creativity research, and personology—these rubrics describe not only the work itself, but also a search for kindred spirits.

These different fields often tunnel through to each other and find useful linkages and illuminating connections. As for whether we will ever really understand creative work, any possible answer to that question depends on the criteria of understanding. For the present, I want only to register one objection to the notion that understanding requires simulation. In the long run, we do not need or want to substitute machines for people. We want to understand ourselves well enough to make our lives better, or at least possible.

In other words, simulation is not necessary for the requisite understanding. At the same time, it may not be sufficient. Even in AI circles the realization is growing that we may be able to write programs that can accomplish certain tasks without our quite understanding how they work. Carried far enough this process will lead to a new science, the psychology of the computer. The computer-generated solution of the 4-color problem in topology led to just such a dilemma. The program was too long and complex for its operations to be checked by humans. But the central idea of all mathematical proof is that every step must be open to inspection and found valid. Here instead, mathematicians had to have *faith* in the computer. Every simulation is really a man-machine interaction, in which it is not easy to decide who or what put which into what or whom. This point emerged as a central problem in a dissertation at M.I.T. on the simulation of the composition of an animated film telling a version of the Cinderella story. "Who made the film?" remained the unanswered question (Kahn, 1979).

THE IDEA OF PROGRESS, TIME PERSPECTIVE, AND THE FEELING OF PERSONAL AGENCY

Who made the film?

We might well ask a question more portentous for the future of all environments in which human development might take place. If the nuclear arms race and other species-destructive patterns continue their accelerated growth, our future looks very dim. The waging of war will become more and more automated. Then the question will arise in the minds of any that remain: Who or What made the war?

Developmentally, this future is now upon us. The world in which adolescents and young adults live is one in which the risk of species self-destruction looms large. When I grew up academically, we learned about feelings of helplessness and despair as part of psychopathology. Now it is *reasonable* to feel helpless and without a future. More than one reasonable position being possible, I do not go so far as to say it is *un*reasonable to feel hopeful and to be future-oriented. But at the present rate of events that day may come.

The objective bases for such questions and feelings are part of the everyday environment of every young person. Those young people who are consciously aware of this profound historical change in the developmental process can reasonably say "If I grow up..."instead of "When I grow up..."

The ecological system that forms the largely unspoken environmental premise for our developmental theories is one in which cultural stability is the rule, and familial stability, if not the rule is the norm. Much of education, especially in the United States, is built on the idea of upward social and educational mobility as a distinct possibility for everyone. The internalization of such societal models that permit growing up hopefully is an integral part of the production system of our societies, and is also inherent in our theories of development.

We do not only premise the idea of individual progress within our theories, we also assume that it is part of the growing person's own mental equipment. The child may say "When I grow up I want to be an astronaut." We expect all sorts of changes in the last word of that sentence. But we do not have a place in our theories for a normal developmental pattern in which its first word changes to "If..."

Closely related to this sense of stability, futurity, and hope is the feeling of personal agency. The growing person needs to feel that some of what happens in the world is due to his own purposeful actions (Gruber, 1984). According to Piaget and Inhelder (1969), even the experience of an objective causal texture of the environment begins as a projection of this feeling of personal agency. In the long run, for the young adult, this sense of effectiveness must reach beyond moment to moment activity and shape the emergence of longer term perspectives. We call this a *sense of purpose.*

To sum up this argument: (1) without a sense of personal agency there can be no meaningful idea of maturity; (2) intellectual growth takes place within a social-affective-historical framework that creates the possibilities for the feeling of personal agency; (3) threats to species survival provide the ultimate attack on this feeling of agency; (4) confronting these threats means taking *personal responsibility* to act toward their abatement. Without such confrontation the whole idea of personal maturity is called into question.

One of the major ideas behind this essay is that developmental theory must be responsive to historical change. Although this is not a new idea (see Fischer and Bullock, 1984), it needs more vigorous pursuit and more precise representation in theoretical work.

Upoem was written for my daughter when she was a small girl, I included it in the talk on which this chapter is based only to suggest that we developmentalists had not thought enough about the idea of progress. In the 18 months since our Symposium, the nuclear arms race has continued and other threats to human survival have deepened. None of them have lessened. My daughter's son was born during our Symposium. As I write, he is now at the age when he can produce the one-word utterance, "Doggie," when he meets a squirrel or a horse. I want him to grow up in a world where, when he and his fellows meet their Russian counterparts, they will all feel, "There can be only one side— Humanity."

If developmental theory must be responsive to historical change, scientific criteria for cognitive-social developmental progress must from now on include the changes in patterns of human thought and in patterns of personal identity necessary to bring this utterance about.

8

Methodological Considerations in Young Adult Cognitive Development Research

Robert A. Mines

The chapters in this book represent a wide array of theoretical models and phases of research on young adult intellectual development. This concluding chapter discusses the psychometric and design issues that warrant consideration in future research endeavors. Statistical application and issues have been recently reviewed (Applebaum and McCall, 1984) and are not presented in this chapter.

THEORETICAL CONSIDERATIONS

The majority of the models in this volume are based on stage assumptions (chapters, Arlin, Basseches, King, Kitchener, Rest). The model presented by Fischer and Kenny and the perspective provided by Gruber are not stage models per se; however, many of the theoretical considerations discussed in this section are still applicable. A number of theoretical issues surrounding stage concepts in developmental psychology are recapitulated in the subfield of young adult cognitive development. The list of issues includes, but is not limited to:

1. Presence and direction of change (Wohlwill, 1973),
2. Rate of change (Wohlwill, 1973),
3. Continuity versus discontinuity of change (Fischer, this volume),
4. Sequences of unequal length (Wohlwill, 1973),
5. Age/educational level confounding (Wohlwill, 1973),
6. Quantitative versus qualitative change (Applebaum and McCall, 1984),
7. Hierarchical arrangement of stages (Commons and Richards, 1984).

Presence and Direction of Change

Cognitive stage models assume that change in level or stage occurs in a theoretically predictable direction. Examples of the presence and direction of change include more complexity, better problem-finding skills, higher levels of abstraction, dialectical reasoning, more complexity of metaphysical or epistemological assumptions, and postconventional moral reasoning.

The possibility that developmental change may be occurring is established in the initial phase of a research program with cross-sectional designs. The presence and direction of change is established with longitudinal data. The Reflective Judgment (Kitchener, this volume) and Moral Reasoning (Rest, this volume) models have the only longitudinal data to date. Change does occur, albeit slowly and in small increments, within these two models. Longitudinal research is under way on some of the other models (e.g., Arlin, Fischer). It is necessary to establish the presence and direction of change along the lines predicted by the model as a basic premise of development.

Rate of Change

The rate of change allows for the establishment of the optimal and typical time spent at a given stage or level. Rate of change information is obtained through longitudinal data collection. The rate of change information has applied implications. For example, programs designed to accelerate stage progression may not be successful because of natural limits to the rate of change. This issue is discussed further in the section on optimal versus natural functioning.

The rate of change from one stage or level to another also has direct implications for young adult cognitive development research. The rate of change may cover a longer time frame than that studied using young adults. Research on models where the rate of change is slow will need to expand the data base to include older adults in order to establish the rate of change through the stages. In addition, rate of change will affect the timing of repeated measures. If the rates of change are slow, then developmental spurts may be missed on some longitudinal designs.

Continuity versus Discontinuity

Some suggest that a basic premise of cognitive stage models is that the stages are discrete reasoning processes in which the upper levels incorporate the elements of the lower level (Commons and Richards, 1984). They argue, stages should be discontinuous rather than continuous. An alternative point of view, presented by Davison, King, Kitchener, and Parker (1980) suggests that "stage sequence can be represented as a continuous developmental dimension of individual differences in reasoning." Furthermore, they argue that as an individual's developmental level increases, the probability of giving a particular stage response increases until it reaches a maximum at that stage, at which point it begins to decrease.

Some models presented in this volume provide data from which one could infer that aspects of young adult cognitive development may be continuous (i.e.,

Reflective Judgment, Moral Judment). On the other hand, discontinuities have also been demonstrated in Fischer's research. These differences in the data on continuity versus discontinuity can be accounted for in various ways:

1. Some aspects of young adult cognitive development may actually be continuous, some discontinuous.
2. The differences may be an artifact of the assessment methodology and data reduction techniques used since authors develop their assessment techniques and scoring procedures based on their assumptions of continuity and discontinuity. For example, if there is a trend toward more complexity in the phenomena of interest and the model is based on a continuous assumption, the assessment methodology will represent the data as continuous, when, in fact, it may be discontinuous. To clarify the continuity/discontinuity aspects of a given model, the researchers should develop both continuity and discontinuity methodologies to adequately test their assumptions.
3. The differences may be due to content familiarity and extent of skills in a given content area (Fischer, this volume). Davison et al. (1980) proposed that the individual uses given stage responses with increasing probabilities until an equilibrium is reached. In other words, as familiarity with content increases, so does the probability that the response will occur, assuming the individual has initially attained the necessary stage structure. This point of view rests on the assumption that the individual is familiar with the content and has the skills inherent in reasoning about a given test item with said content. Fischer's work indicates that differences in skills and content familiarity can account for variation in developmental test performance. The skill and content familiarity differences need to be controlled in order to assume the longitudinal or cross-sectional results are due to developmental differences.
4. The differences in the data could be a function of the timing of assessment. For example, in longitudinal designs, discontinuities may be occurring and the researchers are not finding them due to infrequent assessment.

The continuity/discontinuity assumptions have a direct bearing on the selection of the scales used in the assessment techniques used to study the models. The assumptions the theorists make about continuity/discontinuity also lead to different statistical treatment of the data obtained. These issues are discussed further in the psychometric section.

Sequences of Unequal Length

Are all the stages or levels of a given model equal in terms of time required to consolidate the stage, or equal in terms of the theoretical "distance" between the stages? The time and distance issues affect measurement and design selection as well as having theoretical implications regarding the continuity/discontinuity issue. The length of time required for acquisition of a stage poses no difficulty if all of the intervals are equal. This is highly unlikely and presents a problem for longitudinal research designs, as the timing of the repeated measures is typically standardized (e.g., one year; two year intervals). Variation in the timing of development between stages may be artificially obscured through standardized assessment intervals. We may need more flexibility in our longitudinal designs in order to find whether maturational consolidation differences exist. For example, subgroups of a sample could be assessed at different intervals rather than assessing the entire sample at once.

The theoretical distance between the stage levels has a direct bearing on scale development. The stages or skills probably do not represent equal amounts of psychological phenomena. None of the theorists in this volume assume the stages or skills represent equal distances. This leaves the researcher with nominal or ordinal scales as possibilities for instrument development. The advantages and disadvantages of these two scale choices are discussed in the psychometric section.

Age/Educational Level Confounding

The young adult cognitive development research is directly confounded along age and education levels in most studies. This confounding is a result of studying samples who are in an educational setting, such as undergraduate and graduate schools, where age is typically associated with a given educational level. It is only at the upper ends of the models (Kitchener, King, Rest, this volume) that preliminary data have been acquired to separate the effects of these variables. Another way to look at the age and education confounding is to view it as a natural versus optimal environment interaction effect. The individuals who attend college or graduate school could be considered as having exposure to an optimal environment for developing higher level reasoning processes. Those individuals with equal intellectual ability who have not attended college or graduate school should not demonstrate higher levels of reasoning, as the natural environment typically does not provide demands for complex reasoning. This results in a lower stage functioning than would probably occur under optimal environmental conditions. (See Fischer's chapter for an extended discussion of natural versus optimal condition effects.) In fact, the data presented in this book provides support for the view that adults who have been in environments (i.e., higher education) that require the skills measured by these models are further advanced than those adults having gone into other environments after high school.

Quantitative versus Qualitative Change

By definition, changes in stages or levels are qualitative. The qualitative assumption has scaling implications. Wohlwill (1973) stated the quantitative/qualitative issue in the form of the question of whether or not a behavior is measurable along a quantitative scale. The models of young adult cognitive development (with the exception of Fischer) presented in this volume typically do not meet the quantitative behavior criteria because the structure of the stage is imposed on any set of content. It is the manner in which the individual reasons about a problem that is of interest, not the answer per se. Often the quantitative approach assumes that right and wrong answers exist, in the scoring systems used, when many of the assessment situations present problems that have better or worse answers which are not subject to strict quantitative scoring assumptions. They may fit a more or less of something quantitative assumption or may be qualitative in nature. Thus, treating the data from these models as if they were quantitative may have problems. Wohlwill (1973) noted that attempts to quantify qualitative data through the use of group incidence scores obscures the abruptness or smoothness of stage change, as well as rate and time of change. The quantification of qualitative data may artificially present a picture of continuity.

Hierarchical Arrangement of Stages

The models which define the cognitive processes as stages or levels have the burden of demonstrating that the stages are hierarchically arranged. The ordering of the stages in the models should have an internal coherence that can be demonstrated conceptually first and then tested empirically. Commons and Richards (1984) propose that cognitive models meeting the criteria for stages have a "discrete, irreflexive, inclusive order" consisting of task demands arranged hierarchically that become qualitatively more complex.

The demonstration of hierarchical arrangement includes three phases. The first phase is based on the theoretical and logical consistency of the stages or levels of descriptions. It should be apparent from reading the theoretical explication of the logic of the stage order that the order is sequential and hierarchical. If the order is not apparent then testing for a hierarchical arrangement is questionable. The second phase employs the use of cross-sectional or experimental designs which test for differences between groups that theoretically should be at different stages. The cross-sectional and experimental design methodologies provide intergroup difference data on the hierarchical arrangement of the stages. The groups who are predicted to score higher actually do score higher. Davison (1977) has described and tested an alternative method for demonstrating the sequentiality of stages using a qualitative unfolding model. It has been used to test the sequentiality of the models of Harvey, Hunt, and Schroeder, and Loevinger (Davison, et al., 1980) and Reflective Judgment (King, Kitchener, Davison, Parker and Wood, 1983). It allows the researcher to compare the strength of the stage ordering across the model. The methodologies in the second phase allow the researcher to determine if theoretically predicted differences occur between groups or if there is a coherence to the stage responses within an individual (e.g., Davison et al., 1980).

Fischer, Hand, and Russell (1984) and Commons and Richards (1984) provide a third means of demonstrating the hierarchical arrangement. They have proposed changing the task demands so that each level or stage is assessed by an increasingly more complex task designed specifically for the stage or level. Wohlwill (1973) discussed this approach as a Guttman scale in which the individual should be able to pass items or tasks up to the level of functioning.

The most conservative test of hierarchical arrangement is to study individual changes over time, therefore, phase three involves the longitudinal study of the individual's progression through the stages. Without longitudinal data, one cannot say that intergroup differences are due to developmental factors nor can one say that the cluster of stage scores is due to the hierarchical arrangement of the scores. It is only from the study of individual change over time that sequentiality and hierarchical arrangement can be attributed with confidence.

Summary

To what extent have the models in this book addressed the theoretical issues or met the theoretical assumptions? It is clear that the data from all of the models point to the conclusion that young adults reason more complexly, use increasingly abstract categories, exhibit a progression in the assumptions about knowledge used in justifying beliefs, and to a lesser extent, use dialectical concepts, indicating that the theoretical requirements regarding concepts, sequentiality, and hierarchical arrangement have been met to varying degrees.

The continuity/discontinuity issue is based on the assumption that the demonstration of discontinuity confirms that qualitative differences exist between levels. The continuity/discontinuity requirement has been addressed in different ways by the theorists. Kitchener, Rest, and Basseches assume their data is ordinal and represents varying degrees of stage usage, arranged sequentially and hierarchically. On the other hand, Fischer provides a methodology and supporting data for a discontinuity interpretation of his model. The continuity/discontinuity component to the models may be accounted for in different ways.

First, the continuity data may be an actual reflection of the complexity of adult reasoning and discontinuity assumptions are unnecessary. At any given time, an adult will exhibit a variety of responses in thinking through a problem which would support a continuity perspective. Second, the complex stage responses may be an artifact of imprecise scoring criteria, resulting in various stage responses exhibited in a subject's data set leading to the erroneous conclusion that the model is continuous. This point can be determined by looking at the levels of agreement among raters of the data.

Imprecise scoring categories or scoring rules will result in mediocre or poor interrater agreement and reliability. The raters end up assigning more than one stage response to a subject. Resolving the scoring differences through the use of a mean for example, will give the impression of continuity when the result is due to scoring rule or category imprecision.

Third, the complex stage models may also have a discontinuity aspect to them, however, to date, discontinuity methodologies have not been applied to the complex stage models, thus, the continuity conclusions may be premature.

The "rate of change" is a subset of the continuity/discontinuity problem. On the one hand, a slow gradual rate of change appears to occur in the reflective judgment and moral reasoning longitudinal research. On the other hand, Fischer's (this volume) model provides evidence of plateaus and spurts in specific cognitive skill domains. It would be quite interesting to test the slow change models with a "discontinuity methodology" such as Fischer's, to see if the slow, gradual change data continued to hold up. If the slow, gradual change models are not supported, then the previous differences may have been due to the optimal/natural testing condition differences.

The length of time it takes to move through a stage or an entire model is in many respects, not critical to demonstrate in the validation phase of a research model. The length of time becomes more important in applied research once the theory has validity data to support it. In addition, individual differences in intelligence may set floor and ceiling effects on stage acquisition and rate of progression through the stages. At this time, based on Kitchener's work (this volume), it appears the length of time for change to occur is long (one or two years) and is probably incomplete at the mid-twenties, even among intelligent, highly educated people.

Age/education level confounding is found throughout the young adult cognitive development research. Where data exist which empirically separate the age versus education level and controls for intelligence (Lawson, 1980; Strange, 1978), it appears that higher cognitive processes develop in the context of optimal environments such as higher education. Those adults in noneducational environments apparently are not challenged nor taught more complex reasoning processes in order to solve problems in those settings.

It is very difficult, if not impossible, to separate theoretical issues from psychometric and methodological issues. The burden of verifying or disconfirming the theoretical issues falls in the psychometric and methodology domains. As noted in the theoretical section, many of the issues could not be clearly resolved because of psychometric or methodological confounding. The next section focuses on psychometric issues related to young adult cognitive development research.

PSYCHOMETRIC CONSIDERATIONS

The psychometric qualities of the instruments used to assess the models of young adult cognitive development form the foundation on which the models are refined and built. Without a careful consideration of the psychometric issues, the validity of the models may never be adequately established. The following content areas are discussed in this section:

1. Unit of analysis
2. Scales of measurement (quantitative vs qualitative)
3. Scoring methods
4. Measurement task (preference, production)
5. Natural versus optimal conditions for assessment.

Unit of Analysis

What is the unit of analysis? The models in this book have used a variety of units of analysis. The units of analysis have included specific skills (Fischer), categorization of subsets of a process (Basseches), endorsement of stage prototypic responses (Rest), qualitative differences in responses (Arlin), qualitative differences in subsections of protocols (Kitchener), and an entire body of writing including notes and published work (Gruber). The unit of analysis should be consistent with the theoretical coherence of the model, the assumption of continuity/discontinuity, and assumptions regarding quantitative versus qualitative scaling.

The unit of analysis can become a source of error in interpreting data if it has been defined in a manner which is inconsistent with the theoretical coherence of the model. For example, if the model is descriptive of an entire sequence of thought, such as dialectical reasoning, then the entire response should be evaluated as a whole rather than broken down into subcategories. Breaking the unit of analysis into subcategories rather than using the whole response leads to tenuous interpretations within the context of the theory because it is the gestalt of the response that forms the qualitative aspect of the process.

In some cases, other units of analysis may also be of value, even though they may not be theoretically consistent. A good example is the use of the P-score in the moral reasoning research. The P-score has been used to show the percent of principled stage usage in cross-sectional and longitudinal research. This type of data allows inferences to be made about stage change and sequential progression.

Scales of Measurement

The type of scaling chosen to measure cognitive development should follow directly from the assumptions about the unit of analysis and nature of the data (i.e., quantitative versus qualitative). Two types of scaling, nominal and ordinal, warrant consideration in assessing young adult cognitive development. The use of nominal categories in a Guttman-type scale is a conservative approach to demonstrating the sequencing and hierarchical arrangement of stages. It is assumed that the cognitive processes can be defined precisely and discretely in order to develop a Guttman-type scale. Fischer (this volume) uses highly specific skills with Guttman-type scaling to demonstrate discontinuities, sequencing, and hierarchical arrangement.

Models that have multifaceted stage descriptions may sacrifice precision in terms of scaling for richness in terms of the complexity of the subject's response. It has been a common practice to treat multifaceted data as if the scales were at least ordinal. The ordinal data can be used to demonstrate sequencing and the hierarchical arrangment of the model. For example, Davison et al.'s (1980) unfolding model for analyzing predominate and adjacent stage usage is one technique for demonstrating the hierarchical arrangement and sequencing of complex stage data derived from ordinal scales.

The Guttman-type scale, however, offers greater precision and certainty about the sequencing and hierarchical arrangement of the stages. On the other hand, it is very difficult to find cognitive reasoning models than can be defined so the Guttman-type scales can be used. The ordinal scaling offers more flexibility for obtaining and analyzing data on complex models while sacrificing some degree of certainty about the sequencing and arrangement because of the individual differences and measurement error that exist when assessing multifaceted stage phenomena.

Scoring Methods

In addition to identifying the unit of analysis and appropriate scaling procedures, the researcher must decide how to represent the responses for analysis purposes. The scoring method has a direct impact on the inferences regarding stage or level. To date, the methods which have been used include the highest stage response, the model stage response, the mean level of stage usage, the percentage of highest stage exhibited, the use of cutting scores, strong scalograms procedures, and nominal-descriptive methods (Mines, 1982).

These methods all have merits and limitations. Using the highest stage response or percentage of highest stage utilized is acceptable when a stage can be clearly exhibited and the subject's motivation to produce the highest stage can be assured. Cognitive stage acquisition may be uneven or vary by content domain, thus, the use of the highest responses or percentage of highest stage may lead to interpretation problems if a subject's motivation to perform is not optimal or if the highest stage is interpreted as typical rather than maximal functioning.

The use of the mean or the mode underestimates the highest stage or level and assumes that the scaling meets the criteria for continuity and quantifiability. The mean eliminates the stage or level variance, resulting in a conservative estimate of stage functioning. The use of the mean or mode obscures decalage problems across test items, as well as motivation to produce on a given item. Complex cognitive stage models will not be adequately represented by a mean or a modal score.

The ogive rules of cumulative distribution have not been applied to the models discussed in this book, although Loevinger (1976) used ogive rules with her model. The ogive rules use the distribution of responses rather than the mean, median, or mode. The ogive rules take the distribution of scores into account and yet represent the distribution of scores with a single stage that does not convey the stage or level variance exhibited in the assessment. The ogive rules give a picture of stage usage that is higher than the typical performance, but lower than the optimal performance (Davison et al., 1980).

Fischer, Hand, and Russell (1984) suggested that the data reduction problem could be minimized through the use of a strong scalogram analysis. This procedure specifies a skill or task that a young adult at a higher cognitive stage or level should be able to demonstrate and a young adult at a lower level should not be able to demonstrate. A separate task is designed for each level. This eliminates many of the scoring method problems described previously as the criterion for acquisition as defined in a yes/no dichotomy. It also eliminates the problem of using one task or test to describe the entire range of a cognitive development model. This approach is appropriate for investigating specifically defined skills. It would be difficult to use it on a global reasoning process model without redefining the stages in terms of specific skills.

The selection of a scoring method is directly related to the phase of research a model is in, as well as the specific purpose of a given study. The simple versus complex stage assumptions of the model have direct bearing on the scoring method. Simple stage models are amenable to Guttman-type representations. Complex models can be represented as a mean, percentage of stage usage, or ogive rules depending on what the researcher is interested in (e.g., a conservative estimate of functioning, optimal functioning). If the researcher is interested in investigating exceptional cognitive development, then a process description is sufficient as a score would be meaningless. The scoring method should be selected to represent the phenomena of interest as accurately as possible.

Measurement Task Differences

Rest (1979c) discussed the differences between production and recognition tasks. Production tasks (e.g., reflective judgment interview, dialectical reasoning interview) are designed so the subject must produce the stage or level reasoning. They give a conservative estimate of level of functioning and are limited by the young adult's motivation to perform at his/her highest level If the subject is fatigued or not motivated to do well, a production task will more frequently underestimate the young adult's cognitive development level. The recognition task allows the subject to mark a prototypic response that most closely agrees with his/her point of view on the issue (e.g., Defining Issues Test). Rest (1979c) noted that the subject can recognize or understand higher stage responses before he/she is capable of producing the response. The recognition task provides data that is a liberal estimate of the subject's functioning.

Fischer (this volume) suggested that the type of measurement task (verbal response, written response, object manipulation), familiarity with the task, and length of the task affects the subject's response. For example, in the Mines (1980) study, mathematics and psychology/sociology students were compared on the Reflective Judgment Interview (RJI) (see Kitchener, this book). The mathematics students had higher academic ability scores than the psychology/sociology students. After statistically controlling for the academic ability, the psychology/ sociology students scored significantly higher on reflective judgment. One interpretation was the psychology/sociology students were further advanced on the Reflective Judgment model than one would predict, based on their academic ability. An alternative explanation was that RJI elicits a verbal response, requiring a subject to think out loud in a complex manner about an ill-structured problem. It was informally observed that the psychology/sociology students had better verbal communication skills than the mathematics students. The results, therefore, could have been an artifact of verbal facility. It is possible that the outcome may have been different if the student was able to write a response or if the student were given adequate time to research the problem and present a response.

Task familiarity contributes to variation in subject performance (Fischer, this volume). On any of the cognitive models on which a subject is asked to respond to an unfamiliar question or task, the subject may not perform as well as she/he is capable of because of information deficits, memory capacity, skill deficits, or performance anxiety. None of these may have a developmental stage or level basis to them. The usual interpretation would be that subject A was performing at a given developmental level, when other factors may be operating.

The length of the task, in terms of the response required or latency of response allowed, has a direct effect on the richness of the response. The models presented in this book address complex thinking processes; allowing fifteen minutes to an hour to respond to the task may not allow the subject an adequate time frame or response length to exhibit a complex thinking process. How many times in one's professional capacity does one have only one hour to analyze, evaluate, and present a synthesis on a complex or ill-structured problem? Thus, the attentuated time or format may hinder the subject's ability to respond in a manner comparable to the upper levels of the model.

In order to establish the upper limits of these models, it would be interesting to vary the test formats and time frames. Gruber's (see Chapter 7, this book) intensive case study approach is an example of one techinque that does allow the upper ends to be examined.

Natural versus Optimal Test Conditions

Fischer (this book) addressed the problem of task familiarity and the recognition versus production problem from the standpoint of natural versus optimal conditions. Under natural conditions, the subject is given a task or problem without any practice allowed or instruction as to what type of response is expected.

Under optimal conditions, the subject is first given the task and then instructed as to the better procedure for working on the task or problem and then retested. Then if the subject performs at a lower stage or level, it can be concluded with greater certainty that the performance was not an artifact of the assessment process. In fact, Fischer has compelling data on arithmetic skills, in which he is able to demonstrate performance differences due to natural versus optimal environments. The majority of the data reported in this book was obtained under natural conditions, in which the subjects did not necessarily have prior information concerning the processes involved, the nature of the problem, or the task expectations. Thus, the results may be underestimates of the performance levels of the samples.

Summary

The models in this book have defined the unit of analysis in a variety of ways. In certain cases (e.g., dialectical reasoning, reflective judgment) the unit has been defined as a paragraph or a statement when the actual theoretical description includes the entire thought process used in thinking about a problem. Using smaller thought units is a questionable strategy because the raters must infer the smaller unit is related to a more complex process, thus, increasing the potential for error. This type of rater error can be minimized by articulating the decision rules for scoring smaller thought units and demonstrating the thought units' relationship to the entire thought sequence. Gruber's (this book) "evolving systems" approach takes entire lines of reasoning as the unit of analysis, thus avoiding the problem of defining the unit of analysis in a manner inconsistent with a model's theoretical assumptions. In looking at specific skills, Fischer (this book) also has defined the unit of analysis in a manner which is observable, descriptive, and replicable.

The quantitative/qualitative scale of measurement issue is directly related to the demonstration of the hierarchical arrangement of the stages or levels. Future research will need to define the levels with sufficient precision to allow qualitative scales to be derived in order to minimize other sources of measurement error.

The scoring procedures and the task requirements used to represent and assess the models should follow directly from the model's description of the process. Creativity and innovation may be needed to find ways to adequately sample complex reasoning processes. For example, Gruber's methodology has promise in this regard.

Finally, the optimal versus natural testing conditions issue has a direct bearing on the validation of the model. Each approach provides a different view of a model and the incidence of different stages in the sample. Another way of considering the use of optimal or natural conditions relates to whether one is interested in the best performance a subject is capable of or an estimate of how a subject might perform in naturally occurring situations. Continued research on the models in this volume should consider the use of both optimal and natural methodologies as a means of extending our understanding of the young adult cognitive processes.

CONCLUSIONS

The study of young adult cognitive development is still in its infancy. On the theoretical level, the models and techniques presented in this volume represent a variety of cognitive skills and processes. The array of skills and processes offers a richness to the study and understanding of young adult cognitive development that has been related to the Piagetian perspective, yet has gone beyond it.

The state of the art on the empirical level indicates that within the traditional paradigm, the majority of research is still in the descriptive, cross-sectional phase. The moral reasoning and reflective judgment research have longitudinal data as well. Gruber and Fischer have challenged researchers within the traditional paradigm to reconsider the assumption of linear development. Fischer provides microsequence data on discontinuities across domains as one view. Gruber presents a challenge to consider multiple lines of development interacting with a variety of environments as another view.

Psychometrically, the young adult cognitive development researchers should re-examine the assumptions about the unit of analysis, methods of representing the data, and the statistical treatment of the data derived from nominal scales. The line of work (Fischer) on optimal versus natural environments, and task familiarity provides a direct method of eliminating error due to the absence of task familiarity or knowledge.

The ecological validity of the models needs to be investigated. Ultimately, the important question that influences all of our lives is how adults think about complex problems such as nuclear war, relationships, careers, and so on. Without ecological validity, we may end up fiddling while Rome burns. Psychology is replete with examples of research exhibiting strong internal validity while studying trivial phenomena. We need to work to insure that this criticism will not be made of the young adult cognitive development research.

The work on the models presented in this book has moved beyond the purely speculative or theoretical phase. In order for the models in this book to be seriously considered in developmental psychology, however, the researchers must attend as much to the empirical validation as they have attended to theory building because the data base on most of the models is limited. The Piagetian tradition provided the foundation for the work presented in this book. The post-Piagetian research is well underway, but with a great deal to be done before we can answer Gruber's question, "Which way is up?" (Gruber, this volume).

Bibliography

Ackerman, S.P. 1978. "Relationship of Dogmatism for Formal Operations." Ph.D. dissertation, University of Georgia, *Dissertation Abstracts International 39*, 3460A.

Adelson, J. 1972. "The Political Imagination of the Adolescent." In *Twelve to Sixteen: Early Adolescence*, edited by J. Kagan and R. Coles. New York: Norton.

Adorno, T.W. and Horkheimer, M. 1979. *Dialectic of Enlightenment*. Translated by John Cumming. London: NLB.

Apostle, L. 1979. "Construction and Validation in Contemporary Epistemology." Paper presented at the Archives de Jean Piaget, Geneva, *6*, #47.

Applebaum, M.I. and McCall, R.B. 1984. "Design and Analysis in Developmental Psychology." In *Handbook of Child Psychology*, edited by P.H. Mussen. New York: Wiley and Sons.

Arlin, P.K. 1974. "Problem Finding: The Relation Between Selected Cognitive Process Variables and Problem Finding Performance." Unpublished Ph.D. dissertation, University of Chicago.

―― 1975. "Cognitive Development in Adulthood: A Fifth Stage?" *Developmental Psychology 11*, pp. 602-6.

―― 1975-76. "A Cognitive Process Model of Problem Finding." *Educational Horizons 54*, pp. 99-106.

―― 1977. "Piagetian Operations in Problem-Finding." *Developmental Psychology 13*, pp. 247-98.

―― 1984a. "Adolescent and Adult Thought: A Structural Interpretation." In *Beyond Formal Operations: Late Adolescent and Adult Cognitive Development*, edited by M.L. Commons, F.A. Richards, and C. Armon, pp. 258-71. New York: Praeger.

―― 1984b. *The Arlin Test of Formal Reasoning*. New York: Slosson Educational Publishers.

Armstrong, M. 1980. *Closely Observed Children*. London: Writers and Readers.

Aronfreed, J. 1968. *Conduct and Conscience*. New York: Academic Press.

Bandura, A. 1977. *Social Learning Theory*. Englewood Cliffs, N.J.: Prentice-Hall.

Barrett, D.E. and Yarrow, M.R. 1977. "Prosocial Behavior, Social Inferential Ability, and Assertiveness in Children." *Child Development 48*, pp. 475-81.

Barron, F. and Harrington, D.M. 1981. "Creativity, Intelligence, and Personality." *Annual Review of Psychology 32*, pp. 439–76.

Bart, W., Frey, S. and Baxter, J. 1979. "Generalizability of the Ordering Among Five Formal Reasoning Tasks by an Ordering-Theoretic Method." *Child Study Journal 9*, pp. 251–59.

Basseches, M. 1979. "Beyond Closed-System Problem Solving: A Study of Metasystematic Aspects of Mature Thought." Ph.D. dissertation, Harvard University. *University Microfilms International*, Ann Arbor, MI.

—— 1980. "Dialectical Schemata: A Framework for the Empirical Study of the Development of Dialectical Thinking." *Human Development 23*, pp. 400–421.

—— 1984. *Dialectical Thinking and Adult Development*, Norwood: Ablex.

Bayley, N. 1970. "Development of Mental Abilities." In *Carmichael's Manual of Child Psychology*, edited by P.H. Mussen. New York: Wiley.

Bebeau, M.J., Rest, J.R. and Yamoor, C.M. 1983. "Profession-Specific Tests of Ethical Sensitivity: An Example in Dentistry." Paper presented at the Annual Convention of the American Educational Research Association, Montreal, Canada.

Biggs, D.A., Schomberg, S.F. and Brown, J. 1977. "Moral Judgment Development of Freshmen and Their Pre-College Experiences." *OSA Research Bulletin 17*, University of Minnesota Press.

Biggs, J. and Collis, K. 1982. *A System for Evaluating Learning Outcomes: The SOLO Taxonomy*. New York: Academic Press.

Blasi, A. 1980. "Bridging Moral Cognition and Moral Action: A Critical Review of the Literature." *Psychological Bulletin 88*, pp. 1–45.

Bohr, N. 1934. *Atomic Theory and the Description of Nature*. New York: Macmillan.

Brabeck, M. 1983. "Critical Thinking Skills and Reflective Judgment Development: Redefining the Aims of Higher Education." *Journal of Applied Developmental Psychology 4*, pp. 23–24.

—— in press. "Longitudinal Studies of Intellectual Development During Adulthood: Theoretical and Research Models." *Journal of Research and Development in Education*.

Brabeck, M. and Wood, P.K. 1983. "A Longitudinal Study of Well and Ill-Structured Problem Solving in College Age Women." Unpublished manuscript.

Braine, D.S. and Rumain, B. 1983. "Logical Reasoning." In *Cognitive Development*, edited by J.H. Flavell and E.M. Markman, vol. 3, 4th ed. pp. 231–62. New York: Wiley.

Brainerd, C.J. 1978. "The Stage Question in Cognitive-Developmental Theory." *Behavioral and Brain Services 2*, pp. 173–213.

Bransford, C. 1973. "Moral Development in College Students." Unpublished manuscript, St. Olaf College.

Broadhurst, B.P. 1980. "Report: Defining Issues Test." Unpublished manuscript, Colorado State University.

Broughton, J.M. 1975. "The Development of Natural Epistemology in Years 10–16." Ph.D. dissertation, Harvard University.

—— 1978. "Development of Concepts of Self, Mind, Reality, and Knowledge." In *Social Cognition*, edited by W. Damon, In *New Directions for Child Development*, No. 1, pp. 75–100, San Francisco: Jossey Bass.

—— 1981. "Piaget's Structural Developmental Psychology: Function and the Problem of Knowledge." *Human Development 24*, pp. 257–85.

—— 1984. "Not Beyond Formal Operations But Beyond Piaget." In *Beyond Formal Operations: Late Adolescent and Adult Cognitive Development*, edited by M.L. Commons, F.A. Richards, and C. Armon, pp. 395–411. New York: Praeger.

Brown, A.L., Bransfors, J.D., Ferrara, R.A. and Campione, J.C. 1983. "Learning, Remembering, and Understanding." In *Handbook of Child Psychology* vol. 3, 4th ed. edited by P.H. Mussen, In *Cognitive Development*, edited by J.H. Flavell and E.M. Markman. New York: Wiley.

Bullinger, A. and Chatillon, J.F. 1983. "Recent Theory and Research of Genevan School." In *Handbook of Child Psychology*, vol. 3, 4th ed. edited by P.H. Mussen, In *Cognitive Development*, pp. 231–62. New York: Wiley.

Carlson, R. 1970. "Where is the Person in Personality Research?" *Psychological Review 67*, pp. 203–19.

Case, R. 1978. "Intellectual Development from Birth to Adulthood: Neo-Piagetian Perspective." In *Children's Thinking: What Develops?* edited by R.S. Siegler. Hillsdale, N.J.: Erlbaum.

—— 1980. "The Underlying Mechanism of Intellectual Development." In *Cognition, Development, and Instruction*, edited by J.R. Kirby and J.B. Gibbs. New York: Academic Press.

Cattell, R.B. 1963. "Theory of Fluid and Crystallized Intelligence: A Critical Experiment." *Journal of Educational Psychology 54*, pp. 1–22.

Chap, J.B. and Sinnott, J.D. 1977–78. "Performance of Institutionalized and Community-Active Old Persons on Concrete and Formal Piagetian Tasks." *International Journal of Aging and Human Development 8*, pp. 269–78.

Chi, M.T.H. 1978. "Knowledge Structures and Memory Development." In *Children's Thinking: What Develops?* edited by R.S. Siegler. Hillsdale, N.J.: Erlbaum.

Churchman, C.W. 1971. *The Design of Inquiring Systems: Basic Concepts of Systems and Organizations*. New York: Basic Books.

Clayton, V. and Overton, W.F. 1976. "Concrete and Formal Operational Thought Processes in Young Adulthood and Old Age." *International Journal of Aging and Human Development 7*, pp. 237–45.

Coder, R. 1975. "Moral Judgment in Adults." Unpublished Ph.D. dissertation, University of Minnesota.

Colby, A., Kohlberg, L., Gibbs, J. and Lieberman, M. 1983. "A Longitudinal Study of Moral Judgment." *Monographs of the Society for Research in Child Development 48*.

Colby, A. and Kohlberg, L. in press. *The Measurement of Moral Judgment: A Manual and Its Results*. New York: Cambridge Press.

Commons, M.L. and Richards, F.A. 1984a. "A General Model of Stage Theory." In *Beyond Formal Operations: Late Adolescent and Adult Cognitive Development*, edited by M. Commons, F.A. Richards and C. Armon, pp. 226–34. New York: Praeger.

—— 1984b. "Systematic, Metasystematic and Cross-Paradigmatic Reasoning: A Case for Stages of Reasoning Beyond Formal Operations." In *Beyond Formal Operations: Late Adolescent and Adult Cognitive Development*, pp. 92–119. New York: Praeger.

Commons, M.L., Richards, F.A. and Armon, C. 1984. *Beyond Formal Operations: Late Adolescent and Adult Cognitive Development*. New York: Praeger.

Commons, M.L., Richards F.A. and Kuhn, D. 1982. "Metasystematic Reasoning: A Case for Levels of Reasoning Beyond Piaget's Stage of Formal Operations." *Child Development 53*, pp. 1058–69.

Crowder, J.W. 1976. "The Defining Issues Test and Correlates of Moral Judgment." Unpublished M.A. Thesis, University of Maryland.

Damon, W. 1977. *The Social World of the Child.* San Francisco: Jossey Bass.

Davison, M.L. 1977. "On a Metric, Unidimensional, Qualitative Unfolding Model for Attitudinal or Developmental Data." *Psychometrika 42*, pp. 523–48.

—— 1979. "Testing a Unidimensional, Qualitative Unfolding Model for Attitudinal or Developmental Data." *Psychometrika 44*, pp. 179–94.

Davison, M.L., King, P.M., Kitchener, K.S. and Parker, C.A. 1980. "The Stage Sequence Concept in Cognitive Social Development." *Developmental Psychology 16*, pp. 121–31.

DeLisi, R. and Staudt, J. 1980. "Individual Differences in College Students' Performance on Formal Operations Task." *Journal of Applied Developmental Psychology 1*, pp. 201–8.

Demetriou, A. and Efklides, A. 1979. "Formal Operational Thinking in Young Adults as a Function of Education and Sex." *International Journal of Psychology 14*, pp. 241–53.

Dewey, J. 1959. *Moral Principle in Education.* New York: Philosophical Library.

Dispoto, R. 1974. "Socio-Moral Reasoning and Environmental Activity Emotionality and Knowledge." Unpublished Ph.D. dissertation, Rutgers University.

Dortzbach, J.R. 1975. "Moral Judgment and Perceived Locus of Control: A Cross-Sectional Developmental Study of Adults, Ages 25–74." Unpublished Ph.D. dissertation, University of Oregon.

Dulit, E. 1972. "Adolescent Thinking à la Piaget: The Formal Stage." *Journal of Youth and Adolescence 1*, pp. 281–301.

Dunker, K. 1945. "On Problem Solving." *Psychological Monograph 58,* Whole No. 270.

Durkheim, E. 1961. *Moral Education.* New York: The Free Press.

Edwards, C.P. 1978. "Social Experiences and Moral Judgment in Kenyan Young Adults." *Journal of Genetic Psychology 133*, pp. 19–30.

El-Gosbi, A.M. 1982. "A Study of the Understanding of Science Processes in Relation to Piaget Cognitive Development at the Formal Level, and other Variables Among Prospective Teachers and College Science Majors." Ph.D. dissertation, Universtiy of North Carolina. *Dissertation Abstracts International 43*, 1914A.

Elkind, D. 1962. "Quantity Conceptions in College Students." *Journal of Social Psychology 57*, pp. 459–65.

Ellis, W.T. 1978. "Piagetian Development Level and Sex-Role Identification as Factors in Problem-Solving Performance and Cognitive Style." Ph.D. dissertation, Southern Illinois University. *Dissertation Abstracts International, 38,* 6008A.

El-Sowygh, H.I.Z. 1982. "Performance of a Piagetian Test by Saudi Arabian Students in Colorado Colleges and Universities in Relation to Selected Sociodemographic and Academic Data." Ph.D. dissertation, University of New Mexico. *Dissertation Abstracts International 42*, 3532A-3533A.

Engels, F. 1940. *Dialectics of Nature.* New York: International Publishers.

Ennis, R.H. 1975. "Children's Ability to Handle Piaget's Propositional Logic: A Conceptual Critique." *Review of Educational Research 45*, pp. 1–41.

—— 1976. "An Alternative to Piaget's Conceptualization of Logical Competence." *Child Development 47*, pp. 903–19.

Ericsson, L.A., Chase, W.G. and Faloon, S. 1980. "Acquisition of a Memory Skill." *Science 208*, pp. 1181–82.

Erikson, E.H. 1958. *Young Man Luther*. New York: Norton.

—— 1969. *Gandhi's Truth*. New York: Norton.

Eysenck, H.J. 1976. "The Biology of Morality." In *Moral Development and Behavior*, edited by T. Lickona. New York: Holt, Reinhart & Winston.

Falmagne, R.J. 1975. "Deductive Processes in Children." In *Reasoning: Representation and Process in Children and Adults*. Hillsdale, N.J.: Erlbaum.

—— 1980. "The Development of Logical Competence: A Psycholinguistic Perspective." In *Developmental Models of Thinking*, edited by R. Kluwe and H. Spada. New York: Academic Press.

Feldman, D.H. 1980. *Beyond Universals in Cognitive Development*. Norwood, N.J.: Ablex.

Feuerstein, R. 1979. *The Dynamic Assessment of Retarded Performers: The Learning Potential Assessment Device, Theory, Instruments, and Techniques*. Baltimore: University Park Press.

Feyerabend, P. 1975. *Against Method: Outline of an Anarchist Theory of Knowledge*. London: NLB.

Fischer, K.W. 1980. "A Theory of Cognitive Development: The Control and Construction of Hierarchies of Skills." *Psychological Review 87*, pp. 477–531.

Fischer, K.W. and Bullock, D. 1981. "Patterns of Data: Sequence, Synchrony, and Constraint in Cognitive Development." In *Cognitive Development*, edited by K.W. Fischer, In *New Directions for Child Development*, No. 12. San Francisco: Jossey Bass.

—— 1984. "Cognitive Development in Middle Childhood: Conclusions and New Directions." In *Development During Middle Childhood: The Years from Six to Twelve*, edited by W.A. Collins, pp. 70–146. Washington, D.C.: National Academy Press.

Fischer, K.W., Hand, H.H. and Russell, S.L. 1984. "The Development of Abstractions in Adolescence and Adulthood." In *Beyond Formal Operations: Late Adolescent and Adult Cognitive Development*, edited by M.L. Commons, F.A. Richards, and C. Armon. New York: Praeger.

Fischer, K.W. and Pipp, S.L. 1984. "Process of Cognitive Development: Optimal Level and Skill Acquisition." In *Mechanisms of Cognitive-Development*, edited by R. Sternberg. San Francisco: W.H. Freeman.

Fischer, K.W., Pipp, S.L. and Bullock, D. 1984. "Detecting Discontinuities in Development: Method and Measurement." In *Continuities and Discontinuities in Development*, edited by R. Harmon and R. Emde. New York: Plenum.

Fischer, K.W. & Silvern, L. in press. "Stages and Individual Differences in Cognitive Development." *Annual Review of Psychology*.

Flavell, J.H. 1963. *The Developmental Psychology of Jean Piaget*. New York: Van Nostrand.

—— 1970. "Cognitive Changes in Adulthood." In *Life-Span Developmental Psychology: Research and Theory*, edited by L.R. Goulet and P.B. Baltes. New York: Academic Press.

—— 1971. "Stage Related Properties of Cognitive Development." *Cognitive Psychology 2*, pp. 421–53.

—— 1977. *Cognitive Development*. Englewood Cliffs, N.J.: Prentice-Hall.

—— 1979. "Metacognition and Cognitive Monitoring." *American Psychologist 34*, pp. 906–11.

—— 1982. "Structures, Stages, and Sequences in Cognitive Development." In *Minnesota*

Symposium on Child Psychology, edited by W.A. Collins. Hillsdale, N.J.: Erlbaum.

Flavell, J.A. and Markman, E.M. 1983. "Preface to Volume 3." In *Cognitive Development*, edited by J.A. Flavell and E.M. Markman. New York: Wiley.

Flavell, J.H. and Wohlwill, J.F. 1969. "Formal and Functional Aspects of Cognitive Development." In *Studies in Cognitive Development: Essays in Honor of J. Piaget*, edited by D. Elkind and J. Flavell. New York: Oxford University Press.

Fowler, J.W. 1981. *Stages of Faith*. New York: Harper-Row.

Gallagher, J.M. and Reid, D.K. 1981. *The Learning Theory of Piaget and Inhelder*. Monterey: Brooks/Cole.

Gallia, T.J. 1976. "Moral Reasoning in College Science and Humanities Students: Summary of a Pilot Study." Unpublished manuscript, Glassboro State College.

Galton, F. 1883. *Inquiries Into Human Faculty*. London: Macmillan.

Gardner, H. 1983. *Frames of Mind, The Theory of Multiple Intelligence*. New York: Basic Books.

Gardner, H. and Lohman, W. 1975. "Children's Sensitivity to Literary Styles." *Merrill-Palmer Quarterly 21*, pp. 113–26.

Getzels, J.W. 1964. "Creative Thinking, Problem Solving and Instruction." In *The Sixty-Third Yearbook of The National Society for the Study of Education: Theories of Learning and Instruction*, edited by E. Hilgard. Chicago: University of Chicago Press.

Getzels, J.W. and Csikszentmihalyi, M. 1965. *Creative Thinking in Art Students: An Exploratory Study*. U.S. Office of Education Cooperative Research Report S-080. Chicago: University of Chicago Press.

—— 1976. *The Creative Vision : A Longitudinal Study of Problem Finding in Art*. New York: Wiley.

Gibbs, J.C. and Widamon, K.F. 1982. *Social Intelligence: Measuring The Development of Sociomoral Reflection*. Englewood Cliffs, N.J.: Prentice-Hall.

Gilligan, C. 1978. "In a Different Voice: Women's Conception of the Self and Morality." *Harvard Educational Review 7*, pp. 481–517.

—— 1982. *In a Different Voice: Psychological Theory and Women's Development*. Cambridge, Mass.: Harvard University Press.

Gilligan, C. and Murphy, M. 1979. "Development From Adolescence to Adulthood: The Philosopher and the Dilemma of the Fact." In *Intellectual Development Beyond Childhood*, edited by D. Kuhn. In *New Directions for Child Development*, No. 5. San Francisco: Jossey Bass.

Glaserfeld, E. von and Kelley, M.F. 1982. "On the Concepts of Period, Phase, Stage and Level." *Human Development 25*, pp. 152–60.

Glatfelter, M. 1982. *Identity Development, Intellectual Development, and Their Relationship in Reentry Women Students*. Ph.D. dissertation, University of Minnesota.

Globerson, T. in press. "When Do Structural Changes Underlie Stage Changes: The Case of Mental-Capacity Growth." In *Stage and Structure in Development*, edited by I. Levin and S. Strauss. Norwood, N.J.: Ablex.

Goldiamond, I. 1968. "Moral Development: A Functional Analysis." *Psychology Today 2*, pp. 31-70.

Goolishian, H.W. 1981. "Identification and Treatment of Piaget's Cognitive Levels in a Community College Population." Ph.D. dissertation, University of Massachusetts. *Dissertation Abstracts International, 42*, l058A.

Gould, C. 1978. *Marx's Social Ontology*. Cambridge, Mass.: MIT Press.

Gruber, H.E. 1973. "Courage and Cognitive Growth in Children and Scientists." In *Piaget in the Classroom,* edited by M. Schwebel and J. Raph. New York: Basic Books.

—— 1978. "Darwin's 'Tree of Nature' and Other Images of Wide Scope." In *On Aesthetics in Science,* edited by J. Wechsler. Cambridge, Mass.: MIT Press.

—— 1981. *Darwin On Man: A Psychological Study of Scientific Creativity.* (2nd ed.) Chicago: University of Chicago Press.

—— 1982. "On the Hypothesized Relation Between Giftedness and Creativity." In *Developmental Approaches to Giftedness and Creativity,* edited by D.H. Feldman. San Francisco: Jossey Bass.

—— 1984. "The Emergence of a Sense of Purpose: A Cognitive Case Study of Young Darwin." In *Beyond Formal Operations: Late Adolescent and Adult Cognitive Development,* edited by M.L. Commons, F.A. Richards, and C. Armon. New York: Praeger.

Gruber, H. & Vonèche, J.J. 1976. "Reflexions sur les opérations formelles de la pensée." *Archives de psychologie 44,* pp. 45–55.

—— 1977. *The Essential Piaget.* New York: Basic Books.

Guilford, J.P. 1959. "Three Faces of Intellect." *American Psychologist,* 14, pp. 469–79.

—— 1967. *The Nature of Human Intelligence.* New York: McGraw-Hill.

Haan, N. 1978. "Two Moralities in Action Contexts: Relationships To Thought, Ego Regulation, and Development." *Journal of Personality and Social Psychology 30,* pp. 286–305.

Hand, H.H. 1981. "The Relation Between Developmental Level and Spontaneous Behavior: The Importance of Sampling Contexts." In *Cognitive Development,* edited by K.W. Fischer. In *New Directions For Child Development,* No 12. San Francisco: Jossey Bass.

Hand, H.H. and Fischer, K.W. 1981. "The Development of Concepts of Intentionality and Responsibility in Adolescence." Paper presented at the Sixth Biennial Meeting of the International Society for the Study of Behavioral Development. Toronto, Canada: August.

Hargrove, R.D. 1977. "A Study of the Relationship Between Piagetian Cognitive Developmental Level and Reading Comprehension in College Science Students." Ph.D. dissertation, Rutgers University. *Dissertation Abstracts International, 37,* 7661A.

Harvey, O.J., Hunt, D.E. and Schroder, H.M. 1961. *Conceptual Systems and Personality Organization.* New York: Wiley.

Hayes, A.B. 1981. "An Investigation of the Effect of Dilemma Content on Level of Reasoning in the Reflective Judgment Interview." Ph.D. dissertation, University of Utah.

Hegel, G.W.F. 1965. *The Philosophy of Right* (translated by T.M. Knox), *The Philosophy of History* (translated by J. Sbree). In *Great Books of the Western World,* Vol. 46. Chicago: Encyclopedia Britannica.

Hiley, D.R. 1979. "Relativism, Dogmatism and Rationality." *International Philosophical Quarterly,* 1984.

Hill, G.L.G. 1981. "Piagetian Cognitive Developmental Level, Receptive Language Processing and Visuospatial Skills Among Learning Disabled and Nonlearning Disabled College Students." Ph.D. dissertation, University of South Carolina.

Dissertation Abstracts International, 41, 3490A.

Hoffman, M.L. 1977. "Empathy, Its Development and Prosocial Implications." In *Nebraska Symposium on Motivation,* Vol 25, edited by C. Keasey. Lincoln: University of Nebraska Press.

Honzik, M.P. and McFarlane, J.W. 1973. "Personality Development and Intellectual Functioning from 21 Months to 40 Years." In *Intellectual Functioning in Adults,* edited by C. Eisdorfer and J.E. Blum. New York: Springer.

Horn, J.L. 1976. "Human Abilities: A Review of Research and Theory in the Early 1970s." *Annual Review of Psychology, 27,* pp. 437–86.

—— 1982. "The Aging of Human Abilities." In *Handbook of Developmental Psychology,* edited by B.B. Wolman. Englewood Cliffs, N.J.: Prentice-Hall.

Horz, H., Poltz, H., Parthey, H., Rosenbert, U. and Wessel, K. 1980. *Philosophical Problems in Physical Science.* Minneapolis: Marxist Educational Press.

Inhelder, B. and Piaget, J. 1958. *The Growth of Logical Thinking From Childhood to Adolescence.* London: Routledge & Kegan Paul.

Jameson, F. 1971. *Marxism and Form: 20th Century Dialectical Theories of Literature.* Princeton: Princeton University Press.

Jaques, E., Gibson, R.O. and Isaac, D.J. 1978. *Levels of Abstraction in Logic and Human Action.* London: Heinemann.

Jay, M. 1973. *The Dialectical Imagination.* Boston: Little, Brown & Co.

Jones, E. 1957. *The Life and Work of Sigmund Freud,* Vol. 3. New York: Basic Books.

Kahn, M.K. 1979. *Creation of Computer Animation from Story Descriptions.* Unpublished Ph.D. dissertation, MIT.

Karmiloff-Smith, A. and Inhelder, V. 1974. "If You Want to Get Ahead, Get a Theory." *Cognition 3,* pp. 195–212.

Kaseman, T.C. 1980. *A Longitudinal Study of Moral Development of The West Point Class of 1981.* West Point, NY: Department of Behavioral Sciences and Leadership, U.S. Military Academy.

Keating, D.P. 1980. "Thinking Processes in Adolescence." In *Handbook of Adolescent Development,* edited by J. Adelson, pp. 211–46. New York: Wiley.

Kegan, R.G. 1982. *The Evolving Self.* Cambridge, Mass.: Harvard University Press.

Keller, E.F. 1983. *A Feeling for the Organism: The Life Work of Barbara McClintock.* San Francisco: Freeman.

Kenny, S.L. 1983. "Developmental Discontinuities in Childhood and Adolescence." In *Levels and Transitions in Children's Development,* edited by K.W. Fischer. *New Directions for Child Development,* No. 21. San Francisco: Jossey Bass.

Kilminster, R. 1979. *Praxis and Method: A Sociological Dialogue with Lukacs, Gramsci, and the Early Frankfurt School.* London: Routledge & Kegan Paul.

King, P.M. 1978. "The Development of Reflective Judgment and Formal Operational Thinking in Adolescents and Young Adults." Ph.D. dissertation, University of Minnesota. *Dissertation Abstracts International 38,* 7233A.

—— 1983. *Reflective Judgment Questionnaire.* Technical Report #1. Bowling Green State University.

King, P.M. and Kitchener, K.S. 1984. "Reflective Judgment Theory and Research: Insights into the Process of Knowing in the College Years." Unpublished manuscript.

King, P.M., Kitchener, K.S., Davison, M.L., Parker, C.A. and Wood, P.K. 1983. "The Justification of Beliefs in Young Adults: A Longitudinal Study." *Human Development 26,* pp. 106–16.

King, P.M. and Parker, C.A. 1978. "Assessing Intellectual Development in the College Years." A report of the Instructional Improvement Project, 1976–1977. Unpublished manuscript, University of Minnesota.

Kitchener, K.S. 1978. "Intellectual Development in Late Adolescents and Young Adults: Reflective Judgment and Verbal Reasoning." Ph.D. dissertation, University of Minnesota.

—— 1983a. "Cognition, Metacognition and Epistemic Cognition: A Three-Level Model of Cognitive Processing." *Human Development 4*, pp. 222–32.

—— 1983b. "Educational Goals and Contemporary Models of Reflective Thinking." *Educational Forum 48*, pp. 75–95.

—— 1983c. "Human Development and the College Campus: Sequences and Tasks." In *Measuring Student Development*, edited by G.R. Hanson. *New Directions for Student Services*. San Francisco: Jossey Bass.

Kitchener, K.S. and King, P.M. 1981. "Reflective Judgment: Concepts of Justification and Their Relationship to Age and Education." *Journal of Applied Developmental Psychology 2*, pp. 89–116.

Kitchener, K.S., King, P.M., Davison, M., Parker, C. and Wood, P. in press. "A Longitudinal Study of Moral and Ego Development in Young Adults." *Journal of Youth and Adolescence.*

Kitchener, K.S., King, P.M. and Wood, P.K. 1984. "A Longitudinal Study of Epistemic Cognition in Young Adults." A paper presented at the American Psychological Association meeting, Toronto, Canada.

Kitchener, K.S. and Kitchener, R.F. 1981. "The Development of Natural Rationality: Can Formal Operations Account For It?" In *Social Development in Youth: Structure and Content*, edited by J.A. Meecham and N.R. Santelli. Basel: Karger.

Kitchener, K.S. and Wood, P.K. 1984. "Development of Concept of Justification in German University Students." Unpublished manuscript.

Kohlberg, L. 1969. "Stage and Sequence: The Cognitive-Developmental Approach to Socialization." In *Handbook of Socialization Theory and Research*, edited by D. Goslin. Chicago: Rand McNally.

—— 1973. "Collected Papers on Moral Development and Moral Education." Cambridge, Mass.: Moral Education & Research Foundation.

—— 1971. "Continuities in Childhood and Adult Moral Development Revisited." In *Life-Span Development Psychology: Personality and Socialization*, edited by P.B. Baltes and K.W. Schaie. New York: Academic Press.

—— 1980. "High School Democracy and Educating for A Just Society." In *Moral Education: A First Generation of Research and Development*, edited by R.L. Mosher. New York: Praeger.

Kohlberg, L. and Armon, C. 1984. "Three Types of Stage Models Used in the Study of Adult Development." In *Beyond Formal Operations: Late Adolescent and Adult Cognitive Development*, edited by M. Commons, F. Richards and C. Armon. New York: Praeger.

Kosok, M. 1972. "The Formalization of Hegel's Dialectical Logic." In *Hegel: A Collection of Critical Essays*, edited by A. MacIntyre. Garden City, N.Y.: Anchor.

Kramer, D.A. 1983. "A Post-Formal Operations? A Need For Further Conceptualization." *Human Development 44*, pp. 45–55.

Krebs, R.L. 1967. "Some Relations Between Moral Judgment, Attention, and Resistance to Temptation." Unpublished Ph.D. dissertation, University of Chicago.

Kuhn, D. and Brannock, J. 1977. "Development of the Isolation of Variables Scheme in Experimental and 'Natural Experiment' Contexts." *Developmental Psychology 13,* pp. 9–14.

Kuhn, D. and Ho, V. 1980. "Self-Directed Activity and Cognitive Development." *Journal of Applied Developmental Psychology 1,* pp. 119–33.

Kuhn, D., Langer, J., Kohlberg, L. and Haan, N.S. 1977. "The Development of Formal Operations in Logical and Moral Judgment." *Genetic Psychology Monographs 95,* pp. 97–188.

Kuhn, T.S. 1962. "The Structure of Scientific Revolutions." In *International Encyclopedia of Unified Science,* vol. 2 no.2. Chicago: University of Chicago Press.

—— 1970. *The Structure of Scientific Revolutions,* 2nd ed. Chicago: University of Chicago Press.

Labouvie-Vief, G. 1982. "Dynamic Development and Mature Autonomy: A Theoretical Prologue." *Human Development 25,* pp. 91–105.

Lakatos, I. 1978. *The Methodology of Scientific Research Programs.* Cambridge: Cambridge University Press.

Lawrence, J.A. 1977. "Review and Rationale for Moral Judgment Process Research Using the Defining Issues Test and the Stimulated Recall Techniques." Unpublished manuscript, University of Minnesota.

Lawson, J.M. 1980. "The Relationship Between Graduate Education and the Development of Reflective Judgment: A Function of Age or Educational Experience." Ph.D. dissertation, University of Minnesota.

Leiser, D. 1982. "Piaget's Logical Formalism for Formal Operations: An Interpretation in Context." *Developmental Review 2,* pp. 87–99.

Loevinger, J. 1976. *Ego Development: Conceptions and Theories.* San Francisco: Jossey Bass.

London, P. 1970. "The Rescuers: Motivational Hypotheses About Christians Who Saved Jews From the Nazis." In *Altruism and Helping Behavior,* edited by J. Macaulay and E.L. Berkowitz. New York: Academic Press.

Lovell, K. 1961. "A Follow-up Study of Inhelder and Piaget's 'The Growth of Logical Thinking.' " *British Journal of Psychology 52,* pp. 143–53.

Mackworth, N.H. 1965. "Orginality." *American Psychologist 20,* pp. 51–56.

Magaña, H.A. 1982. "An Evaluation of the Differential Impact of a Developmental Curriculum on Students with Varying Personality Profiles." In *Character Development in College Students,* edited by J.M. Whiteley, Schenectady, N.Y.: Character Research Press.

Mandel, E. 1973. *An Introduction to Marxist Economic Theory.* New York: Pathfinder Press.

Maqsud, M. 1977. "The Influence of Social Heterogeneity and Sentimental Credibility on Moral Judgments of Nigerian Muslim Adolescents." *Journal of Cross-Cultural Psychology 8,* pp. 113–22.

Martarano, S.C. 1977. "A Developmental Analysis of Performance on Piaget's Formal Operations Tasks." *Developmental Psychology 13,* pp. 666–72.

Maruyama, M. 1963. "The Second Cybernetics: Deviation-Amplifying Mutual Causal Processes." *American Scientist 51,* pp. 164–79 and 250–56.

Marx, K. 1967. "Writings of the Young Marx on Philosophy and Society." edited by L.D. Easton and K.H. Guddat. Garden City: Anchor.

Marx, K. and Engels, F. 1955. *The Communist Manifesto.* New York: Appleton-Century Crofts.

McCall, R.D., Eichorn, D.H. and Hogarty, P.S. 1977. "Transitions in Early Mental Development." *Monographs of the Society for Research in Child Development 42.*

McCall, R.B., Meyers, E.D. Jr., Hartman, J. and Roche, A.F. 1983. "Developmental Changes in Head Circumferences and Mental Performance Growth Rates: A Test of Epstein's Phrenoblysis Hypothesis." *Developmental Psychobiology 16,* pp. 457–68.

McGeorge, C. 1977. "Some Correlates of Principled Moral Thinking in Young Adults." *Journal of Moral Education.*

Meecham, J. 1983. "Wisdom and the Contest of Knowledge: Knowing That One Doesn't Know." In *On The Development of Developmental Psychology,* edited by K. Kuhn and J.A. Meecham. Basel: Karger.

Mentkowski, M. and Strait, M.J. 1983. "A Longitudinal Study of Student Change in Cognitive Development and Generic Abilities in an Outcome-Centered Liberal Arts Curriculum." Final report to the National Institute of Education.

Merton, R.S. 1945. "Sociology of Knowledge." In *Twentieth Century Sociology,* edited by G. Gurvitch and W.E. Moore. New York: Philosophical Library.

Miller, G.A., Galanter, E. and Pribam, K.H. 1960. *Plans and the Structure of Behavior.* New York: Holt, Rinehart & Winston.

Mines, R.A. 1980. "Levels of Intellectual Development and Associated Critical Thinking Skills in Young Adults." Ph.D. dissertation, University of Iowa.

—— 1982. "Student Development Assessment Techniques." In *Measuring Student Development,* edited by G.R. Hanson. San Francisco: Jossey Bass.

Minsky, M. 1977. "Game-System Theory." In *Thinking: Readings in Cognitive Science,* edited by P.W. Johnson-Laird and P.C. Wason. Cambridge: Cambridge University Press.

Mischel, W. and Mischel, H. 1976. "A Cognitive Social-Learning Approach to Morality and Self-Regulation." In *Moral Development and Behavior,* edited by T. Lickona. New York: Holt, Rinehart & Winston.

Mortorano, S. 1975. "Formal Operations Thinkings: Now You See It, Now You Don't." Paper presented at the Society for Research in Child Development Convention, Denver, Colorado.

Moshman, O. 1979. "Development of Formal Hypothesis-Testing Ability." *Developmental Psychology 15,* pp. 104–12.

Muhs, P.J., Hooper, F.H. and Papalia-Finlay, D. 1980. "Cross-Sectional Analysis of Cognitive Functioning Across the Life-Span." *International Journal of Aging and Human Development 10,* pp. 311–33.

Murphy, J.M. and Gilligan, C. 1980. "Moral Development in Late Adolescence and Adulthood: A Critique and Reconstruction of Kohlberg's Theory." *Human Development 23,* pp. 77–104.

Neimark, E.D. 1975a. "Intellectual Development During Adolescence." In *Review of Child Development Research,* edited by F.D. Horowitz. Chicago: University of Chicago Press.

—— 1975b. "Longitudinal Development of Formal Operations Thought." *Genetic Psychology Monographs 91,* pp. 171–225.

—— 1979. "Current Status of Formal Operations Research." *Human Development 22,* pp. 60–67.

Neisser, U. 1976. "General, Academic and Artificial Intelligence." In *The Nature of Intelligence*, edited by L.B. Resnick. Hillsdale, N.J.: Erlbaum.

Nessleroade, J.R. and Baltes, P.B. 1974. "Adolescent Personality Development and Historical Change—1970–1972." *Monographs of the Society for Research in Child Development 39*.

Newell, A., Shaw, J.C. and Simon, H.A. 1962. "The Processes of Creative Thinking." In *Contemporary Approaches to Creative Thinking*, edited by H.E. Gruber, G. Terrell and M. Wertheimer. New York: Atherton.

Nisbett, R.E. and Wilson T.D. 1977. "Telling More Than We Can Know: Verbal Reports on Mental Processes." *Psychological Review 84*, pp. 231–59.

O'Brien, D. and Overton, W.F. 1982. "Conditional Reasoning and the Competence-Performance Issue: A Developmental Analysis of a Training Task." *Journal of Experimental Child Psychology 34*, pp. 274–90.

Ollman, B. 1971. *Alienation*. Cambridge: Cambridge University Press.

Olson, D., Basseches, M. and Richards, F.A. 1981. "Dialectical Thinking as a Post-Formal Operational Level of Cognitive Organization: The Development of a Comprehensive and Preference Instrument." Unpublished research report, Cornell University.

Overton, W.F. 1984. "World Views and Their Influence on Psychological Theory and Research: Kuhn-Lakatos-Lauden." In *Advances in Child Development and Behavior*, edited by H.W. Reese. New York: Academic Press.

Parete, J.D. 1979. "Formal Reasoning Abilities of College Age Students: An Investigation of the Concrete and Formal Reasoning Stages Formulated by Jean Piaget." Ph.D. dissertation, Ohio State University. *Dissertation Abstracts International 39*, 6006A.

Perkins, D.N. 1981. *The Mind's Best Work*. Cambridge, Mass.: Harvard University Press.

Perry, W.G. 1970. *Forms of Intellectual and Ethical Development in the College Years*. New York: Holt, Rinehart & Winston.

Piaget, J. 1941. "Le Mécanisme du Développement Mental et les Lois du Groupement des Opérations." *Archives de Psychologie, Geneve 28*, pp. 215–85.

—— 1952. *The Origins of Intelligence in Children*. New York: Norton.

—— 1953. *Logic and Psychology*. Manchester, U.K.: Manchester University Press.

—— 1957. "Logique et Equilibre Dans les Comportements de Sujet." *Etudes d'Epistemologie Genetique 2*, pp. 27–118.

—— 1955. *The Moral Judgment of the Child*. Translated by M. Gabain. New York: The Free Press. Originally published, 1932.

—— 1970. *Piaget's Theory*. In *Carmichael's Manual of Child Development, Vol. 1*, edited by R.H. Mussen. New York: Wiley.

—— 1971. *Biology and Knowledge*. Chicago: University of Chicago Press. Originally published, 1967.

—— 1972. "Intellectual Evolution From Adolescence to Adulthood." *Human Development 15*, pp. 1–12.

—— 1978. *The Development of Thought*. Oxford: Blackwell.

Piaget, J. and Inhelder, B. 1969. *The Psychology of the Child*. New York: Basic Books.

Podgoretskaya, N.A. 1979. "A Study of Spontaneous Logical Thinking in Adults." *Soviet Psychology 17*, pp. 70–84.

Polkinghorne, D.E. 1983. *Methodology for The Human Sciences: Systems of Inquiry*. Albany, N.Y.: State University of New York Press.

Popper, K. 1959. *The Logic of Scientific Discovery.* New York: Basic Books.

—— 1963. *Conjectures and Refutations: The Growth of Scientific Knowledge.* New York: Harper & Row.

Provine, W. 1971. *The Origins of Theoretical Population Genetics.* Chicago: University of Chicago Press.

Rawls, J. 1971. *A Theory of Justice.* Cambridge, Mass.: Harvard University Press.

Rest, J. 1973. "Patterns and Preferences in Moral Judgment." *Journal of Personality 41,* pp. 86–109.

—— 1975. "Longitudinal Study of the Defining Issues Test: A Strategy for Analyzing Developmental Change." *Developmental Psychology 11,* pp. 738–48.

—— 1977. "Development in Moral Reasoning, Liberal-Conservative Ideology, and Conceptualizing Politics." Unpublished manuscript, Stanford University.

—— 1979a. *Development in Judging Moral Issues.* Minneapolis: University of Minneapolis.

—— 1979b. "The Impact of Higher Education on Moral Judgement Development." Minnesota Moral Research Project (330 Burton Hall, University of Minnesota, Minneapolis, MN 55455).

—— 1979c. "Revised Manual for the Defining Issues Test." Minnesota Moral Research Project.

—— 1981. "The Impact of Higher Education on Moral Judgment Education." Paper presented at the convention of the American Educational Research Association, Los Angeles, April.

—— 1983. "Morality." In *Cognitive Development,* edited by J.H. Flavell. In *Handbook of Child Psychology,* edited by P.H. Mussen, New York: Wiley.

Rest, J.R., Cooper, D., Coder, R., Masanz, J. and Anderson, D. 1974. "Judging the Important Issues in Moral Dilemmas—An Objective Test of Development." *Developmental Psychology 10,* pp. 491–501.

Richards, F.A. and Commons, M.L. 1984. "Systematic, Metasystematic, and Cross-Paradigmatic Reasoning: A Case for Stages of Reasoning Beyond Formal Operations." In *Beyond Formal Operations: Late Adolescent and Adult Cognitive Development.* New York: Praeger.

Riegel, K.F. 1973. "Dialectic Operations: The Final Period of Cognitive Development." *Human Development 16,* pp. 346–70..

Roberge, J.J. and Flexer, B.K. 1979. "Further Examination of Formal Operational Reasoning Abilities." *Child Development 50,* pp. 478–84.

Ross, R.J. 1973. "Some Empirical Parameters of Formal Thinking." *Journal of Youth and Adolescence 2,* pp. 167–77.

Sakalys, J.A. 1982. "Effects of a Research Methods Course on Nursing Students' Research Attitudes and Cognitive Development." Ph.D. dissertation, University of Denver.

Schmidt, J.A. 1983. "The Intellectual Development of Traditionally and Nontraditionally Aged College Students: A Cross-Sectional Study with Longitudinal Follow-up." Ph.D. dissertation, University of Minnesota.

Schomberg, S.F. 1975. "Some Personality Correlates of Moral Maturity Among Community College Students." Unpublished manuscript, University of Minnesota.

Schon, D. 1963. *The Displacement of Concepts.* Cambridge: Tavistock Press.

Schroeder, H., Driver, J. and Steufert, S. 1967. *Human Information Processing.* New

York: Holt, Rinehart & Winston.

Schwartz, S.H. 1977. "Normative Influences on Altruism." In *Advances in Experimental Social Psychology, Vol.10,* edited by L. Berkowitz. New York: Academic Press.

Schwebel, M. 1972. *Logical Thinking in College Freshmen.* Final Report, Project No O-B-105 (Grant No OEG-2-7-0039, 509).

—— 1975. "Formal Operations in First-Year College Students." *The Journal of Psychology 91,* pp. 133–41.

Selman, R.L. 1980. *The Growth of Interpersonal Understanding.* New York: Academic Press.

Shaklee, H. 1979. "Bounded Rationality and Cognitive Development: Upper Limits on Growth?" *Cognitive Psychology 11,* pp. 327–45.

Shantz, C.U. 1983. "Social Cognition." In *Cognitive Development,* edited by J.H. Flavell and E.M. Markman, in *Handbook of Child Psychology, 4th ed.,* edited by P.H. Mussen. New York: Wiley.

Sheehan, N.W. 1977. "An Examination of Selected Performance Factors and Correlates of Piagetian Logical Functioning in Elderly Women." Ph.D. dissertation, University of Wisconsin-Madison. *Dissertation Abstracts International 37,* 4656B-4657B.

Shoff, S.P. 1979. "The Significance of Age, Sex, and Type of Education on the Development of Reasoning in Adults." Ph.D. dissertation, University of Utah.

Siegler, R.S. 1976. "Three Aspects of Cognitive Development." *Cognitive Psychology 8,* pp. 481–520.

Simon, H.A. 1957. *Models of Man.* New York: Wiley.

—— 1978. "Information-Processing Theory of Human Problem Solving." In *Handbook of Learning and Cognitive Processes, Vol. 5: Human Information Processing,* edited by W.K. Estes. Hillsdale, N.Y.: Erlbaum.

—— 1979. "Information Processing Models of Cognition." *Annual Review of Psychology 30,* pp. 363–96.

Sinclair, H. 1977. "Recent Developments in Genetic Epistemology." *The Genetic Epistemologist: Quarterly Newsletter of the Jean Piaget Society 6,* pp. 1–3.

Sinnott, J.D. 1975. "Everyday Thinking and Piagetian Operativity in Adults." *Human Development 18,* pp. 430–43.

—— 1981. "The Theory of Relativity: A Metatheory for Development?" *Human Development 24,* pp. 293–311.

—— 1984. "Post-Formal Reasoning: The Relativistic Stage." In *Beyond Formal Operations: Late Adolescent and Adult Cognitive Development,* edited by M.L. Commons, F.A. Richards and C. Armon. New York: Praeger.

Sinnott, J.D. and Guttmann, D. 1978. "Piagetian Logical Abilities and Older Adults' Abilities to Solve Everyday Problems." *Human Development 21,* pp. 327–33.

Slovic, P., Fischoff, M. and Lichtenstein, S. 1977. "Behavioral Decision Theory." *Annual Review of Psychology 28,* pp. 1–39.

Smith, A. 1937. *An Inquiry into the Nature and Causes of the Wealth of Nations.* New York: Modern Library.

Spearman, C.E. 1927. *The Nature of Intelligence and the Principles of Cognition.* London: Macmillan.

Spelke, E., Hirst, W. and Neisser, U. 1976. "Skills of Divided Attention." *Cognition 4,* pp. 215–30.

Staub, E. 1978, 1979. *Positive Social Behavior and Morality, Vol. I and II*. New York: Academic Press.

Sternberg, R.J. and Davidson, J.E. 1983. "Insight in the Gifted." *Educational Psychology 18*, pp. 51-57.

Stone, C.A. and Day, M.C. 1978. "Levels of Availability of a Formal Operational Strategy." *Child Development 49*, pp. 1054-65.

Strange, C.C. 1978. "Intellectual Development, Motive for Education, and Learning Styles During the College Years: A Comparison of Adult and Traditionally Age College Students." Ph.D. dissertation, University of Iowa.

Strange, C.C. and King, P.M. 1981. "Intellectual Development and Its Relationship to Maturation During the College Years." *Journal of Applied Developmental Psychology 2*, pp. 281-95.

Suppe, F. 1977. "The Search for Philosophical Understanding of Scientific Theories." In *Structure of Scientific Theories*, edited by F. Suppe. Chicago: University of Illinois.

Terman, L.M. 1973. *Concept Mastery Test Manual*. New York: Psychological Corporation.

Thoma, S.J. and Davison, M.L. 1983. "Moral Reasoning Development in Graduate Eduation." *Journal of Applied Developmental Psychology 4*, pp. 227-38.

Thurston, L.L. 1936. *Primary Mental Abilities*. Chicago: University of Chicago Press.

Tomlinson-Keasey, C. 1972. "Formal Operations in Females From Eleven to Fifty-Four Years of Age." *Developmental Psychology 6*, p. 364.

Tomlinson-Keasey, C. and Keasey, G.B. 1974. "The Mediating Role of Cognitive Development in Moral Judgment." *Child Development 45*, pp. 291-99.

Turiel, E. 1969. "Developmental Processes in the Child's Moral Thinking." In *Trends and Issues in Developmental Psychology*, edited by P. Mussen, J. Langer and E. Covington. New York: Holt, Rinehart & Winston.

Volker, J. 1980. *Moral Reasoning and College Experience*. Unpublished M.A. thesis, University of Minnesota.

—— 1984. *Moral Sensitivity in Counseling-Psychology Students*. Ph.D. dissertation, University of Minnesota.

Vu, N.V. 1978. "Piaget's Formal Operations and the Acquisition of the Probability and Correlation Concepts of Graduate Students." Ph.D. dissertation, Southern Illinois University. *Dissertation Abstracts International 38*, 6030A-6031A.

Waddington, C.H. 1957. *The Strategy of the Genes*. London: Allen & Unwin.

Wechsler, D. 1958. *The Measurement and Appraisal of Adult Intelligence*. Baltimore: Williams & Wilkins.

Welfel, E.R. 1982. "How Students Make Judgments: Do Educational Level and Academic Major Make a Difference?" *Journal of College Student Personnel 23*, pp. 430-97.

Welfel, E.R. and Davison, M.L. 1983. "Four Years Later: A Longitudinal Study of the Development of Reflective Judgment During The College Years." Unpublished manuscript.

Werner, H. 1957. "The Concept of Development From a Comparative and Organismic Point of View." In *The Concept of Development*, edited by D.B. Harris. Minneapolis: University of Minnesota.

Wertheimer, M. 1945. *Productive Thinking*. New York: Harper & Row.

Westfall, R.S. 1980a. *Never At Rest: A Biography of Isaac Newton*. Cambridge:

Cambridge University Press.

—— 1980b. "Newton's Marvelous Years of Discovery and Their Aftermath: Myth versus Manuscript." *Isis 71,* pp. 109–21.

White, K.M. and Ferstenberg, A. 1978. "Professional Specialization and Formal Operations: The Balance Task." *The Journal of Genetic Psychology 133,* pp. 97–104.

Whitehead, A.N. and Russell, B. 1925–1927. *Principia Mathematica.* Cambridge: Cambridge University Press.

Whiteley, J. 1982. *Character Development in College Students.* Schenectady, N.Y.: Character Education Press.

Wilson, E.O. 1975. *Sociobiology: The New Synthesis.* Cambridge, Mass.: Harvard University Press, Belknap Press.

Wittkower, R. and Wittkower, M. 1963. *Born Under Saturn: The Character and Conduct of Artists, A Documented History from Antiquity to the French Revolution.* New York: Norton.

Wohlwill, J. 1973. *The Study of Behavioral Development.* New York: Academic Press.

Wood, P.K. 1983. "Inquiring Systems and Problem Structure: Implications for Cognitive Development." *Human Development 26,* pp. 249–65.

Woodward, C. in preparation. "The Aesthetic of Science: Robert B. Woodward, Organic Chemist." In *Creative People at Work: 12 Cognitive Case Studies,* edited by D.B. Wallace and H.E. Gruber.

Yamoor, C.M., Bebeau, M.J. and Rest, J.R. 1983. "Preliminary Estimates of the Reliability and Validity of a Dental Ethical Sensitivity Test." Paper presented at the Annual Convention of the American Educational Research Association, Montreal, Canada.

Zajonc, R.B. 1980. "Feeling and Thinking: Preferences Need No Inferences." *American Psychologist 35,* pp. 151–75.

Author Index

Subject Index

abstract: categories, 139; mapping, 67, 75; system, 67, 75; thinking, 75; tier, 74

abstraction, 58, 64–69, 73–75, 127

accomodation, 49

adolescence, 5, 6, 16, 20, 32, 57, 58, 62, 64, 74, 97, 99

adolescent, 24, 58, 59, 67, 73, 74, 88, 113, 116, 132; cognition, 23, 27; reasoning, 5–6, 20; thinking, 17; thought 5, 25

adult: cognition, 26–28, 32; decision making, 28; reasoning, 5–6, 20, 21, 33; thinking, 5, 19, 55; thought, 5, 20, 21, 27, 29

affect, 124

age/education confounding, 137, 140

analysis: combinatorial, 3; dialectical, 37–41, 45–46, 49; formal, 38–41; formalistic, 41; metacognitive, 19–20; multiple regression, 101–2; of results, 117; skill-theory, 62, 69; statistical, 109; unit of 90, 141, 142, 145, 146

aptitudes: differentiation of, 15

aroused affects, 93

assessments: conditions, 141; creative, 17; developmental, 16,17; difficulties, 17; methodologies, 17, 21, 136; procedures, 17, 20, 21; techniques, 136; timing, 136; tools, 21

assimilation, 19, 49, 77, 80

assumption, 77, 80; cognitive, 86; epistemological, 45, 80; simple versus complex stage, 143; stage, 134; theoretical, 139, 145

awareness of consequences, 93

"bounded rationality," 28

case study, 112

ceiling effects, 140

change: continuous, 61–62, 71, 72; developmental, 58, 69, 72; direction, 134–35; discontinuous, 62; historical, 132; level, 134; longitudinal, 81; quantitative versus qualitative, 137–38; rate of, 135, 140

closed system, 47–48, 50

cluster: hypothesis, 72; scorees, 139; of spurts, 71–72

cognition, 19, 27, 49, 114; adolescent, 27; adult, 26–28, 32; epistemic, 76; social, 93; young adult, 22, 23, 28, 29, 32

cognitive: activity, 46; development, 18, 20, 23, 28, 40, 46, 54, 55, 57, 60, 64, 74, 92, 114, 116, 118, 134, 140, 141, 143, 146,; adult, 1, 2; developmental definition, 24–25; developmental level, 58; developmental model, 25; developmental research, 57; disequilibrium, 52; equilibrium, 53; functioning, 75; growth, 25, 114; inquiry, 46; level, 58–59, 72–73; operations, 24, 93; organizations, 33, 46, 50; processes, 32, 46, 116,146; processing, 18, 21; process model, 22–24; process variables, 22, 24; research, 70; schemata, 49; science, 25, 26, 128–29; strategies, 20, 76; structures, 46; transformation, 96

combinatorial analysis, 3; system, 3, 5

competence-performance distinction, 16

complex: developmental, 16; problems, 146; processes, 144, 145; stage model, 21, 142

components: moral, 93–96

composite scores, 14
concept, 35; displacement of, 26, 28–31;
  of frames, 26; moral, 64; stage, 90
Concept Mastery Test, 87, 88
concrete operational, 2
concrete operations, 4, 47, 58
conditions: natural versus optimal,
  144–45
conservation, 49
consistency: theoretical and logical, 138
consolidation, 72
constitutive: relationship, 36, 37, 41, 43,
  45, 46, 48
content: area, 16, 21, 136, 140;
  familiarity, 136
contextual relativism, 45
continuity, 135–36, 139–42
continuous, 59–63, 69, 70, 72;
  developmental dimension, 135
contraction, 27–30, 32; correlative, 4
creode, 117–118
creative: effort, 129; individual, 118;
  lives, 126, 128; people, 125–27;
  person, 124–25, 127–28, 131; work,
  122–26, 128–31

data: multifaceted, 142; reduction, 136,
  143; representation, 146
decalage, 142
decision making, 28
Defining Issues Test, 97, 143
definition of specific operators, 26
design issues, 134
"determination from above," 125
development, 83; cognitive, 18, 20, 23,
  28, 40, 46, 55, 57, 61, 64, 74, 92,
  114, 137–38, 140, 146; divergent,
  118; ego, 33, 55; ethical, 51; faith,
  55; human, 131; intellectual, 51, 88,
  114, 134; linear, 146; moral, 55, 91,
  92, 97, 99, 105–6, 114; multi-
  directional, 117; sequentiality 85;

social-personality, 95; socio-cognitive,
  54
developmental: assessment, 16; change,
  58, 69, 72, 135; characteristics, 53;
  differences, 136; direction, 45; issues,
  113; level, 57, 62–64, 75, 135;
  prerequisites, 24; processsess, 23; progress, 112, 117; question, 26;
  sequence, 60–61, 73, 91, 121; spurts,
  62; tasks, 114; transformation, 35–36,
  39, 41, 45–48; variables, 24
deviation amplifying system, 125
dialectic, 35–56; operations,
  25,28,116–17
dialectical: analysis, 37–41, 45, 46, 49;
  approach, 38, 40, 41; concepts, 139;
  epistemologies, 35, 37; model, 48, 50;
  movement, 46; ontologies, 35, 37;
  perspective, 31, 39, 46; philosophical
  perspective, 34–35; process, 41, 46,
  49, 53; reasoning, 141, 143, 145;
  schemata (DS) , 30, 42–48, 51, 52,
  55; thinking, 33, 34, 37, 40–56
differences, 84–85; individual, 91, 93;
  qualitative, 84; quantitative, 84;
  scoring, 139
differentiation, 36, 43, 46, 72, 81; of
  aptitudes, 15
dilemma, 60, 80–83, 90–91, 98, 111,
  114, 131; moral, 61, 97
discontinuity, 57–59, 63, 69–74, 135–
  36,139–41, 146
discontinuous, 62
discovered problems, 22, 23, 25, 26, 32
discovery-oriented, 28
disequilibrium, 45
displacement of concept, 26, 28–31
distance: issue, 136; theoretical, 137
distribution: bimodal, 70
DIT, 97–99, 102-3, 105, 109-11
divergent thinking, 24
DS framework, 45–46

unified model, 26, 28
unique phenomena, 125
unit of analysis, 90

validity, 91, 140; data, 140; ecological, 146; internal, 146; studies, 126
value-relativist, 52
variability, 83; individual, 83; intersubject, 83; intrasubject, 16; performance, 16; subject, 17; of tasks, 21
variables: classical cognitive, 23; cognitive process, 22, 24; content domains, 16; demographic, 99; developmental, 24; environmental, 90; explanatory, 16; moral judgment, 110; performance, 16; recognition versus production, 144; task, 16
variance, 143; stage, 142
variation, 71

young adult: cognition, 22, 23, 28, 29, 32; reasoning, 33; thought, 25, 27

About the Authors

Dr. Patricia K. Arlin is on the Faculty of Education at the University of British Columbia. Her current work is in the area of problem finding in adolescents.

Dr. Michael Basseches is a Post-Doctoral Fellow in the psychology department at Clark University and a Fellow of the Clinical Developmental Institute in Belmont, MA.

Dr. Kurt W. Fischer is on the psychology faculty at the University of Denver. One of his recent works is with A. Lazeron, titled *Human Development from Conception to Adolescence*, 1984.

Dr. Howard E. Gruber currently holds the Chair of Genetic Epistemology at the University of Geneva, Switzerland. He is the author of *Darwin on Man: A Scientific Study of Scientific Creativity*, 1981.

Ms. Sheryl L. Kenny is a doctoral student at Cornell University. Her recent publications include, "Developmental Discontinuities in Childhood and Adolescence," in K.W. Fischer (ed.), *Levels and Transitions in Children's Development*, 1983.

Dr. Patricia M. King is on the faculty of the College Student Personnel Department at Bowling Green State University. Her recent work includes "The Justification of Beliefs in Young Adults," *Human Development 26*, 1983, 106–16.

Dr. Karen S. Kitchener is on the Counseling Psychology faculty at the University of Denver. Her most recent work includes "A Longitudinal Study of Moral and Ego Development in Young Adults." *Journal of Youth and Adolescence*, in press.

Dr. Robert A. Mines is on the Counseling Psychology faculty at the University of Denver. His recent work includes an article entitled "Psychometric Considerations in the Assessment of Student Development." *Journal of College Student Personnel*, 1985.

Dr. James R. Rest is on the faculty at the University of Minnesota. His most recent work includes the chapter on Morality in P.H. Mussen (ed.), *Handbook of Child Psychology*, 1983.